COMMERCIAL REGULATION AND JUDICIAL REVIEW

Commercial Regulation and Judicial Review

Edited by
JULIA BLACK, PETER MUCHLINSKI
AND PAUL WALKER

·HART·
PUBLISHING
OXFORD
1998

Hart Publishing
Oxford
UK

Distributed in the United States by
Northwestern University Press
625 Colfax
Evanston
Illinois
60208-4210 USA

Distributed in Australia and New Zealand by
Federation Press Pty Ltd
PO Box 45
Annandale, NSW 2038
Australia

Distributed in Netherlands, Belgium and Luxembourg by
Intersentia, Churchillaan 108
B2900 Schoten
Antwerpen
Belgium

Hart Publishing is a specialist legal publisher based in Oxford, England. To
order further copies of this book or to request a list of other publications
please write to:

Hart Publishing, 19 Whitehouse Road, Oxford, OX1 4PA
Telephone: +44 (0)1865 434459 or Fax: (0)1865 794882
e-mail: hartpub@janep.demon.co.uk

British Library Cataloguing in Publication Data
Data Available

ISBN 1-901362-65-5 (cloth)

Typeset in 10pt Sabon
by Hope Services
Printed in Great Britain on acid-free paper
by Bookcraft Ltd, Midsomer Norton.

Contents

Table of Cases

Table of Legislation

1

Introduction

JULIA BLACK* AND PETER MUCHLINSKI**

The rapid growth of judicial review litigation is well noted in public law circles.[1] Commercial lawyers, however, are beginning to find that they have to dust down their notes on judicial review, for this strange beast is now entering their midst. Articles on judicial review are appearing in academic and practitioner journals in finance, banking, company and commercial law. The bemusement with which judicial review is greeted is sometimes palpable. Who can seek review and on what basis? Will review provide a new decision on the actual substance of your case from the court, or is review more limited? Is the decision maker subject review or not? Does the challenge have to be in public or private law proceedings? Finding clear answers is often frustrating: the grounds of review are notoriously open textured; it is almost impossible to advise clients categorically what is or is not illegal, irrational, or procedurally unfair. Remedies are discretionary and damages rarely awarded. The growth in commercial judicial review does not only affect commercial actors and their lawyers, however; it affects those who are making the decisions which are being subjected to challenge. Regulators are increasingly finding that they are having to defend their decisions in court. The exact nature of the impact of such challenges is difficult to measure, but it cannot fail, at least, to affect the way in which decisions are presented.

It was with the aim of exploring the issues associated with judicial review in the commercial context that the LSE and Brick Court chambers held the series of seminars out of which this book arises.[2] The contributions to the book examine the incidence and role of judicial review in different areas of regulation, and explore the problems which commercial regulation poses for public law and those which public law poses for commercial actors. The book is aimed both at those for whom judicial review is a new phenomenon as well as public lawyers who have perhaps noted the growing rise of regulatory respondents in judicial review actions, but who seek a wider discussion of its role in commercial regulation.

---

* London School of Economics.
** London School of Economics and Professor-elect, Queen Mary and Westfield College.

[1] L. Bridges, G. Mezsaros and M. Sunkin, *Judicial Review in Perspective* (Cavendish, London, 1995 2nd ed).
[2] LSE Law Department and Brick Court Chambers seminar series organised by the editors, April-May 1997.

The intention of this Introduction is to provide an overview of the broader context in which the contributors' more detailed discussions occur. It will first set the scene by identifying the principal features of the regulatory environment in which litigation is occurring. It will then examine why companies and others may seek review, what they have to show and what they can hope to gain. The third part will explore broader issues as to the appropriate role of judicial review in the commercial context, and ask whether there are any particular features of commercial regulation which demand an approach which is any different from that which judicial review takes in other areas. Finally, it will draw out some of the challenges which commercial regulation and judicial review pose for each other at present, and those which may arise in the future.

SETTING THE SCENE

The development of contemporary approaches to commercial regulation must be seen in the light of the "market revolution" instituted by the last Conservative government.[3] The change in the nature of the relationship between the state and the market which constituted that revolution was marked by privatisation, liberalisation, the reform of existing regulatory structures and the creation of new ones. The shift from state to private ownership of the utilities was coupled with the setting up of regulatory offices to oversee the efficient working of the resulting markets.[4] A new, mixed, statutory and self-regulatory framework was created for the supervision of the financial services industry.[5] Markets were liberalised and then regulated: TV broadcasting, for example, was deregulated through the setting up of the Independent Television Commission and the franchising auction system.[6]

Such developments have in themselves created new pressures for the effective review of administrative action.[7] The establishment of specialised regulatory

---

[3] See generally R. Baldwin, *Regulation in Question: The Growing Agenda* (Merck Sharp & Dohme Ltd, London, 1995);

[4] See further Colin Scott's chapter in this volume; and generally C.D. Foster, *Privatization, Public Ownership and the Regulation of Natural Monopoly* (Blackwell, Oxford, 1992); T. Prosser, *Law and the Regulators* (Clarendon Press, Oxford, 1997); M. Bishop, J. Kay and C. Mayer, *The Regulatory Challenge* (OUP, Oxford, 1995); J. Kay, C. Mayer and D. Thompson, *Privatization and Regulation: The UK Experience* (Oxford, OUP, 1986).

[5] The regulatory context explored by Martyn Hopper in this volume.

[6] See further M. Cave and P. Williamson, "The Reregulation of British Broadcasting" in Bishop, Kay and Mayer, *op.cit.* p.160; C. Marsden, *Multimedia Multinationals and the Regulation of UK Digital Television*, forthcoming.

[7] Pressures for accountability have also arisen in areas of commercial activity which are subject to non-statutory regulation. In particular, the activities of sports regulators, whose governing bodies have given rise to problems of accountability for many years, have come under increased scrutiny as sport acquires a commercial significance far beyond that envisaged by the founders of such bodies. *Law v National Greyhound Racing Club Ltd* [1983] 1 WLR 1302; *R v Disciplinary Committee of the Jockey Club ex p Aga Khan* [1993] 2 All ER 853; *R v Football Association Ltd ex p Football League Ltd* [1993] 2 All ER 833.

bodies demands not only that these bodies act to secure the often conflicting goals which legislation assigns them, but also that the regulators remain accountable, given the public interest aspects of their activities, and that they act fairly, in view of the far reaching consequences of their powers.[8]

To an extent other administrative bodies have been charged with the role of "regulator of regulators". In particular, the role of the competition authorities as arbiters of both good market practice and good regulatory practice has been significantly enhanced. The Office of Fair Trading (OFT) and the Monopolies and Mergers Commission (MMC) have been given specific remits to police competition in certain privatised and deregulated industries, and to exercise a watching brief over the competitive effects of the activities of financial services regulators.

But often there is no body before which challenge to a regulatory decision can be made. The court is then the only option. And even if there is such a body, that "regulator of regulators" can expect its decisions to be challenged in court. However those who turn to judicial review perhaps seek something which the court cannot, or is not meant to, provide: a new decision on the merits. Judicial review can be a powerful but limited weapon. It cannot provide the full accountability which may be sought, accountability that would often be better found through other means.[9] That it is asked to provide such accountability, however, can pose the court with a significant challenge.

Moreover, the development of new institutional structures in which commercial regulation occurs have created a regulatory environment which could not have been envisaged in the unitary theory of the constitution espoused by Dicey.[10] The current range of bodies exercising regulatory powers includes both statutory and non-statutory entities, rule-making and supervisory bodies, disciplinary systems and guardians of workable competition who operate sometimes through rules, but more often through contractual vehicles such as licences or franchises. Not all of these structures or instruments are traditionally thought of as susceptible to review, yet they are part of a regulatory function which is in a broad sense public.[11] How judicial review should respond to them has become a significant area of debate.

CHALLENGING REGULATORS VIA JUDICIAL REVIEW

In the last few years, judicial review actions have been brought against, inter alia, the MMC, the OFT, each of the Director Generals of Water, Electricity,

---

[8] See further Baldwin *op.cit.*

[9] These limitations have been noted by many; for recent discussions see C. Harlow and R. Rawlings, *Law and Administration* (Weidenfeld and Nicolson, London, 1997), R. Cranston, "Reviewing Judicial Review" in G. Richardson and H. Genn (eds), *Administrative Law and Government Action* (OUP, Oxford, 1995).

[10] See further Craig *op.cit.*, Ch.1.

[11] For an historical perspective on the question see P.P. Craig, "Constitutions, Property and Regulation" [1991] Public Law 538.

Telecommunications, each of the financial services regulators, the Takeover Panel, Lloyds, the Stock Exchange, the Bank of England, the Independent Television Commission and the director of passenger rail franchising. However, the success rate is not high, at least if measured in terms of remedies granted. Yet the costs are, with estimates ranging from around £50,000 to £60,000 for a straightforward case, to anything up to or over £100,000 for a more complex one.[12] So why then do companies, and others, seek review?

There is no systematic empirical evidence on which to base an answer, but a number of reasons can be suggested. Most obviously, as noted above, judicial review may be the only formal means which exists to challenge the decision, and there can be much at stake. Often, the decision concerns a central aspect of business strategy: whether or not the company obtains the franchise or licence is of core significance to its commercial development. Alternatively, the company may be in an on-going relationship with the regulator, and seeks to challenge a decision either because of its immediate impact or because of the impact which it could have for the future.[13] There may also be strong tactical reasons for seeking review, even in the absence of a favourable decision. The mere fact of applying for leave can be used as a bargaining counter in regulatory negotiations. Alternatively or in addition, seeking review can be simply a way of publicising one's case: what Marsden has termed "vanity" judicial review.[14] Significant publicity can attach (or be engineered to attach) to judicial review. The two stage process of leave and hearing can in fact assist this publicity: gaining leave is often reported as a victory even though the final decision goes against the applicant.

How then can one access these potential benefits: who can bring an action, on what grounds, and what remedies are available?[15] Briefly, judicial review proceedings can be brought by anyone with "sufficient interest" in the matter to which the application relates.[16] This has been given an increasingly broad interpretation, and pressure groups and concerned individuals have been given standing to bring judicial review.[17] Third parties can participate, and all proceedings must be served on those directly affected.[18] Review can be brought against bodies exercising statutory powers and those exercising a "public" or

[12] G. McBain, "Commercial Judicial Review", *Commercial Lawyer*, February 1996, 50 at 51.

[13] For examples see A. Lidbetter, "Judicial Review in the Company and Commercial Context" (1995) *BJIBFL* 62.

[14] C. Marsden, "Judicial Review of the Channel 5 TV Licence Award: ITC Excercises "Model Care"" (1996) *Nottingham LJ* 86.

[15] For full discussion see P.P. Craig, *Administrative Law* (Sweet and Maxwell, London, 1994, 3rd ed), H.W.R Wade, *Administrative Law* 7th ed, (Oxford, OUP, 1994), P. Cane, *An Introduction to Administrative Law* (Clarendon Press, Oxford, 1995, 2nd ed), M. Supperstone and J. Goudie (eds), *Judicial Review* (Sweet and Maxwell, London, 1998, 2nd ed).

[16] Order 53 r 3(7).

[17] *R v IRC ex p. National Federation of Self Employed and Small Businesses* [1982] AC 617; *R v SS for Employment* ex p. *EOC* [1994] 1 All ER 910; *R v Inspectorate of Pollution, ex p. Greenpeace (No.2)* [1994] 4 All ER 329; *R v Foreign Secretary, ex p. World Development Movement* [1995] 1 All ER 389.

[18] O. 53 r 5(7).

"governmental" function.[19] The applicant has to seek leave to bring the action, and must do so within a maximum of three months of the decision which is the subject of the challenge being made.[20]

To succeed, the applicant has to show that the body has acted illegally, irrationally or in a manner which is procedurally unfair. The central tenet of judicial review, however, is that it is just that: review and not appeal. The court will consider whether the body acted ultra vires or made an error of law, or whether it took into account irrelevant considerations or failed to take into account relevant considerations, whether it acted in bad faith or with an improper motive, whether it acted irrationally or failed to follow a fair procedure in the circumstances. It will not act as an appellate body, and will not overturn a decision simply because it disagrees with it. Of course, whether or not that is in fact just what the court does do is a matter of significant debate.

If any of the grounds for review are shown, then the court has a discretion whether or not to grant a remedy. The remedies available are that the decision may be quashed (certiorari), action may be required (mandamus) or prevented (prohibition/injunction) or the legal position clarified (declaration). Damages are only awarded where there is some existing private law cause of action, however; there is no right to damages for "maladministration".

ISSUES IN THE CURRENT DEBATE

This bald description of the availability of judicial review hides a wealth of contention, and the question of how those principles have been applied with respect to different commercial regulators forms a large part of the discussion of the subsequent chapters. In order to provide some context to that discussion, however, it is worth exploring in more depth the question of what the approach of the courts should be when called upon to review the actions of commercial regulators. In considering this question, we may question the longer term impact that an action in judicial review, successful or otherwise, may have on the regulator's performance of its functions. However, given the lack of any detailed analysis of such an impact, we are left only with anecdotal evidence.[21] This is unfortunate, as much of the debate, particularly on the broader questions of the role and scope of judicial review, adopts quite particular assumptions as to the nature of that impact.

The issues which are raised particularly (although not uniquely) in the context of commercial regulation are threefold: whether a particular body should

[19] *R v Panel on Takeovers and Mergers, ex p Datafin plc and another* [1987] 1 All ER 564; *R v Disciplinary Committee of the Jockey Club, ex p Aga Khan* [1993] 2 All ER 853.
[20] The combined effect of O.53 r 4 and s.31(6) Supreme Court Act: *R v Dairy Produce Quota Tribunal, ex parte Caswell* [1990] 2 AC 738.
[21] See further G. Richardson and M. Sunkin, "Judicial Review: Questions of Impact" [1996] Public Law 79.

be subject to review; if that body is reviewable, then what intensity of review should apply and how we should assess that intensity; and what are the respective merits of public and private actions.

To review or not to review?

There is first the fundamental question of whether the regulator is or should be subject to judicial review. This question is not unique to the commercial context, but can be particularly pertinent because of the particular institutional forms that commercial regulation can take. As to whether the regulator is subject to review, the legal position currently is that statutory bodies, and those which are not statutory but in which there is sufficient governmental interest in their function, are subject to review.[22] If the body is integrated into a governmental or statutory system of regulation, then it will be held to be public. Thus the Takeover Panel, the Securities and Investments Board, the financial services self regulatory organisations, the Stock Exchange, the Advertising Standards Council and the British Pharmaceutical Association have all been held to be subject to review.[23] The legal dividing line between public and private bodies is far from clear, however: the Insurance Ombudsman is not subject to review,[24] and although the disciplinary committee of Lloyds has been held to be reviewable,[25] the courts have held that decisions concerning actions to be taken relating to losses cannot be challenged by judicial review.[26] Issues arise therefore of the consistency of the courts' approach, and significant questions still remain as to exactly the basis on which the courts will hold a body to be subject to review. For example, just how far does a body have to be integrated into an overall system of regulation to be held to be subject to judicial review? Does the presence of some institutional features, such as a contractual relationship with members, or voluntary submission to the body's jurisdiction, mean that it is always deemed to be private?[27]

The issue of whether a non-statutory or self regulatory body is subject to review are difficult enough, as Martyn Hopper shows in Chapter 3. The question of whether self regulatory bodies *should* be subject to review is even more intractable, but is worth exploring briefly. Broadly speaking the arguments in favour and against the extension of review to such bodies break down into a

---

[22] For discussions see J. Black, "Constitutionalising Self Regulation" (1996) 59 MLR 24, Craig, *op.cit.*, Cane, *op.cit.*

[23] *R v Panel on Takeovers and Mergers, ex p Datafin* [1987] 1 All ER 564; *R v Advertising Standards Authority, ex p The Insurance Service plc* (1990) 2 Admin LR 77; *R v Code of Practice Committee of the British Pharmeceutical Society, ex p Professional Counselling Aids Ltd* (1990) 3 Admin LR 697; *R v Stock Exchange, ex p Else* [1993] 1 All ER 420; *R v SIB, ex p IFAA*, Times 18 May 1995; *R v Lautro, ex p Ross* [1993] 1 All ER 545.

[24] *R v Insurance Ombudsman Bureau, ex parte Aegon Life*, The Times, 7 January 1994.

[25] *R v Lloyd's Disciplinary Committee, ex p Posgate*

[26] *R v Lloyd's, ex p Briggs* [1993] Lloyd's LR 176.

[27] See further Black, *op.cit.*

number of groups. One type of argument in favour of judicial review of such bodies is rooted in the need to control abuse of power. The role of judicial review, it is argued, is to regulate all forms of power; any exercise of power, public or private, by state or companies should be subject to principles of 'liberty, fair dealing and good administration'.[28] Narrower forms of the power argument focus either on the amount of power exercised, and urge review of the exercise of monopoly power,[29] or on the nature of the power being exercised. The latter borrow implicitly or explicitly from the ideas of corporatism or neo-corporatism in other social science disciplines and find the justification for review to be the actual delegation by the state to the regulator of the state's power to regulate.[30]

Other types of argument focus on the social or civic function of self regulatory bodies, and see such bodies not simply as instruments of power but as systems of self government and, as such, as *loci* of civic participation in political life.[31] The role of the courts in this context is to act as mediators between the interests of individuals and the norms of the community, determining the community's central values and upholding them, even if this appears to intrude on the autonomy of an individual or group. This essentially republican argument echoes with those who emphasise the role of the courts in developing and applying constitutional principles and protecting individual rights based on common law values.[32] Review of self regulators would thus on these arguments be justified on the basis that it was necessary to ensure that in their internal processes they acted in accordance with community norms and values, respecting each individual's freedoms, rights and ability to participate fully in the self-governing process.

---

[28] G. Borrie, "The Regulation of Public and Private Power" [1989] Public Law 552 at p 559. See also Lord Woolf, 'Public Law – Private Law: Why the Divide?' [1986] Public Law 220 and `Droit Public – English Style' [1995] Public Law 57; D. Oliver, "Is the *Ultra Vires* Rule the Basis of Judicial Review?" [1987] Public Law 543.

[29] D. Pannick, 'Who is Subject to Judicial Review and in Respect of What?' [1992] Public Law 1.

[30] See, eg P. Cane, 'Self Regulation and Judicial Review' (1986) Civil Justice Quarterly 324; P. Streeck and P. Schmitter, "Community, Market, State – And Associations? The Prospective Contribution of Interest Governance to Social Order" in P. Streeck and P. Schmitter (eds), *Private Interest Government: Beyond Market and State* (Sage, London, 1985).

[31] P. Michelman, 'Foreword: Traces of Self-Government' (1986) 100 *Harvard LR* 4 at 73; C. Sunstein, *After the Rights Revolution: Reconceiving the Regulatory State* (Harvard UP, Harvard, 1990) p 35.

[32] T.R.S. Allan, 'The Limits of Parliamentary Sovereignty' [1985] Public Law 614; 'The Limits of Parliamentary Sovereignty' (1988) 104 LQR 422 and *Law, Liberty and Justice* (OUP, Oxford, 1993); see also D.J. Galligan, *Discretionary Powers* (OUP, Oxford, 1986) and A. Hutchinson, *Dwelling on the Threshold: Critical Essays on Modern Legal Thought* (1988), 92. For an account of the 'community' image of judicial review which these writers represent, see Cotterrell, 'Judicial Review and Legal Theory' in Richardson and Genn, *op.cit*. A "rights-based" approach to judicial review is also argued for by some current senior judges in their extra judicial writings: N. Browne-Wilkinson, "The Infiltration of a Bill of Rights" [1992] Public Law 397; J. Laws, "Is the High Court the Guardian of Fundamental Constitutional Rights?" [1993] Public Law 59; id., "Law and Democracy" [1995] Public Law 72; id., "The Constitution: Morals and Rights" [1996] Public Law 622; S. Sedley, "The Sound of Silence: Constitutional Law without a Constitution" (1994) 110 *LQR* 270.

On the opposite side of the debate, the arguments against the application of judicial review to non statutory regulators tend to focus both on the conceptual strain that may result if the principles of judicial review are extended to all self regulating bodies and the desire to protect the body's autonomy from court or state interference. The concern of the legal or conceptual argument is that such an extension may damage the coherence of the principles of judicial review: principles of fairness, rationality or legality which were fashioned and developed to control action by government, and indeed the remedies which are available, simply cannot be applied to the actions of all those who exercise significant power without doing considerable violence to those very same principles.[33]

The autonomy arguments are wider ranging, and take two forms, not often distinguished. The legal dominion argument focuses on the legal autonomy of the body, and argues that to impose judicial review would be to subject the body to legal norms and interpretations of its own rules which would be inappropriate. This argument has both practical and principled dimensions, and it is one to which we will return below in considering the appropriate degree or intensity of judicial review. In practical terms, it is argued that such judicial imperialism can have detrimental impacts on the area which it is trying to regulate. In terms of principle, the argument seeks a recognition of legal pluralism. It argues that the unitary conception of law in which judicial review is rooted should give way to a pluralistic conception which recognises the operation of other spheres of legal relations.[34] The argument is thus that self regulatory bodies are "mini-legal systems" which should be allowed to formulate and apply their own rules; the courts should recognise the plurality of such systems and not seek to 'cast the net of legal logic'[35] over them.

The legal autonomy argument is echoed in that for the political autonomy of such bodies. The political autonomy argument is again one to which we will return below, and it stresses the desirability of preserving the body's autonomy from interference in its decision making. It also has practical and principled aspects. In its practical form it stresses the damage to the body's effective operation that would be consequent on the application of judicial review: the lack of speed or finality in making decisions, the lack of expertise on the part of the courts to be able to assess the decision, the lack of knowledge or awareness of the impact that their decision might have. In terms of principle then in its application to non-statutory bodies the argument has a neo-liberal hue: self regulatory bodies represent a sphere of private relations which should be free from state interference, the state should simply provide the facilitative framework in which the body can operate.[36]

---

[33] See for example the comments of Rose J in *R v Football Association, ex p Football League* [1993] 2 All ER 833 and 849.

[34] H. Arthurs, 'Rethinking Administrative Law: A Slightly Dicey Business' (1979) 17 *Osgoode Hall* LR 1.

[35] J. Dickinson, *Administrative Justice and the Supremacy of Law in the United States* (Harvard UP, Harvard, 1927) p 126.

[36] See for example, F. Hayek, *Law, Legislation and Liberty*, vol. 3 (Routledge, London, 1982).

The intensity of review

Simply determining that the body is or should be public and subject to judicial review does not end the debate, however. The question then arises as to the appropriate degree of intensity of review which should apply to the body's decisions. Should statutory and non-statutory bodies be subject to different intensities of judicial review? Should commercial regulators be subjected to a less intense form of review than other administrative bodies? The extent to which commercial regulators are subjected to a less intense form of review and in what respects is considered more fully by Paul Walker in Chapter 6. The question which is addressed here is the broader one of what approach the courts should take in exercising their review function. This is relevant in the context of commercial regulation but again is not unique to it.

Arguments for judicial restraint in the exercise of the review function, or at least a certain form of restraint, in part echo those of legal and political autonomy set out above. In particular, considerable emphasis is often placed on the expertise of the regulatory or administrative body. Such focus on the body's expertise is often used in two ways: both to emphasise in practical terms who is best placed to make the best decision, court or regulator, and also to suggest that such expertise confers legitimacy on the regulator's decisions, reducing if not eliminating the need for judicial intervention.[37]

Arguments for judicial restraint also have a procedural dimension. They focus on the appropriateness (or rather lack of it) of litigation as a means of determining the issues which are typically raised in an action for judicial review. These arguments are often as much about the broad issue of the appropriate role of courts in the decision making of public bodies as they are about the more particular questions of the appropriateness of principles of legality, rationality or procedural fairness. The arguments are essentially that the intrinsic nature of adversarial hearings is to reduce what is a multi-faceted issue in the determination of which there may be no outright winners or losers into a bi-polar dispute which takes on the character of a zero-sum game. The consideration of the question is framed by the interests of the two parties, and the decision led simply by the evidence they present before the court.[38]

Finally, separately or in addition to the above, arguments for judicial restraint rely on the constitutional principle of parliamentary sovereignty. Decried by some as a "fig leaf" which public law would do well to dispose of,[39] the

[37] See Cranston, *op.cit.*; R. Baldwin and C. McCrudden, *Regulation and Public Law* (Weidenfeld and Nicolson, London, 1987); for judicial statements which follow this line see for example the comments of Lords Goff and Templeman in *R v ITC, ex p TSW Ltd, The Times* 30 March 1992.

[38] This argument appears in a number of places, but for perhaps the most sophisticated and relatively recent discussion see J. Allison, "The Procedural Reason for Judicial Restraint" [1994] Public Law 453.

[39] Laws *op.cit.* (1995); see also M. Hunt, *Using Human Rights Law in English Courts* (Hart Publishing, Oxford, 1997).

principle has remarkable resilience and a not inconsiderable following.[40] The principle urges at least a certain form of restraint in that it would restrict the role and operation of judicial review to the upholding of parliamentary intent. Moreover, Parliament has given certain powers to those bodies to perform certain functions; those powers were not given to the courts, and it is not for the courts to exercise powers of which they are not the donee.[41] Nevertheless, such bodies have to be kept within the "four corners" of the legislation, and the courts are the sole determiners of the meaning of legal rules and of the scope of the body's powers.

On the other hand, it is argued that the principle of parliamentary sovereignty should not be the main or indeed sole determinator of the scope and principles of judicial review. Rather the principles of judicial review, and indeed that of parliamentary sovereignty, are common law principles, fashioned by the courts. Moreover, they include a recognition of certain individual rights, including those of fairness, due process and rationality, and embody and reflect wider societal values and norms.[42]

It could be thought that the latter group of arguments would lead to more intensive review than the former. This would be a slightly misleading characterisation. It is suggested that we cannot simply put arguments which are based in the principle of parliamentary sovereignty or expertise on one side and those which are rooted in a "rights" or "community values" perspective on the other, and label the former restrictive and the latter interventionist. Although this is often done, it is not quite accurate. Rather the different forms of argument should be seen as advocating particular roles for the courts which in some respects are more interventionist, but in others more restrictive. So although both the parliamentary sovereignty and the expertise arguments, for example, are often characterised as urging judicial restraint,[43] the former would in some situations require judicial intervention whereas the latter would not. This is particularly as the parliamentary sovereignty argument is often, implicitly or explicitly, linked with the legal dominion argument. Taken together the sovereignty and dominion arguments would insist on the courts exercising tight control over the interpretation of statutory or regulatory provisions, whereas the expertise argument would allow a greater margin of appreciation for such bodies to adopt their own interpretations, within the limits of rationality.[44] An argument rooted in community values (sometimes characterised as interventionist) could lead to a similar position on this point as the expertise argument, although for different reasons.

---

[40] For a recent restatement see Lord Irvine of Lairg, "Judges and Decision Makers: The Theory and Practice of *Wednesbury* Review" [1996] Public Law 59, and further C. Forsyth, "Of Fig Leaves and Fairy Tales: The *Ultra Vires* Doctrine, the Sovereignty of Parliament and Judicial Review" (1996) 55(1) *CLJ* 122.

[41] See Lairg, *op. cit.*, Wade *op.cit.*,

[42] See references cited at n 32.

[43] Lairg, *op.cit.*.

[44] This argument is developed more fully by Julia Black in Chapter 7.

So in considering the issue of the appropriate role of judicial review, we should be wary of using a broad brush in labelling certain approaches as always and in every respect ones of judicial "restraint" or "intervention". But in using such labels, the question also arises of how we measure "intervention": is any overturning of a regulator's decision intrusive or interventionist? Or only certain types? What of decisions which expand the scope of the regulator's jurisdiction?[45] The overturning of a regulatory decision may on its face appear to be "interventionist", but in practice it may have little impact on the continuing operation of the regulator; conversely, an action in judicial review, even if unsuccessful, indeed even if it does not proceed beyond the leave stage, may have a considerable impact. Only with the benefit of a specialist understanding and knowledge of the regulatory system and of the impact of a particular decision on the operation of the adminstrator or regulator can assessments of the degree to which judicial review is "interventionist" convincingly be made.

The merits of public or private actions

Finally, there are the more specific arguments of which is a preferable form of action for an individual litigant to take: one in private or one in public law. As Michael Swainston discusses in Chapter 4, public law actions may in many respects pose advantages for a litigant; it may also be their only option. They may not be in a contractual relationship with the regulator; in the case of disciplinary hearings they may not be in an employment relationship and so employment rules would not apply; or there may be no appeal process from the regulator or adminstrator's decision. The rules on standing are becoming increasingly relaxed, with principles of representative and public interest standing being developed,[46] although there may still be limits on the extent that particular groups, for example, shareholders in utility companies, could challenge regulatory decisions.[47] There are also opportunities for third parties to join themselves to an action.[48] Further, the remedies available may in some circumstances be more preferable for the applicant (for example certiorari to quash a disciplinary decision which had removed a person's licence to work at a particular occupation), although on the other hand damages are rarely awarded, and in any event are not available for a public law wrong.

Public law litigation is also speedier than actions in private law, with the average length of a case being 18 months.[49] Short time limits require litigation to be started promptly and within a maximum of three months; there are usually no

[45] For example, *R v DGES, ex p Redrow Homes, The Times* 21 February 1995.

[46] P. Cane, "Standing Up for the Public" [1995] Public Law 276; further C. Harlow and R. Rawlings, *Pressure Through Law* (1992).

[47] See *R v Stock Exchange, ex p Else, op.cit.*, and for criticism, Martyn Hopper, Chapter 3.

[48] RSC O 53 r5(3), or to be heard, r 9(1) (eg *R v Customs and Excise Commissioners, ex p Eurotunnel plc* 1995 COD 291).

[49] Bridges, Mezsaros and Sunkin, *op.cit.*

lengthy processes of discovery or cross examination. Further, the granting of leave gives the applicant early on in the process a greater indication of the merits of his case than he would have at the start of a private law action. Finally, as noted above, granting of leave may also confer considerable tactical advantages, publicising the applicant's grievance, and perhaps improving its negotiating stance with the regulator.

ISSUES PARTICULAR TO COMMERCIAL REGULATION

Judicial review raises issues which range from grand questions of constitutional theory such as the appropriate scope of judicial review and its role relating to administrative and regulatory action, down to the technical, and tactical, issues of which type of action, one in public law or one in private law, is available or most advantageous to this particular individual in this particular case. These issues are equally as pertinent in the context of commercial regulation as they can be in other areas of judicial review. But does judicial review of commercial regulators raise issues which are distinct from those which arise in the context of judicial review as a whole? Is there a particular feature or set of features which means that judicial review in the commercial sphere should or does operate differently from the way in which it operates in the context of, for example, housing, immigration, social security, or planning?

There are certainly differences in the number of cases which are brought in these different contexts. However, commercial judicial review, although a growing area, is not an important one in numerical terms. As the work by Bridges, Sunkin and Meszaros shows, judicial review litigation principally concerns homelessness, immigration and crime.[50] Applications for leave by commercial litigants however have a significantly higher success rate (70% compared with an average of 38%),[51] although this may simply be because commercial applicants will usually be able to afford specialist legal advice in drafting their applications, and of course does not necessarily translate into a higher success rate in gaining the final judgement.

That said, as Harlow and Rawlings note, statistics do not of themselves tell the full story. They cannot measure the ripple effect: the impact of a judgement beyond its particular facts, nor do they attest to the impact that the mere potential of review may have on a regulator's decision making processes.[52] Clearly the incidence of commercial judicial review is growing, and it has involved some high profile cases. But to reiterate, does judicial review of those regulating commercial activities need to be exercised in a manner or on a basis which is distinct from the exercise of the general judicial review jurisdiction?

[50] *ibid.*
[51] *ibid.*
[52] Harlow and Rawlings, *op cit* at 537.

There are several arguments which could be put forward as giving rise to that need. It could be argued that certain principles should drive judicial review in the commercial context. The commercial environment in which regulators and firms operate could mean that principles, for example, of economic efficiency or the needs of commercial activity should either exclude or drive the definition of what principles should govern the conduct of such regulators. However, it is difficult to see why this should be so: the aim of regulation need not necessarily be to ensure economic efficiency, and indeed regulation is frequently characterised by broad, and often conflicting, objectives which range far beyond that of economic efficiency.[53] Why economic efficiency should be the goal that judicial review seeks to ensure is not clear. Moreover, judicial review has its own principles which may operate in tension with that of economic efficiency, notably those of procedural fairness.[54]

It could be argued that there is a need for a judicial "light touch" to be applied with respect to commercial regulators. As noted, whether or not this is in fact occurring is considered by Paul Walker in Chapter 6. As to whether it should occur, a number of arguments or considerations could be put forward, many of which draw on those outlined above.[55] It could be argued that commercial regulators have been deliberately given powers which are broadly defined, conferring on them considerable discretion to determine themselves the extent to which intervention in the market mechanism is necessary or desirable. Clearly, the more discretion that is given to the regulator the greater is its capacity to intervene in the economic process that it is charged with overseeing. The more accountable the regulator is under the law the narrower (in theory) is its discretion. An excessive subjection of commercial regulators to judicial review would be contrary to an expressed intent to confer discretion on them. This argument can also be put in terms of expertise. Intensive judicial review may render regulators more cautious and as a result less effective in using their expertise to protect workable market relations. The commercial aims of regulation should therefore be given a wide margin of appreciation so that the regulator can freely achieve control over the market, often in ways that the participants may find disagreeable.

On the other hand, it could be argued that the substantive aims of the regulator should be subjected to an overarching set of principles of good administration, even where this may reduce effective regulatory power. Again briefly following through the discussion set out above, it could be argued that good administration is a basic constitutional concept that cannot be qualified. Further, the "light touch" approach to judicial review could be a mask for

<hr/>

[53] In relation to utilities regulators, for example, see Prosser, *op.cit.*
[54] On the tensions between (*inter alia*) efficiency, effectiveness and due process see Baldwin and McCrudden, *op.cit.*, and R. Baldwin, *Rules and Government* (Clarendon Press, Oxford, 1995). An example of the tensions between legal principles and regulatory objectives is provided by the *Scottish Power* case: see further Colin Scott's discussion in Chapter 2, and at [1997] Public Law 400.
[55] And on which see further Harlow and Rawlings, *op.cit.*, chs 1-4.

abuses of private property rights that a free society could not accept. (Paradoxically, however, the current doctrines of review may lead to what some would perceive to be such a result, as the *Allerdale* case, discussed by Christopher Clarke and Catharine Otton-Goulder in Chapter 5, illustrates.)[56]

It may also be further argued that judicial review could play a particularly valuable role in the context of commercial regulation by guarding against "industry capture". The industries that are being regulated are generally those which display features of natural monopoly (eg gas, water, electricity, rail transport), or the need for prudential supervision in the public interest (as with financial services), for example. These industries are also part of the global economy. It is part of the wider strategy of the firms involved to act increasingly as multinationals. As such issues of wider public and political concern are being handled by regulators, who are, in effect, the nationally-based regulators of a wider transnational business system. It may be essential for good governance and public responsiveness for these bodies to be subjected to scrutiny not just by market players but by the wider public to ensure that proper the regulation of markets is actually taking place. Judicial review may provide the only forum in which decisions could be formally challenged, and the courts could play a role in overseeing the decision-making process from the perspective of rationality and legality, and ensuring that decisions are made which are not simply pandering to special interest at the expense of wider public policy goals.[57]

The arguments of discretion, expertise and the need to ensure accountability or protection of rights are apposite but not unique to the commercial context. Thus far, it is suggested, we have found no arguments from *principle* which suggest that the features of commercial regulation are such that those arguments should be resolved in any particular way. Does the commercial context impose *practical* demands on decision making which call for a particular judicial approach: are there pragmatic reasons why a judicial "light touch" should be applied? A consideration often put forward as justifying such an approach is the need for speed in decision making.[58] This need may exist in particular instances, but it is hard to see why there is necessarily and always any greater need for urgency in the commercial context than in that of housing or asylum, for example. Another justification which is frequently put for a "light touch" is that encouraging review actions could encourage tactical litigation.[59] This may well be the case; commercial actors rarely have the same self-limiting financial restraints as individual litigants, and there may well be commercial advantage to be gained from tactical litigation on the part of applicants. This argument

---

[56] *Credit Suisse v Allerdale Borough Council* [1996] 3 WLR 894 (CA).
[57] The apparent motivation for the action in *R v Water Services, ex p Oldham MBC and others*, 20th February 1998 (held that the DGWS should have used his enforcement powers against firms which introduced "budget payment units" as the use of such payment systems could involve the disconnection of water supply without the statutory safeguards being applied).
[58] For example, *R v Takeover Panel, ex p Guinness* [1990] 1 QB 146.
[59] It was to discourage this that Lord Donaldson emphasised in *Datafin* that the courts' relationship with the Panel should be "historic" rather than contemporaneous.

however applies to any litigation, public or private, and the leave requirement is in part designed to limit such tactics.

So the answer to the question: what is so special about commercial judicial review, is: nothing. The questions posed by commercial judicial review are posed in the context of judicial review more generally, and there is no aspect of the commercial context which suggests that they should be answered in a particular way. Those answers have still to be found in a deeper political theory.[60] However a number of factors combine in the area of commercial regulation to ensure that it provides a particularly challenging context for judicial review.

First, the structures and instruments that characterise much commercial regulation are not ones which fit conveniently into traditional categories of "public" and "private". Commercial regulation frequently combines institutional structures and legal instruments which are familiar subjects of private law with a function which is the usual subject of public law. Judicial review (and indeed aspects of private law) are having to adapt to meet this new hybridity. The need for and the nature of this adaptation are discussed further by Colin Scott and Julia Black in Chapters 2 and 7 respectively.

Second, commercial judicial review involves applicants who are far removed from those found in the more typical areas of judicial review. The combination of powerful corporate interests and changing rules on standing has lead some to predict that a new, public interest model of judicial review is emerging.[61] Thus Rawlings argues that not only will judicial review proceedings tip further in the direction of collective legal action, "but that increasingly they will be populated by a compendium of powerful repeat players... concerned to ensure that relevant precedents do not cut across collective interests, and further to use litigation strategically in the development of long term policy strategies."[62] It can be anticipated that powerful commercial actors will increasingly seek judicial review in an attempt affect the operation of the regulation by securing strategically important decisions on the operation of regulatory processes and the interpretation of legal rules and other regulatory instruments. This will require the courts to engage to an even greater extent with the existing systems of commercial regulation, and in places develop a better understanding of them.

If judicial review of commercial regulation raises no new constitutional issues, then what is the debate about? Is it that things are being treated as susceptible to public law principles when they should be dealt with as a matter of private law or vice versa? Perhaps, but as the principles of public and private law in places are starting to converge[63] this cannot be the whole problem. Is it that the courts are imposing norms, interpretations or principles which are contrary

[60] See further P.P. Craig, *Public Law and Democracy in the US and the UK* (OUP, Oxford, 1992).
[61] Harlow and Rawlings, ch 17.
[62] R. Rawlings, "Courts and Interests" in I. Loveland (ed), *A Special Relationship? American Influences on Public Law in the UK* (Clarendon Press, Oxford, 1995), 113.
[63] For discussion see D. Oliver "Common Values in Public and Private Law and the Public Private Divide" [1997] Public Law 630; on the interaction of public and private law principles in the commercial context see further Julia Black's chapter in this volume.

to those of the regulatory system? In part: this can and does occur. As the different chapters show, particularly those of Martyn Hopper, Colin Scott and Julia Black, the courts can simply misunderstand the system that is being reviewed, a misunderstanding which can have unfortunate consequences both for the regulatory system and for the coherence of judicial review itself.

It is in this argument of misunderstanding that we perhaps find the principal concern. That concern is often not so much about the constitutional role of the courts vis a vis regulatory bodies (although it is partly that), but about the appropriate role of the legal system as a whole. When we complain about judicial review we are often just complaining about law; what is often really wanted is a "law free zone". The disadvantages of judicial review that are always listed in the debate: "what should the appropriate role of judicial review be", viz. lack of speed or flexibility, the potential for tactical play between parties, the nature of the adversarial process as bi-polar, a zero sum game, are not unique to judicial review but are simply features of litigation per se. Those disadvantages would not disappear were the applicable principles of law applied as part of private as opposed to public law, for it is not so much a particular set of legal principles which is being criticised as law itself. Thus the plea for "non-interventionist" judicial review is often at root a plea to remove law from the field altogether. Judicial review is simply one manifestation of the increasing role played by law and legal values in regulation, a role which some would resist. It is this important theme, the juridification of regulation, which is pursued by Colin Scott in Chapter 2.

PROSPECTS FOR THE FUTURE

What then are the prospects for judicial review in the commercial context in the next few years? There is no reason to suppose that the growth in commercial judicial review will stop, and many reasons to suggest that it will continue. The liberalisation of the standing rules and the increasing awareness of pressure groups, companies, and their legal advisors, of the potential benefits to be gained from seeking review are all likely to be factors in that expansion.

It may also be that new grounds become available through the importation into the national context of grounds used in the European, notably that of proportionality,[64] and the incorporation of the European Convention on Human Rights will also undoubtedly have an impact.[65] Both of these will apply across the whole spectrum of judicial review, but the introduction of the Convention could have a particular impact on commercial regulation. The potential impact of article 6 on disciplinary proceedings is already engendering much debate amongst regulators and legal practitioners. Further, it could be that article 1 of

---

[64] For a full discussion see Craig, *op.cit.*; P.P. Craig and G. de Burca, *EU Law: Cases and Materials* (Sweet and Maxwell, London, 1996).

[65] For a discussion of the impact of the Convention thus far see Hunt, *op.cit.*

the first Protocol on the peaceful enjoyment of private possessions becomes used in litigation as an argument for resisting regulation. The extent to which an analogous provision in the US Constitution has been used to challenge regulatory decisions on the basis that they are an unconstitutional "taking" of property has been significant. Any parallel development could have a substantial impact on the operation both of judicial review and of commercial regulation if it were to be accepted.[66]

It may also be that the scope of judicial review will expand to include privatised utilities.[67] Such bodies would then fall within the definition of public authorities for the purposes of the Human Rights Bill.[68] The application of judicial review principles to such companies would have a significant impact on their operation. It would also add a new dimension to the corporate governance debate, but that is a separate issue.[69] These are just two directions in which commercial judicial review may go; there may be others which a more prescient commentator would include. But at least one thing can be said with assurance: that the principles of public law will become more familiar to commercial lawyers and their clients.

[66] See C. McCrudden, "The Use of "Super-Mandates" and the Purposes of Regulation" in C. McCrudden (ed), *Regulation and Deregulation: Policy and Practice* (OUP, Oxford, forthcoming).

[67] A privatised utility has been held to be subject to judicial review in Northern Ireland, and a privatised utility has been held to be an emanation of the state for the purposes of direct effect: *Griffin v South West Water Services Ltd* (1995) IRLR 15.

[68] Human Rights Bill, clause 6.

[69] Privatised utilities have already received special consideration in the Greenbury Report on Directors' Remuneration (1995).

2

The Juridification of Regulatory Relations in the UK Utilities Sectors

INTRODUCTION

Privatisation of the United Kingdom utilities sectors over the last fifteen years has been accompanied by a marked change in the way in which these sectors are viewed by lawyers, and in the relationship of these sectors with the legal system more generally. During the period of public ownership of the utilities sectors organisational and supply relationships were governed almost exclusively by bureaucratic methods, with very little involvement of lawyers or recourse to the legal framework within which the services were managed and provided.[1] The descriptive argument of this chapter is that the UK utilities sectors are witnessing processes of juridification. Juridification describes a process by which relations hitherto governed by other values and expectations come to be subjected to legal values and rules—"the tendency to formalize all social relations in juridical terms".[2] Such a process creates the risk that law will overstep the mark beyond which its contribution to structuring the way in which relations are managed ceases to be useful. In that event law risks being ignored or being destructive either of activities which it seeks to control or of the legitimacy of

* Law Department, London School of Economics and Political Science. I am grateful to participants at the CNRS/ESRC Conference "Ten Years of Research on Communication", Chantilly, Apr. 1996, and at the London School of Economics and Brick Court Chambers Seminar Series, "Commercial Regulation and Judicial Review", London, Apr. 1997, and to Cosmo Graham, Aileen McHarg, Tony Prosser, Gunther Teubner and the editors for comments on earlier drafts of parts of this chapter. I remain responsible for errors and infelicities.

[1] See B. Schwartz and H.W.R. Wade, *The Legal Control of Government: Administrative Law in Britain and the United States* Oxford University Press, Oxford, 1972), at 37–41, cited in C. Harlow and R. Rawlings, *Law and Administration* (2nd edn., Butterworths, London, 1997), at 312–13. The decision of the House of Lords in *Bromley London BC* v. *Greater London Council* [1983] 1 AC 768 provides a rare example of a judicial intervention in the decisions affecting a public corporation, the London Transport Executive, and interpreting the obligations of the statute under which it was established and operated. See the discussion in A. Ogus, *Regulation: Legal Form and Economic Theory* (Oxford University Press, Oxford, 1994), at 274–6.

[2] M. Loughlin, *Legality and Locality—The Role of Law in Central–Local Government Relations* Oxford University Press, Oxford, 1996), at 369. Loughlin suggests that the British state tradition generally is characterised by a "largely non-juridified structure of administrative law", at 379.

law itself—the so called "regulatory trilemma".[3] Though the most visible indicators of juridification are instances of litigation, whether judicial review or other forms of action, they are just the tip of the iceberg. The seepage of law into the management of relationships in the utilities sectors is also indicated by the more hidden but growing presence of lawyers at each stage of negotiating commercial and regulatory relationships, the increasing use of more formal processes of information gathering and enforcement, and the hidden growth of technical regulatory rules expressed in a variety of legal and sub-legal instruments.[4]

The descriptive claim that the utilities sectors are becoming juridified calls for a number of distinct forms of critical analysis. First, the main body of the chapter is devoted to an examination of the most visible indicator of juridification—the marked increase in incidences of litigation. Though much of the analysis is concerned with judicial review of decisions of public authorities, the inclusion of contractual disputes recognises that contracts have been deployed in the utilities sectors to meet the regulatory purposes of government policy-makers, regulators and/or dominant firms seeking to exercise some form of regulatory power over the market.

Secondly, we need to understand why law is taking on greater importance in the utilities sectors following privatisation. The main factor in increasing the importance of law in the utilities sectors has been the processes of liberalisation which have developed some years after privatisation in most of the utilities sectors. Liberalisation has had the effect of multiplying the number of players participating in each sector (both regulatory and commercial) and tended to threaten the consensual, bureaucratic models of provision and regulation which carried over from the era of public ownership. Increasingly these more numerous players are seeking to test their rights and obligations against the legal frameworks of each sector.

The final issue for analysis is to understand the potential impact of juridification. While the impact might be understood in the instrumental terms of interfering with the efficiency of expert regulation, or improving the accountability of non-elected regulatory authorities, we question whether such straightforward instrumental effects for law are credible. The limits of legal understanding of the utilities sectors are amply demonstrated by the analysis of the case law, within which the needs of the legal system to categorise aspects of provision and regulation in terms which the law recognises leads to outcomes which are difficult to understand and process from the perspective of the utilities sectors. Understood at a theoretical level it is possible for law to support organic processes within the utilities sectors which might enhance regulatory efficiency

---

[3] G. Teubner, "Juridification—Concepts, Aspects, Limits, Solutions" in G. Teubner (ed.), *Juridification of Social Spheres* (Walter de Gruyter, Berlin, 1987), 3–48 at 3–5.

[4] J. McEldowney, "Law and Regulation: Current Issues and Future Directions" in M. Bishop, J. Kay, and C. Mayer (eds.), *The Regulatory Challenge* (Oxford University Press, Oxford, 1995) 408–22 at 418–9.

or accountability, or to damage them through the over-ambitious claims of the legal system to be able to control processes which fall outside its particular organising rationales and objectives.

ADMINISTRATIVE LAW

Administrative law governing regulatory relations in the utilities sectors has a number of distinct sources. Most visible are the somewhat limited provisions of the various statutes governing the powers and duties of ministers and regulatory offices.[5] For example, the Telecommunications Act 1984 sets out the basic responsibilities of the Director General of Telecommunications to monitor and collect information about telecommunications activities,[6] enforce licence conditions,[7] and to investigate complaints.[8] In carrying out these duties the Director General shares a responsibility with the Secretary of State to secure the provision of telecommunications services sufficient "to satisfy all reasonable demands" and "to secure that any person by whom such services fall to be provided is able to finance the provision of those services".[9] Further duties to promote the interests of "consumers, purchasers and other users", "to maintain and promote effective competition", "to promote efficiency and economy" among the service providers and to promote research[10] are expressed in such terms as to be secondary responsibilities.

The chief powers possessed by the Director General are to enforce licence conditions (noted above), modify licence conditions[11] and to collect information from licensees and others.[12] The main statutory procedural duties applying to the exercise of these powers are the duty to hold a 28-day consultation on any proposed licence modification,[13] and the requirement of 28 days' notice prior to the issuing of any provisional or final order against a licensee in respect of an alleged licence breach.[14] In each case the director has a duty to consider representations and objections from the licensee affected and from third parties. In the case of a provisional or final order the licensee has a limited right to appeal to the High Court on grounds either that it is *ultra vires* or that procedural

---

[5] The Office of Telecommunications (Oftel) established by the Telecommunications Act 1984, the Office of Gas Supply (Ofgas) established by the Gas Act 1986, The Office of Electricity Supply (Offer) established by the Electricity Act 1989, the Office of Water Supply (Ofwat) established by the Water Act 1989, superceded by the Water Industry Act 1991, and the Office of the Rail Regulator (ORR) established by the Railways Act 1993.

[6] Telecommunications Act 1984, s.47.

[7] *ibid.*, s.17.

[8] *ibid.*, s.49.

[9] *ibid.*, s.3(1).

[10] *ibid.*, s.3(2).

[11] *ibid.*, ss.12, 13.

[12] *ibid.*, s.53.

[13] *ibid.*, s.12(2).

[14] *ibid.*, s.17(3).

requirements were not satisfied.[15] It is a characteristic of the utilities regimes in general that they were designed with a view to restricting the scope for legal challenges to regulatory decisions. The issuing of orders is, in theory, of great importance, since it is this and not the breach of a licence condition itself, which triggers the right of the Director General to enforce the order through the court, and the right of third parties adversely affected by the breach to claim damages. In practice Oftel made little use of its formal enforcement powers before 1996, reflecting the close and consensual nature of relations with British Telecom, its principal regulatee. The ultimate sanction against a licensee, the revocation of its licence, is reserved to the Secretary of State through provisions in the licence.

It is within such statutory frameworks that licences, authorisations, appointments and franchises were granted to the various telecommunications, gas, electricity, water and railway companies which provide utilities services to the public. These latter instruments contain the chief obligations of the companies. Though generally issued by the Secretary of State (or the regulator, if the powers are delegated), they are subject to oversight and modification at the initiative of the various regulators (within the constraints noted below). The legislation and licences between them empower the regulators to issue orders in respect of breach of licence conditions and determinations of various forms of dispute both between licensees (for example in the case of telecommunications interconnection[16]) and between licensees and their customers.[17] Additionally various sub-legal instruments, or instruments of "soft law", have been developed.[18] These include circular letters from regulators to the licensees,[19] guidelines issued by regulators,[20] and codes of practice, developed by licensees with the encouragement of the regulators, for example governing relations between companies and their customers.

Alongside the statutory framework is the general common law which applies to the administrative activities of public bodies such as regulatory offices. Thus ministers and regulatory offices, and perhaps also dominant firms (see below), may be subjected to judicial review of administrative action on grounds of illegality, unfairness or irrationality. Notwithstanding the rather limited duties in respect of consultation and transparency contained within the statutory frameworks, of which the Telecommunications Act 1984 (noted above) is an exemplar, in practice the regulatory offices, led by the Office of Telecommunications,

[15] Telecommunications Act 1984, s. 18.
[16] Licence Issues to British Telecommunications plc (1984, as amended), Condition 13.
[17] E.g. Telecommunications Act 1984 (as amended by Competition and Service (Utilities) Act 1992) ss. 27F–27I.
[18] The term "soft law", widely used in discussion of European Community legal instruments, refers to legally non-binding instruments which are, nevertheless intended, to have normative effect: R. Baldwin, *Government and Rules* (Oxford University Press, Oxford, 1995), at 226–30, 248–52.
[19] E.g., the "Dear Regulatory Director" and "Dear Managing Director" letters issued by Ofwat.
[20] Notably the Oftel *Guidelines on the Operation of Fair Trading Condition* (Oftel, London, 1997) which are to some degree modelled on the European Commission *Guidelines on the Application of EEC Competition Rules in the Telecommunications Sector* [1991] OJ C233/2.

have developed more elaborate procedures for consultation on licence modifications than required by the legislation.[21]

To view administrative activity through the lens of judicial review brings with
it particular effects. A loosening of principles of standing and greater use of
social science data in litigation have mitigated some of the problems of the private-law model of adjudication on which judicial review actions were historically based.[22] Loughlin goes further, suggesting that a distinctive model of
public law adjudication has developed in recent years, which reduces some of
the worst problems of viewing what are essentially public policy disputes from
a litigation perspective. He notes that:

> "the scope of the action is not exogenously given but is shaped by the parties; the party
> structure is not rigidly bi-polar but amorphous; fact inquiry is predictive and legisla-
> tive rather than historical and adjudicative; relief is forward-looking, flexible and with
> important consequences for absentees; the remedy is not imposed but negotiated; its
> administration requires the continuing participation of the court; the judge plays an
> active role throughout; and the action concerns a grievance about the operation of
> public policy."[23]

But we may question whether such adaptation reflects a wish within the judi-
ciary to be better equipped to adjudicate in judicial review cases or an unrealis-
tic belief that the courts are better equipped than they in fact are to understand
the effects of the application of its supervisory jurisdiction for the actors in the
sectors concerned.

There are two important aspects to the litigation which has occurred. First
the pattern of cases indicates the circumstances under which litigation occurs.
This analysis suggests that licence enforcement decisions remain largely subject
to a consensual model as between regulator and licensee, and that litigation is
used by third parties to prise open procedures which are relatively opaque and
which lead to unsatisfactory conclusions for such third parties. At the level of
regulatory enforcement pressure for greater formality also comes from the concerns of third parties, who need reassuring that dominant firms are being
policed, for example in relation to consumer obligations or anti-competitive
conduct. Conversely the modest incidence of recent actions brought by licensees
against their regulators in respect of licence modification suggests that in this
area of regulatory activity the consensual model is beginning to break down.
Such a breakdown in the consensual model may be a response to changes in
market structure, and thus the behaviour of regulators and regulatees in the face
of liberalisation. In the telecommunications sector the willingness and capacity

---

[21] See Oftel, *Improving Accountability: Oftel's Procedures and Processes* (Office of
Telecommunications, London, 1997); National Audit Office, *The Work of the Directors General of
Telecommunications, Gas Supply, Water Services and Electricity Supply* (House of Commons Paper
No. HC 645, Session 1995–6).
[22] G. Richardson and M. Sunkin, "Judicial Review: Questions of Impact" [1996] *Public Law*
79–103 at 86.
[23] M. Loughlin, n. 2 above, at 403.

of BT to litigate may also be a spill-over from its success in challenging ministerial rule-making through litigation in respect of the government's European Community obligations. Paradoxically the self-regulatory aspect of telecommunications regulation has been the least consensual when measured against the relatively high incidence of litigation to challenge self-regulatory decisions.

The second question that is raised by the litigation which has occurred is to what extent any pattern is discernible in the approach taken by the courts to the extent and manner of any intervention in regulatory decisions. There is a view that the courts take a more restrictive attitude to judicial review in cases involving commercial regulation.[24] This is evidenced by the fact that though the courts are willing to expand the ambit of their supervision of regulatory activities, for example to cover self-regulatory bodies,[25] they take a non-interventionist approach to the substantive activities of the regulatory body. This contrasts with the greater willingness to intervene in decisions of ministers and local authorities. This may partly be explained by a juridical conception of regulators as independent and expert bodies.[26] Paradoxically the courts may show greater respect for non-democratic institutions than for democratic ones. Consequences of this restrictive approach have been said to include the general non-availability of the prerogative orders, application of stringent time limits, and application of restrictions on discovery and cross-examination to cases involving challenges to regulators, whether brought by judicial review or some other form of action.[27] Overall, though we may form a view as to the characteristics of any particular decision, a pattern is difficult to detect.

The discussion which follows in this section explores key regulatory events and relationships, in order to secure an understanding of which regulatory issues have been contested through litigation. It starts with the issuing of licences, a process which has attracted virtually no litigation. The discussion proceeds to the two central regulatory issues, in terms of relations between regulators and firms, the enforcement and modification of licences. These processes provide the central powers through which regulators seek to secure the desired behaviour of their regulatees. The final three parts of this section focus on others with actual or potential importance in the regulatory landscape, ministers in respect of their powers to issue guidance or directions to regulators, and their powers to make rules through statutory instruments, and self-regulatory bodies which have a growing importance with the marketing of utility services in liberalised markets. Inevitably, discussion within an administrative law framework of the key functions and relationships in the utilities sectors focuses on

---

[24] R. Gordon, "Declaratory Judgements and Judicial Review". Paper presented at IBC conference, *Rights and Remedies in Regulated Industries*, London, 1995. See also the discussion of this issue in the chapters by Hopper and Walker in this volume.

[25] *R. v. Panel on Takeovers and Mergers, ex p. Datafin* [1987] 1 QB 815.

[26] See, e.g., the judgment of Lord Denning MR in *Laker Airways v. Department of Trade* [1977] 2 WLR 234; R. Baldwin, "A British Independent Regulatory Agency and the 'Skytrain' Decision" [1978] *Public Law* 57.

[27] Gordon, n. 24 above.

those exercising public power. Thus one of the weaknesses of the administrative law lens is that the substantial private power held by utilities firms through their possession of information, and through their market power, is almost completely obscured.[28]

Issuing of Licences

The decisions of the President of the Board of Trade concerning whom to license in the telecommunications sector have never been subjected to judicial review, nor have any other licensing decisions in the utilities sectors privatised since 1980. This is not surprising as the licensing procedure is opaque. Since the ending of the BT–Mercury Duopoly, the government has, in principle, been willing to license all applicants who meet financial criteria for public telecommunications operators' (PTO) licences. Though provided for in the licensing instruments licence revocation is not a plausible sanction against a utility firm, because it is so drastic and because it is likely to affect customers adversely, and no licence has yet come up for renewal.

The closest form of litigation to this issue has been concerned with the issue of broadcasting licences for the regional ITV broadcasters. These licences are used to allocate valuable monopoly rights in competitive bidding. The form of competition anticipated by these licensing procedures is different from that which applies in the case of gas, electricity and telecommunications, since the broadcasting licensee is competing for the field, and once it has won the franchise it has the exclusive control of it. In this respect it is closer in character to railway franchising under the Railways Act 1993. It is understandable that the moment at which the franchise is awarded should be more liable to litigation, given that the award of a monopoly follows, than is the case in other sectors. Attempts to challenge such decisions have, however, been unsuccessful. The principle that the licensing authority should, in certain circumstances, give reasons for decisions, set out by the House of Lords in relation to the ITC,[29] has not been applied to the licensing functions of ministers. The principle set down in the *TSW* case was to apply to cases where an existing licence holder was applying for a new licence. No such renewal cases have yet occurred in the utilities sectors. In future the reasons for a ministerial or agency decision in respect of the grant of licences could be subject to a freedom of information application,[30] making future challenges to decisions easier.

---

[28] C. Scott, C. Hall and C. Hood, "Regulatory Space and Institutional Reform: The Case of Telecommunications" in P. Vass (ed.), *CRI Regulatory Review 1997* (Centre for the Study of Regulated Industries, London, 1997).

[29] See *R. v. ITC, ex p. TSW Broadcasting Ltd* [1996] EMLR 291. Nothwithstanding the importance of this House of Lords decision to the broadcasting sector, it was only reported four years after the decision.

[30] See the Government White Paper "Your Right to Know" (Cm 3818, Dec. 1997).

Recent litigation concerning broadcasting licences arose following the award of the Channel 5 licence. In *R v Independent Television Commission, ex p. Virgin Television Ltd*[31] Virgin challenged the franchising process through an application for judicial review on the ground that the successful applicant had been able to modify its bid, in respect of the shareholders' funding commitment, between application and award, and that the decision that Virgin failed to meet the quality threshold was irrational. Two other companies were also affected by the decision of the ITC. New Century was the only other bidder which met the quality threshold, while UKTV was in the same position as Virgin, having failed to meet the quality threshold. Both were refused leave to apply for judicial review because they each were pursuing the first ground of Virgin's application. Each was also refused leave to appear during the course of Virgin's application. But at the hearing the Divisional Court did permit the other two firms to be heard. Recognising the limitations of the traditional assumptions of judicial review, Henry LJ said that "judicial review being often concerned with the identification of a public wrong, the conventional adversarial approach may often be too narrow".[32] The Divisional Court held that the request by the ITC for further information and provision of such information as to the finances of the successful applicant, Channel 5 Broadcasting (C5B), was anticipated by the statutory procedure for the issue of licences set down in the Broadcasting Act 1990 and that it was neither illegal nor unfair for such additional information to be provided.

In addressing Virgin's claim that the ITC acted irrationally in finding that Virgin failed to meet the statutory quality threshold, Henry LJ spoke pejoratively of attempts by counsel "to encourage an interventionist frame of mind" which were met by the caution that the court should neither "assume the mantle of the Commission itself (as the decision-making body)" nor "allow itself to become a Court of Appeal from the decision making body when no such provision is made in the Act which created the Commission and vested it with clearly defined powers and duties".[33] Lord Templeman's caution in the *TSW* case (mentioned above) was cited with approval. Henry LJ set out in considerable detail the procedures used by the ITC to assess whether the quality threshold had been met and concluded:

> "It is quite plain that the Commission approached its task of evaluating the application and the evidence provided by Virgin to support it with model care."[34]

Thus the Divisional Court interpreted its supervisory role in respect of the licensing procedure to be a non-interventionist one. Having observed that judicial review procedure lacks rigour, Henry LJ referred to the "'pick-out-a-plum' school of advocacy" as particularly dangerous in the absence of full discovery,

---

[31] [1996] EMLR 319.
[32] At 322.
[33] At 340.
[34] At 345.

cross-examination and the full rigour of pleadings. Henry LJ emphasised[35] that the area of decision-making in question was not simply a quantitative exercise but involved qualitative analysis and judgement: it followed that a heavy burden fell on the applicant. The judicial caution in this case is thus based on a concern that the court will not have sufficient expertise to form a view about the way in which the Commission exercised its statutory duties in respect of the qualitative elements in licensing decisions.

Enforcement of Licences

It is well established that in carrying out licence enforcement functions utilities regulators are subject to judicial review, [36] though to date there has not been a great deal of litigation. The Divisional Court in particular has generally shown itself unwilling to intervene with the discretion of regulators in relation to licence enforcement. This non-interventionist stance has been revealed both in relation to positive actions of the regulator, for example in withdrawing recognition of a Code of Practice which effectively closed down one class of service providers,[37] and the refusal to act to prevent British Telecom using its market power for the similar purpose of regulating the market in sexline services.[38] However, dicta in the *Maystart* case reveal a perception on the part of the Court of Appeal of Oftel's discretion being highly constrained. Simon Brown LJ said of the Director General, in relation to power to enforce BT's licence, or to modify it if it did not cover the undesirable action complained of:

> "Had he any doubts about its desirability, he must inevitably, as it seems to me, have followed the course outlined in his letter, first attempting modification of the licence under section 12, failing which he could have ordered a section 13 reference."

These dicta suggest that, whereas on the wording of the statute Oftel has considerable discretion in ordering priorities, in the Court's view, if the Director General found that the actions of BT acted against the public interest, Oftel would be *obliged* to seek a licence modification, and perhaps then seek an MMC reference if BT did not agree it. This leaves little space for Oftel to come to a view about the adverse public interest consequences of a PTO's activities, but to decide not to act against it because it is not a matter of priority, or because the likely benefit of such action would be too small.[39] It was held that even had there

---

[35] At 341.

[36] R. v. *Director General of Gas Supply, ex p. Smith* (Div. Ct., 1988); McEldowney, n. 4 above, at 419.

[37] See R. v. *Director General of Telecommunications, ex p. Let's Talk (UK) Ltd* (QBD, 6 Apr. 1992).

[38] *Maystart Ltd* v. *Director General of Telecommunications* (Court of Appeal, 17 Feb. 1994).

[39] Cf. Telecommunications Act 1984, s. 16(5) which permits the Director General not to proceed with enforcement of a licence condition where such enforcement would be inconsistent with his duties or the breach is trivial.

been an arguable case (which there was not), the ten-week delay between receipt of Oftel's letter and Maystart's applying for leave was so great that the Court should probably have refused the application in any case. This aspect of the decision indicates a judicial conception of the sector as one in which time may well be of the greatest importance: the requirement in Order 53 rule 4 that applications for leave to move for judicial review must be made promptly will therefore mean that in such cases the applicant would have to show particularly good reason for any delay, even within the three month long-stop period identified in that rule.

This view of regulators as having highly constrained discretion was acted on in a case in which the electricity regulator, Offer, refused to intervene in a dispute between a regional electricity distribution company (Manweb) and a number of house builders who were unhappy at the steep rise in connection charges for new homes levied by the company. A number of the building firms involved referred the dispute to Offer, relying on the provisions of the Electricity Act 1989, which state that any dispute between a licensed supplier and a person seeking supply of electricity may be referred to Offer for determination or reference to an arbitrator.[40] Offer held that the charges were excessive. Subsequently a further group of builders, who had paid the contested connection charges and sat on the sidelines of the dispute referred to Offer, sought to have a determination from Offer that the charges for connection which they had paid were also excessive. Offer refused to make such a determination, claiming that once the charges were paid there was no dispute and it was powerless to intervene.

Schiemann J held that restricting the definition of dispute to "unresolved dispute" or dispute in which payment has not yet been made was to restrict the natural meaning of the words. Therefore Offer would be required to make a determination on the dispute.[41] The decision purports simply to apply the natural meaning of the statute in defining Offer's jurisdiction to resolve disputes. In fact it seems to take a wide view of the legitimate dispute-resolving jurisdiction of Offer and to give the regulator a more substantial role in regulating what are basically contractual disputes than the regulator had felt was appropriate. Thus this represents a more interventionist decision than that applied to the Oftel case noted above.

These decisions do not provide any clear indication as to the circumstances in which a court is likely to intervene. Such interventionist indications as exist are likely to encourage licensees and those affected by regulatory decisions to seek judicial review, as they see courts more actively as providing mechanisms for appeal. Given the concentration of interest concerning the activities of regulators in the regulated firms as compared with third parties, it is surprising that much of the licence-enforcement litigation has been brought by third parties. This suggests that, notwithstanding a modest shift in regulatory practice towards more formal enforcement, the intended consensual regime still remains

[40] Electricity Act 1989, s.23.
[41] R. v. *Director General of Electricity Supply, ex p. Redrow* (QBD, 21 Feb. 1995).

central as regards relations between licensees and regulators, and that third parties, whether new service providers or major customers, fall outside the regime and are likely to escalate disputes to litigation more willingly. Breakdown in consensual relations between licensees and regulators is more evident in relation to licence modification.

Rule-making by Licence Modification

The power of the Director General to modify the conditions contained in the licensing instruments provides, in practice, the main mechanism by which regulatory rules can be amended and supplemented. This is because the main regulatory rules are contained in licences and similar instruments, and the regulators possess few powers to issue more general regulatory rules. The use of licences for the main regulatory rules in the utilities sectors is said to provide a greater protection against the risk that the regulator or a future government might substantially alter the regulatory regime. It was important to the government to demonstrate a commitment to the continuity of the regimes established by the privatising legislation in order to encourage the new investment which privatisation was intended to deliver.[42] Where the existing licence regime does not cover a situation which the regulator thinks ought to be regulated, the only option is to seek to modify the licences of those firms to which the new rule ought to apply. Additionally one of the central planks of the regimes established by the privatizing legislation, the application of price controls in respect of services where a substantial element of monopoly was retained, was framed in such a way that the price controls contained in licences were to expire after four or five years. Such price controls could only be retained (in their original or modified form) through licence modification.

Given the importance of the statutory procedures for modification of licence conditions by the regulators it is perhaps surprising that the first litigation to challenge a regulator's actions only occurred only in 1996, twelve years into the life of the telecommunications regime and seven years after the Electricity Act 1989. It is less surprising when we notice that the statutory regimes were established in such a way as to encourage consensual bargaining between licensees and regulators (though this was apparently not anticipated by the government), and only as the regulators have grown in experience and knowledge of the sectors they oversee have they sought to use licence modifications to make radical changes to the so-called "regulatory contract"[43] established between licensees and regulators by the government on privatisation.

[42] B. Levy, and P. Spiller, *Regulation, Institutions and Commitment* (Cambridge University Press, Cambridge, 1996), at 20.
[43] C. Veljanovski, "The Regulation Game" in C. Veljanovski (ed.), *Regulators and Markets—An Assessment of the Growth of Regulation in the United Kingdom* (Institute of Economic Affairs, London, 1991).

The provisions for licence modification, substantially common to the telecommunications, gas, water, electricity and rail sectors, set out two ways in which licensing instruments can be modified. Modifications may occur by agreement between the regulator and licensee, or without agreement following a reference to the Monopolies and Mergers Commission (MMC). The MMC reference procedure is filled with uncertainty for both sides. The regulator is not restricted to referring the matters contained in the proposed licence modification, but can draw a reference more widely. The MMC is to apply distinct statutory criteria to the evaluation of the matters referred. Provided that the MMC concludes that the matter referred acts against the public interest, and that a licence modification can remedy the matter, the regulator can make any licence modification which appears "requisite" to remedy the matters identified in the report. Thus, as a matter of statute, the regulator is not bound to implement the MMC recommendation as to the nature of the licence modification needed. The time-consuming and uncertain nature of the MMC reference procedure gives both licensees and regulators powerful incentives to reach agreement on proposed licence modifications.[44] Inevitably the bargaining process is somewhat hidden, so that even the best efforts of regulators to make licence modification decisions transparently do not provide a procedure for making regulatory rules for the sectors concerned which is fully inclusive. The power reserved by the Secretary of State to require an agreed modification to be referred to the MMC, designed to guard against capture of the regulator,[45] though requiring the Secretary of State to be kept informed of proposed consensual licence modifications, has never been used.

The interaction of licence-modification procedures with judicial review raises intriguing questions about the extent to which the courts will overlay administrative law principles on the statutory procedures, and how the courts deal with the use by the legislature of an individuated licence modification procedure for the making of rules for a whole sector.[46] Two recent cases have addressed issues relating to the extent to which licence modifications can be used substantially to amend the regulatory regime, and whether a licensee can reopen a consensual modification through a judicial review action. The extent of the regulator's discretion to reject an MMC recommendation has not been addressed by the courts.[47]

---

[44] M. Armstrong, S. Cowan and J. Vickers, *Regulatory Reform* (MIT Press, Cambridge, Mass., 1994), at 360; C. Graham and T. Prosser, *Privatising Public Enterprises* (Oxford University Press, Oxford, 1991), at 213, 230.

[45] This provision was introduced in the 1982 Telecommunications Bill, lost due to the 1983 general election, but retained in the Bill which became the Telecommunications Act 1984. See HC 1982–3, Standing Committee H, vol. VI, 22 Feb. 1983, col. 1180 (Mr Baker).

[46] These issues are more fully addressed in my "Regulatory Discretion in Licence Modifications: *The Scottish Power Case*" [1997] *Public Law* 400–9. See also C. Graham "Regulatory Responses to MMC Decisions" in P. Vass (ed.) *CRI Regulatory Review 1997* (CRI, London, 1997).

[47] But it has been held that the similar powers exercised by the Secretary of State on receipt of an MMC report under the Fair Trading Act 1973 leave the Secretary of State free to disregard the MMC recommendation: *R. v. Secretary of State for Trade, ex p. Anderson Strathclyde plc* [1983] 2 All ER

The *British Telecom* and *Scottish Power* cases were judicial review actions brought by licensees following a consensual modification to their licence conditions.[48] The essence of British Telecom's case was that the modification of its licence to include within it a general prohibition on anti-competitive conduct was *ultra vires,* because it denied to BT the protection of an individual licence modification and the possibility of an MMC reference for each instance of anti-competitive conduct not covered by BT's licence which Oftel sought to regulate. Scottish Power's case was that the Director General of Electricity Supply should have reopened the consensual modification to the Scottish Power licence when the MMC recommended a more favourable licence modification in the case of the other Scottish electricity company, Scottish Hydro-Electric. In each case the licensees were seeking to challenge by judicial review licence modifications which they had consented to under the statutory procedure.

The modification to which BT had agreed was part of a package of changes introduced by Oftel which actually reduced the burden of regulation on British Telecom. The so-called Fair Trading Condition (FTC) was seen by Oftel as a necessary accompaniment to a series of relaxations in regulation which had seen the removal of the RPI+2 cap on BT's line rental charges, the reduction in the scope of the retail price cap from more than 60 per cent of BT's revenue to about 25 per cent, and a plan to replace annual consultation over BT's interconnection charges, hitherto set by Oftel, with a wholesale price cap which would operate automatically without the need for regulatory bargaining. These changes gave BT greater market freedom in relation to pricing, and carried with them the risk that BT would use its monopoly power to act anti-competitively. In the face of such liberalisation the new condition was to compensate for the inadequacies of British competition law, as Oftel saw them.

The FTC licence modification proposed by Oftel (which became Condition 18A of BT's licence) was designed to introduce new norms of conduct based on Articles 85 and 86 of the EC Treaty, prohibiting abuse of dominant position and restrictive agreements with anti-competitive effect. The new Condition 18A would supplement and extend the existing prohibition in Condition 17 of BT's

---

233. The recent decision of the Northern Ireland Electricity Regulator to reject an MMC recommendation in respect of a licence modification for Northern Ireland Electricity (NIE) has triggered a judicial review action, undecided at the time of writing. The background to this litigation is described by A. McHarg, "Reviewing Electricity Price Controls in Northern Ireland" (1997) 8 *Utilities Law Review* 159–63. McHarg's assessment (at 162) is that following the *Anderson Strathclyde* case "unless NIE can persuade a court that the Director General's proposals render it incapable of financing its licensed activities or they are otherwise perverse or irrational, a legal challenge is unlikely to succeed".

[48] *R. v. Director General of Telecommunications, ex p. British Telecommunications plc* Div. Ct., 20 Dec. 1996, unreported, unofficial transcript); *R. v. Director General of Electricity Supply, ex p. Scottish Power* (CA, 3 Feb. 1997, unofficial transcript). I have considered these cases more fully in my published notes, on which parts of the analysis which follows are based: n. 46 above; "Anti-Competitive Conduct, Licence Modification and Judicial Review in the Telecommunications Sector" (1997) 8 *Utilities Law Review* 120–2. See also A. McHarg "A Duty to be Consistent? *R. v. Director General of Electricity Supply, ex p. Scottish Power plc*" (1998) 61 *Modern Law Review* 93–101, at 99–100.

licence on undue preference and undue discrimination. The new licence condition was intended also to give Oftel greater capacity for rapid and effective
enforcement of these new norms. The condition provided that in applying the
Condition the DGT would have regard to European Community jurisprudence
(ECJ decisions, Commission decisions and notices), pronouncements of the
Director General of Fair Trading and Monopolies and Mergers Commission
and any guidelines issued by Oftel. The Condition empowered the DGT to
make an initial determination, after giving BT an opportunity to comment.
Similarly BT was to have an opportunity to comment before the making of a
final determination or order by the DGT. BT might require the DGT to take
into account the views of an Advisory Body, established by Oftel, before making a final determination. The value to BT of this procedure is demonstrated by
the fact that, on the occasion of the making of the first provisional order against
BT for breach of the new condition, a subsequent reference of the matter to the
Advisory Body prevented Oftel from proceeding to a final order, because of a
finding by the Advisory Body that Oftel's conclusion that the condition had
been breached was incorrect.[49]

By bringing a judicial review action, BT was attempting to sever the changes
to the price control regime, which it found acceptable, from the new controls on
anti-competitive conduct, which it did not find acceptable.[50] Considering the
statutory procedure for modifying licence conditions, Phillips LJ expressed the
general principle governing the DGT's discretion in the following terms:

> "The discretion as to the terms of a licence condition must be exercised in accordance
> with the express requirements of the Act and in a manner calculated to promote the
> policy and objects of the Act, as determined from the Act when read as a whole."

This proposition, supported by authority, was supplemented by a further principle:

> "A condition must not be inserted in the licence which is so unclear as to be void for
> uncertainty."

Given that the DGT has a statutory duty, *inter alia*, to "maintain and promote
effective competition" in the telecommunications sector (noted above), BT was
likely to have some difficulty in demonstrating that the exercise of discretion by
the DGT fell outside these principles.

The main substantive grounds of claim put forward by BT were that one way
or another Condition 18A upset the statutory balance between the DGT and
general domestic and EC competition authorities, as set out in the Telecommunications Act 1984, and more generally in other legislation and Treaty obligations. Addressing these claims, which were framed in a number of ways,

---

[49] *Report of the Advisory Body on Fair Trading in Telecommunications: Draft Final
Determination Under Condition 18A of BT's Licence; BT Chargecard Report by ABFTT: Oftel's
Views* (Oftel, London, Dec. 1997).

[50] C. Graham "Judicial Review and the Regulators" (1997) 6 *Utilities Law Review* 107–8, at 107.

Phillips LJ held that the specific powers of the DGT to regulate conduct by reference to modification and enforcement of licences was bound to "do most of the job in that field which would otherwise have fallen to be done, as best it could, under the general powers of the 1973 and 1980 [general competition] Acts". Put slightly differently the more specific telecommunications regime was held to take precedence over the powers exercised by the DGT and by the other competition authorities under general competition legislation. Somewhat different arguments apply to the relationship between Condition 18A and EC competition law. BT argued that to introduce norms based on Articles 85 and 86 created the risk that they would be interpreted differently from Community law, with no mechanism for resolving such conflict. The Court found this assertion devoid of merit. The court might have reflected on the extensive voluntary alignment of domestic competition regimes with EC norms, both within EC Member States and outside, most of which alignments would be open to the same complaint, but none of which have been challenged by the European Commission.[51]

The court accepted that there was a degree of uncertainty about the way in which Condition 18A was framed, notwithstanding Oftel's intention to rely on the European Community jurisprudence to interpret the prohibitions, but rejected BT's claim that this rendered the condition *ultra vires*. This rejection was based on the observation that BT had already to live with some uncertainty about the interpretation of its licence, and Condition 18A did not significantly add to that uncertainty. Phillips LJ's remarks suggested approval for a new licence condition which would save delay and uncertainty associated with the need to modify licences to address specific forms of anti-competitive conduct which could be addressed economically by the new Condition 18A.

The argument which the court found most troubling was BT's claim that the use of general anti-competitive conduct conditions in a licence modification unlawfully by-passed the statutory provision that licence modifications should, where not consented to by the licensee, be subject to review by the MMC and possible veto by the Secretary of State. By removing the need for further licence modification to address specific forms of anti-competitive conduct the DGT was seeking to by-pass this protection to licensees. Phillips LJ responded to this argument in circular fashion, indicating that since BT had agreed to the proposed licence modification, it had had the statutory protection, which is based on consent. The Secretary of State had the power to veto the modification which he had not exercised.

The issue in the *Scottish Power* case was not that the Director General of Electricity Supply (DGES) had failed to implement the MMC proposals in respect of Scottish Hydro-Electric (SHE), the company on whose licence the report was carried out, but rather whether the other company, Scottish Power (SP), which had agreed to the proposed modifications should be permitted to

---

[51] I. Maher, "Alignment of Competition Laws in the European Community" (1997) 16 *Yearbook of European Law* 223–42.

benefit from the more favourable regime proposed by the MMC, through further licence amendment by the DGES. The proposed licence modification which SP had accepted and SHE had rejected concerned the price control on the charges made to franchise customers taking under 100 Kilowatts of supply a year. Because the two Scottish companies both generated and supplied electricity and, in contrast with England and Wales, there was no market element to the determination of supply prices, the generation component of the price control had been fixed in relation to the price paid by regional electricity companies (RECs) in England and Wales. Both the Scottish companies had argued that in modifying the price control in 1995 this component, the Great Britain yardstick (GBY), should be modified to reflect the price the RECs paid in relation to electricity for its smaller customers, a higher figure, rather than an averaged-out figure which included the cheaper electricity it supplied to its larger customers.

When the DGES proposed a modification which retained the GBY in its original form, both companies protested, but whereas SP reluctantly accepted the licence modification, SHE rejected it, forcing a MMC reference. The MMC Report supported the view of SHE that the GBY should be modified as it had proposed to the DGES. The MMC concluded that to fail to modify the GBY would hold the price of supply to the franchise market "below the level which would prevail in a free market" and that this acted against the public interest, as it would prevent the development of competition. Though this would result in increasing SHE's revenue by £18 million a year, £17 million of this would effectively be clawed back in the MMC's modification of the price control on distribution. The DGES implemented the MMC's proposed licence modification fully in respect of SHE. The DGES informed SP that he did not propose to make a further modification of its licence to change the GBY. He noted that the GBY was just one of a number of factors affecting competition in the sector and the MMC had not commented on the implications of its proposed modification that SP and SHE would have different GBYs. The DGES stated that it was not possible to know what attitude the MMC would have taken to SP's position because it was not asked and did not comment on it.

The Court of Appeal (*per* Sir Ralph Gibson) overturned the Divisional Court's decision that the DGES had acted rationally, quashed his decision not to modify SP's licence and remitted the issue back to the DGES for a fresh decision. The court held that the reasons given for the DGES's decision were not valid. In particular the argument made by the DGES that he had had regard to the whole picture, and had concluded that increasing the generation component would upset the revenue and price aspects of the package of modifications which had been agreed by SP, was not a valid reason because he could have proposed additional modifications which would have reduced SP's revenue by corresponding amounts, as happened approximately with SHE. The failure to propose a modification, on the reasons advanced, was both irrational and unfair. The DGES decided not to proceed with an appeal, resolving the dispute with a consensual modification to SP's licence, under which SP secured the benefit of the revised GBY but agreed "to reduce prices to its franchise customers equivalent to 2 per cent of the total annual bill".[52]

Regarding the relationship between regulatory activity and judicial review, in *Scottish Power* the fact that the licensee agreed to the proposed modification is not directly stated to be a ground for refusing to grant judicial review. This absence is puzzling, given the importance in principle of determining whether a licensee given the statutory protection of an MMC reference should be entitled to elect to challenge a regulatory decision by judicial review without availing itself of the statutory procedure.[53] There are considerable resource implications for the regulator in having to reopen issues relating to a set of licence conditions, and corrections to particular aspects of a licence arising from changes in the regulatory environment might ordinarily be made, if thought necessary, by the regulator at some later modification stage.

In general, the *Scottish Power* decision sits uneasily with the Divisional Court decision in *British Telecom*. If the Directors General have a broad discretion to propose licence modifications, subject to the principles laid down by Phillips LJ in *BT* and subject to the protections of the licence modification procedure, it is difficult to see why the review of a proposed modification of one company's licence should affect the duties of the regulator in respect of the licence of another company, beyond the general duty to keep the sector, and therefore licence conditions, under review. The difference in approach appears to be based on differing perceptions of the relationship between regulator and licensee envisaged by the statutory regimes. In *British Telecom* the implicit assumption is that, provided procedural requirements are met and the powers are used to advance the purposes of the statute, the court is unlikely to intervene. In contrast, the *Scottish Power* decision views the relationship between regulator and licensee as one in which the regulator engages not in general policy-making, but rather in individuated decision-making in respect of the particular licensee. The licensee is to be protected not only by the statutory protections of the legislation (notably the right to reject a licence modification and force an MMC reference), but also by the common law doctrines which protect the individual who is the subject of individuated decision-making. Thus SP was, *prima facie*, entitled to have its licence modified to correspond to the modification of SHE's licence and, at the very least, was entitled to a full set of reasons why its licence was not to be so modified.

Executive Rule-Making

Although the British utilities regimes do not provide much scope for executive rule-making, membership of the European Union has resulted in new forms of

---

[52] Office of Electricity Regulation Press Release R22/97, 19 May 1997.
[53] Graham, n. 50 above, at 108.

rule-making, both by the EU institutions and by the UK government, to secure the development of EC policy in relation to the utilities sectors. At both levels these processes have resulted in considerable tension and litigation. Thus British Telecom took its challenge to the manner of implementation of the EC Utilities Procurement Directive through the Divisional Court and Court of Appeal to the European Court of Justice before new regulations were implemented after a further Divisional Court hearing.[54] In similar fashion BT challenged the UK's implementation of the ONP Leased Lines Directive.[55] In each case BT was using judicial review to challenge the way in which its position in the UK market was treated by the UK government, arguing that it should not be burdened with all the duties which attached to dominant monopolists, where, because of the relatively advanced state of liberalisation in the UK, it no longer held legal monopolies in any parts of the sector. A substantial part of the problem has arisen because the EC legislation has been targeted at regimes which are not liberalised, and fit poorly with the liberalised UK regime.[56] Further tension is possible as the UK government takes further steps to implement EC regimes for liberalisation of telecommunications, energy and possibly postal sectors.

The autonomous legislative capacity of the European Commission under Article 90(3) of the EC Treaty has been challenged, substantially unsuccessfully, on three occasions by Member State governments.[57] This legislative power has been used to greatest effect to provide for the liberalisation of the telecommunications sector without the involvement of the other EC institutions. While the Commission has substantially won its legal battles over its competence to issue such general Article 90(3) legislation, political considerations have meant that legislation to liberalize other EC utilities sectors has generally been proposed under Article 100A EC, which requires the co-operation of the Council and the Parliament.[58]

Relations between Agencies and Ministers

There is no strong tradition of independent regulatory agencies in the United Kingdom. Typically, where government has created new agencies, rule-making powers have been substantially retained by the government, together with other

[54] Case C–392/93 R. v. *HM Treasury, ex p. British Telecommunications plc* [1994] 1 CMLR 621 (QBD, CAl); [1996] ECR I-1631 (ECJ).
[55] Case C–302/94 R. v. *Secretary of State for Trade and Industry, ex p. British Telecommunications plc* [1996] ECR I–6417.
[56] A. Hunt, "Regulation of Telecommunications: The Developing EU Regulatory Framework and its Impact on the United Kingdom" (1997) 3 *European Public Law* 93–115, at 110.
[57] Joined Cases 188–90/80 *France, Italy and UK* v. *Commission* [1982] ECR 2545; Case 202/88 *France* v. *Commission* [1991] ECR I–2223; Joined Cases C–271/90 etc, *Spain, Belgium, and Italy* v. *Commission* [1992] ECR I–5833.
[58] C. Scott, "Changing Patterns of European Community Utilities Law and Policy: An Institutional Hypothesis" in J. Shaw and G. More (eds.), *New Legal Dynamics of European Union* (Oxford University Press, Oxford, 1996), at 209.

powers to veto agency decisions and/or to issue guidance or instructions on how agencies are to carry out their tasks. Because of this there is inevitably scope not only for ministers and agencies to dispute their respective roles, but also for third parties to attempt to exploit such relationships. Legislative regimes define the extent to which and manner in which ministers may intervene in the conduct of agency business. For a minister to overstep that boundary or for an agency to refuse to recognise the statutory authority of the minister may result in judicial review. No other route is likely to be open to a third party to achieve its objective.

This potential is well demonstrated by the celebrated *Laker Airways* case.[59] The Civil Aviation Act 1971 empowered the Minister to issue both guidance and directions to the Civil Aviation Authority. The power to issue directions was restricted to ensuring that national security was protected and that UK international obligations were met or international relations maintained.[60] No such limitations were placed on the issue of guidance. Laker was caught up in a change of government and an attempt by an incoming government to end proposals for competition on air routes. The government removed the designation which had been given to Laker and purported to change the policy by issuing guidance requiring the CAA not to license a second operator, save that, within British Airways' sphere of influence, a second operator could be licensed with BA's consent. In a judicial review action by Laker Airways, which had its licence revoked after the issue of the fresh guidance, the Court of Appeal held the guidance to be *ultra vires*, because it sought to change the policy rather than simply amplify, explain or supplement the general objectives.[61] Only directions could be used actually to change the policy, and directions could only be issued in limited circumstances which did not apply in this case. The decision was criticised by Baldwin as failing to recognise the character of the new regulatory agencies, which were not judicial in character and did not therefore need protecting from ministerial intervention.[62] This approach of the Court of Appeal would provide an explanation for a non-interventionist approach to agencies generally as expert bodies, less subject to the kind of irrational decision-making of other public bodies which the courts have become involved in supervising.

A more contemporary case throws up a similar problem, in the form of an agency which failed to follow a lawfully issued direction. At the time of the passage of the Railways Act 1993 there was considerable concern in Parliament that the privatisation of rail routes by means of franchising would result in a considerable reduction in services. To appease Parliament the Secretary of State issued an instruction, as he was empowered to do,[63] to the Office of Passenger Rail

---

[59] *Laker Airways* v. *Department of Trade* [1977] QB 643.

[60] Civil Aviation Act 1971, s. 4.

[61] *Per* Lord Denning MR.

[62] R. Baldwin, "A British Independent Regulatory Agency and the 'Skytrain' Decision" [1978] *Public Law* 57 at 79–80; C. Harlow and R. Rawlings, *Law and Administration* (2nd edn., Butterworths, London,1997) at 83–90.

[63] Railways Act 1993, s.5.

Franchising (OPRAF) that, in setting out minimum service levels for franchisees, OPRAF should base these on the existing British Rail timetable. Thus the government was attempting to free railway operators to make commercial decisions about frequency of service, while at the same time attempting to meet political concerns that service levels should not be reduced. The two objectives were not consistent with each other and collided in OPRAF's franchising decisions. A pressure group brought an application for judicial review against OPRAF in respect of the first franchises on the ground that minimum service levels fell well short of the existing British Rail timetable. In *R. v. Director of Passenger Rail Franchising, ex p. Save Our Railways*[64] the Court of Appeal held that to comply with the instruction changes to timetables permitted by OPRAF could only be "marginal, not significant or substantial" (*per* Sir Thomas Bingham MR). In each case service levels were set below 90 per cent of the old BR timetable, in some cases considerably below, as low as 45 per cent. Five of the seven franchises were held to be clearly unlawful as not complying with the instruction of the Secretary of State. This case is one in which the Secretary of State was rather caught out, in that he used the power to issue instructions in such a way that he was able to reassure Parliament, but in so doing undermined some of the intent of the legislation in providing greater commercial freedom in respect of time-tabling. Perhaps the factor of greatest interest here is that it was a pressure group which was able to exploit this inconsistency through litigation. Their victory, however, was a pyrrhic one, as the minister acted to change the rules, legalising the minimum service levels.[65]

Self-regulation

In the telecommunications sector considerable use has been made of self-regulation, particularly over content and contract conditions for the information services which have been provided by a large number of small companies since the mid-1980s. In *R. v. ICSTIS, ex p. Firstcode*[66] the parties were agreed that the decisions of the Independent Committee on Standards in Telecommunications Information Services (ICSTIS) were subject to judicial review. ICSTIS sought that the grant of leave by Sedley J be set aside on the merits. The decision of Owen J not to set aside the grant of leave was appealed to the Court of Appeal. ICSTIS is a private body, created by a contractual agreement between British Telecom and all other network operators, under which ICSTIS issued a Code governing the activities of Premium Rate Service (PRS) providers such as Firstcode. The Code provided for ICSTIS to determine whether in any particular instances the Code had been breached. The Code

[64] *Independent*, 20 Dec. 1995.
[65] J. Goh, "Privatisation of the Railways and Judicial Review" (1996) 7 *Utilities Law Review* 42–3.
[66] CA, 24 Feb. 1993, Lexis transcript.

recorded that each contract between the network operator and the PRS provider contained a provision obliging the PRS provider to comply with the Code. ICSTIS is independent of BT and other telecommunications firms. Applying the decision of the Court of Appeal in *R. v. Panel on Takeovers and Mergers, ex p. Datafin plc*,[67] Kennedy LJ concluded that ICSTIS was exercising a form of public law jurisdiction, rather than being simply a body whose sole source of power is consensual submission to its jurisdiction. ICSTIS' decisions were therefore judicially reviewable. The basis for this conclusion is not at all clear. We may observe that all PRS providers have to submit to ICSTIS' jurisdiction, but this is only because the providers' contracts with BT and all other network operators include a requirement to abide by the ICSTIS Code. It was precisely Firstcode's argument in this case that its contract with BT had been modified to restrict ICSTIS' jurisdiction in the case of Firstcode. But Russell LJ held that, since ICSTIS' jurisdiction was not dependent on contracts between the provider and ICSTIS, the provisions of any contract between the provider and BT could not affect its jurisdiction. Where a contract could be relevant was in limiting the scope for BT in applying to the provider the sanctions required by ICSTIS. The reasoning on these issues seems to be circular and unsatisfactory.

A stronger argument, which was not referred to in the decision of the court, would be to point out that BT's licence[68] requires there to be a code of practice approved by the Director General of Telecommunications before BT is able to offer its network for use for chatline, interactive game, and live conversation message services. Thus it is clear that the code exists only because of the activity of public officials in issuing, modifying and enforcing licences. This might justify the conclusion that ICSTIS' jurisdiction is a public law one, not dependent on contract, and because of that its activities cannot be fettered by any particular contract. It seems that the Court of Appeal reached its conclusion that ICSTIS was a public body subject to judicial review under conditions in which both parties accepted this premise, and therefore the alternative case was not argued. An alternative view would be to suggest that, since its sanctions are only capable of being implemented by contract, then that is the source of its power. The court overturned the decision to give leave for judicial review on the ground that it was not arguable that the terms of Firstcode's contract with BT could affect ICSTIS' jurisdiction. Thus we find that in applying the principles of public law to this small corner of telecommunications regulation, what seems to be a private body, established by and deriving its jurisdiction from contract, takes on the characteristics of a public law body, with universally applicable jurisdiction.

Though it seems clear that the courts will regard ICSTIS as a body exercising public law functions, and therefore subject to judicial review, the scope of such review is not likely to be as full as would be possible for genuine public authorities exercising statutory powers. In a first instance decision Kennedy J, when

[67] [1987] 1 QB 815.
[68] Condition 33A.

refusing leave to move for judicial review, observed (obiter) that the case concerned interpretation by ICSTIS of the provisions of its own code. This juridical interpretation of a self-regulatory body accords it the status of a "fuller" regulator than it would in the case of Oftel, in the sense that it both makes and enforces the rules.[69] Accordingly Kennedy J would, if necessary, have adopted the general approach of Lord Donaldson in *R. v. Panel on Take-Overs and Mergers, ex p. Guinness*[70] to the effect that in the case of the Takeover Panel illegality would certainly apply where the Panel acted in breach of the general law, but is more difficult to apply in the context of an alleged misinterpretation of its own rules by a body which under the scheme is both legislator and interpreter.

Self-regulation in advertising generally is becoming increasingly important as liberalisation has rendered advertising a very important tool for gaining or retaining market share.[71] British Telecom's advertising campaigns appear to be aimed at keeping the company very much in the public eye, increasing the use of telecommunications by its customers, and proclaiming the significant price reductions which have, in many cases, been imposed by the regulatory framework. For new entrants to the market, advertising is used to make customers aware of the choices of providers in many aspects of the market, and of the significantly reduced prices which, in many cases, they are able to offer when compared with British Telecom. It is inevitable that marketing campaigns in this sector have been subject to large numbers of complaints by competitors, both through the print advertising self-regulator, the Advertising Standards Authority,[72] and through the Independent Television Commission and a self-regulatory unit handling the regulation of commercial broadcast advertising, the Broadcasting Advertising Clearance Centre.

It is not surprising that the pressure being put on advertising regulation should have spilled over into litigation in *R. v. British Advertising Clearance Centre, ex p. Swiftcall*.[73] The applicant, Swiftcall, was a company offering reduced rate international calls via an 0800 number and credit card. The BACC,

---

[69]   *R. v. ICSTIS Ltd, ex p. Telephone Entertainment Service*, 6 Feb 1992, Lexis Transcript. The distinction between "full" and "partial" regulation is more fully explored in C. Hood and C. Scott "Bureaucratic Regulation and New Public Management: Mirror-Image Developments?" 321–45, 336–7.

[70]   [1990] 1 QB 146 (at 159). Lord Donaldson added that an alleged misinterpretation by the Panel of its own rules would only ground a finding of illegality where it was so far removed from the natural and ordinary meaning that a body subject to the rules could be misled.

[71]   Other regulatory issues have also come to the fore, notably the way in which personal data on customers and former customers are used by dominant incumbents to defend market share. Both the Data Protection Registrar and the sectoral regulators for gas and telecommunications have raised concerns about the legality of the use of such information by BT and British Gas.

[72]   Numerous examples of complaints brought under the ASA code by competitors include, e.g., the complaint brought against BT in respect of a national newspaper campaign claiming that its ISDN lines were cheaper than using couriers for firms using a courier at least once a week. The complaint was partially upheld on the grounds that the costs were not clearly set out and that comparisons made were unfair: Advertising Standards Authority (1997) 79 *ASA Monthly Report* 14–15.

[73]   Div. Ct., 16 Nov. 1995, Lexis Transcript. See also *Vodafone Group plc v. Orange Personal Communication Services Ltd* [1997] EMLR 84.

which provides a pre-clearance service for the ITV companies which own it, rejected the advertisment on the ground that it did not inform customers of the total cost of the service, as it neglected to include both the local connection charge and VAT. Swiftcall added information to its advertisement, indicating in general terms that local connection charges and VAT applied and the BACC gave clearance. Subsequently BACC received a complaint from British Telecom about the advertisement, indicating its view that it was still misleading and drawing the BACC's attention to a similar complaint by BT about Swiftcall which was pending with the Advertising Standards Authority. Swiftcall was informed of this complaint and asked to respond. During this correspondence BACC informed Swiftcall that charges quoted would have to include VAT and the local access charge. Swiftcall indicated that it could not include such charges without remaking the advertisement and refused. Swiftcall sought judicial review on the basis that it had a legitimate expectation that it would be permitted to broadcast the advertisement, and that this had been breached. Swiftcall also said that BACC was not acting fairly as between operators, by not requiring BT to include VAT in the calculation of call charges in its advertisement, nor to indicate precisely the basis on which BT discounts applied.

Carnwath J indicated that he was unwilling even to address the two preliminary arguments made on behalf of the BACC; first that it was not a body amenable to judicial review; secondly that the BACC had not actually made a decision. With regard to the second point he thought that the correspondence made it clear what BACC's decision would be, although the parties were only at the stage of exchanging views. Nevertheless the judge was not prepared to intervene in the action of the BACC. He dismissed the substantive basis of the application fairly rapidly, holding that decision makers must be able to change their minds on policy issues, and that in this case there had been no breach of legitimate expectation. He held also that there was no evidence that the BACC had acted unfairly.

It appears from these decisions that self-regulatory bodies, though liable to judicial review where meeting the *Datafin* criteria, are subject to less supervision than would be true of public authorities. The *ICSTIS* cases suggest that the courts will take a less interventionist approach to the interpretation of ICSTIS' rules. The *Swiftcall* case seems to suggest that a lower standard of legitimate expectations will be applied to self-regulatory bodies than would be applied to public authorities. For those who think judicial intervention in regulatory activity to be inherently undesirable, the greater use of self-regulation offers a possible way of limiting the scope of such intervention.

Contractual Disputes

The privatisation and liberalisation of the UK utilities sectors has substantially transformed the nature of legal relationships, such that many matters which were previously governed by bureaucratic or statutory principles are now governed by contracts. This is true not only of relations between utilities suppliers and their customers (with some variation from sector to sector), but also of relations between owners of network facilities and service providers seeking to use those facilities. These latter wholesale relationships were, during the period of nationalised ownership, substantially intra-organisational, and thus bureaucratically governed. Liberalisation has made these new wholesale contracts extremely important, both to dominant incumbents seeking to maintain market position and new entrants seeking to develop market share. The presence of contracts does not of itself suggest that juridification is likely to occur. Socio-legal research on long-term commercial contracts has demonstrated that these relationships subsist without frequent recourse to lawyers or legal rules.[74] But in the utilities sectors it appears that one of the effects of placing so much emphasis on the use of contracts to achieve objectives previously pursued through administrative instruments is to create the risk that the actors will begin to see these relationships in juridical terms, and, to some degree, litigate to determine their rights and obligations.

Where contractual relations are being tested in the courts against the background of the legal framework of the Telecommunications Act 1984 and associated licences, a hybrid contractual form is emerging which has some characteristics of private law and some characteristics of public law. The relations which give rise to litigation arise partly from commercial negotiation and partly from the broader framework of activity within the regulated sector. The effect is for contractual principles to be mediated by the legal principles of the telecommunications sector, but also for the legal principles of the telecommunications sector to be shaped in unexpected ways by the values of contractual litigation.

Contractual disputes are classically regarded as private matters between the two parties. There is a tendency for the courts to see the legal instrument of contract being used "and assume that it is being used in the way the law recognises: as an instrument of exchange between broadly equal parties. In fact, society uses the legal instrument in a multitude of different ways".[75] The consequence of this

---

[74] S. Macaulay, "Non-Contractual Relations in Business" (1963) 28 *American Sociological Review* 55; H. Beale and T. Dugdale," Contracts Between Businessmen: Planning and the Use of Contractual Remedies" (1975) 2 *British Journal of Law and Society* 45; M. Hviid, "Relational Contracts and Repeated Games" in D. Campbell and P. Vincent-Jones (eds.) *Contract and Economic Organisation* (Dartmouth, Aldershot, 1995).

[75] J. Black, "Constitutionalising Self-Regulation" (1996) 59 *Modern Law Review* 24–55 at 42.

is that when contractual disputes are litigated the courts are unable to adapt their approach to the use of contract as a regulatory instrument, or in a regulated sphere, and only look at the respective rights and duties of the two parties, and not at the interests or views of third parties.[76] However, the emergent juridical conception of contractual relations in the telecommunications sector does not seem entirely to fit this classical conception. On the one hand commercial contracts between telecommunications firms have the potential to be shaped by the duties owed by Public Telecommunications Operators (PTOs) under their licences from the Secretary of State, duties traditionally conceived of as being of a public law character, rather than giving rise to private rights. On the other hand there is potential to treat a dispute that is fundamentally about the regulatory regime, that is the exercise of public duties, through the lens of contract law.

Wholesale Contracts

The main experience of wholesale contractual litigation in the telecommunications sector post-privatisation has concerned, first, the terms of interconnection between BT and Mercury Communications Limited (MCL) and, secondly, the rights of the dominant incumbent, British Telecom, to cut off the services provided by it to companies using BT's network to provide premium rate services (PRS) or other types of service to their customers. Both forms of dispute have effectively been litigated as if they were contractual disputes.

One of the most important cases taken in the telecommunications sector is the action by MCL challenging the basis on which BT charged it for interconnection. This issue is absolutely central to the regulation of the liberalizing market, and has been subject to sustained regulatory activity over the past few years. The action was framed as a commercial law case concerning contractual interpretation, though it might equally well have been framed as a judicial review action challenging the interpretation by the regulator of BT's licence obligations in relation to interconnection. In *Mercury Communications Limited* v. *Director General of Telecommunications*,[77] MCL was seeking to challenge Oftel's interpretation of BT's licence in relation to interconnection charges. At issue in the case was the interpretation of Condition 13 of BT's licence which required it to permit interconnection to its network through contract with other licensed

[76] Though the courts are able to look at some issues of public policy in contractual litigation, e.g. relating to illegality and restraint of trade. Legislation such as the Unfair Contract Terms Act 1977 has imported new regulatory principles into contractual litigation.

[77] [1996] 1 All ER 575. The analysis of the case which follows is substantially based on my note: "The Life (and Death?) of *O'Reilly*" (1995) 6 *Utilities Law Review* 20–1. See also A. McHarg, "Regulation as a Private Law Function" [1995] *Public Law* 539–51; P. Craig, "Proceeding Outside Order 53: A Modified Test?" (1996) 112 *Law Quarterly Review* 531–5. Nothwithstanding the importance of this House of Lords decision for public law generally it took nearly a year to reach the law reports.

operators. In the event that BT and an interconnecting operator failed to agree a contract for interconnection the Director General of Telecommunications was empowered to determine the terms of interconnection.[78] In the event that this licence condition was invoked the Director General was required to ensure, *inter alia*, that the interconnecting operator paid for "the cost of anything done pursuant to or in connection with the agreement including fully allocated costs attributable to the services to be provided and taking into account relevant overheads and a reasonable rate of return on attributable assets". Oftel and BT both interpreted this requirement to refer to charging of costs on the basis of the actual use of the network, whereas MCL sought an interpretation on the basis of the total capacity of line used by MCL. To allow capacity charging at this wholesale stage, MCL argued, would give it greater flexibility to establish pricing to its customers which would distinguish it from BT in the market.

At the time at which MCL's case was brought there was in fact an interconnection agreement in place between it and BT. The DGT had issued a determination in December 1993 which, *inter alia*, replicated a clause from the 1985 interconnection agreement which provided that either party might at any time seek a review of the contract with the other party, and where agreement could not be reached a determination could be sought from the DGT, on the same terms as provided for in Condition 13 of BT's licence. The declaration sought by MCL related to the interpretation of the basis for charging which was in the current interconnection agreement and which the DGT *would* make if called upon so to do under clause 29 of the interconnection agreement (which at that time had not actually been incorporated into the interconnection agreement).

Both Oftel and BT sought to have the proceedings brought by MCL struck out. They complained that the way in which the proceedings were brought allowed MCL to avoid the procedural protections given to public authorities by the procedure for judicial review, which requires applicants to seek leave from the Court, and to do so promptly (and in any event within three months). The House of Lords refused to strike out the proceedings.[79] This case marked a significant new point in the trend towards the relaxation of the general principle laid down in *O'Reilly* v. *Mackman*[80] that public law rights may only be pursued through actions for judicial review.[81] By construing the *Mercury* case as involving private law rights, the decision may substantially have undermined the public/private distinction argued for in that case, with the adverse practical consequences which may follow relating to the certainty of regulatory decisions.

[78] Licence Issued to British Telecommunications plc (1984, as amended), Condition 13.5.
[79] But Lord Slynn did say (at 582): "In dealing with the originating summons the trial judge can have regard to, even if he is not strictly bound by, the procedural protection which would be available to a public authority under the provisions of Order 53." For the making of orders by the Director General of Telecommunications, s. 18(3) of the Telecommunications Act 1984 creates an even shorter period, of six weeks, outside which an order cannot be challenged.
[80] [1982] 3 All ER 1124.
[81] See *Roy* v. *Kensington and Chelsea Family Practitioner Committee* [1992] 1 AC 624; Craig, n. 77 above, 531–5.

The primary basis of the action by BT and Oftel to have the action struck out was that the relationships involved between BT, MCL and the DGT were entirely governed by public law, and the action could only properly be brought by way of judicial review (following *O'Reilly* v. *Mackman*[82]). Such a contention had been rejected at first instance and in the Court of Appeal. In the House of Lords Lord Slynn noted the possibility of an exception to the general principle of *O'Reilly* in Lord Diplock's speech, "particularly where the invalidity of the decision arises as a collateral issue in a claim for infringement of a right of the plaintiff arising under private law, or where none of the parties objects to the adoption of the procedure by writ or originating summons".[83] Lord Slynn himself said, "[i]t is of particular importance, as I see it, to retain some flexibility as the precise limits of what is called 'public law' and what is called 'private law' are by no means worked out".[84] Applying this analysis to the case before the House Lord Slynn said that, although it was clear that the DGT was acting under statutory powers, that "does not mean that what the Director General does cannot lead to disputes which fall outside the realms of administrative law any more than a Government department cannot enter into a commercial contract or commit a tort actionable before the court under its ordinary procedures".[85] In this case the provision for determination by the DGT arose because of the *contract* between the parties, "the dispute in substance and in form is as to the effect of the terms of the contract even if it can also be expressed as a dispute as to the terms of the licence".[86] Furthermore, in Lord Slynn's view an action in the Commercial Court might be better suited to resolve an issue of this sort.

MCL's appeal against the striking out action was allowed, and this permitted MCL to proceed with the action and had the potential to unravel many months of consultation over the interconnection regime between the industry and Oftel. Mercury chose not to proceed with the action, as regulatory developments effectively overtook the dispute. In any case the DGT had said publicly that if MCL had succeeded in the action, and this had led to unsatisfactory developments, then he would propose licence modifications to render the regime workable

---

[82] [1983] 2 AC 237. In recommending the reforms to the procedure for judicial review, which occurred in 1977, the Law Commission had anticipated that actions for declarations could still be brought by ordinary action, as well as by the new Ord. 53 procedure. However the courts very rapidly sought to close off the option of an ordinary action, taking the view that the new Ord. 53 procedure lacked the disadvantages of its predecessor and that public authorities ought to be protected by leave requirements and time limits from the uncertainties associated with an ordinary action. See H.W.R. Wade and C.F. Forsyth *Administrative Law* (7th edn., Clarendon Press, 1994), at 680–695.

[83] At 285.

[84] At 581.

[85] The distinction drawn here between administrative law on the one hand and liability of public authorities in contract and tort on the other suggests that his Lordship was not prepared to view contractual and tortious liability of public authorities as administrative law. Such a distinction is not supported by, *inter alia*, Wade and Forsyth, n. 82 above, ch. 20.

[86] At 582.

once more.[87] Perhaps the more important aspect of the House's decision was the encouragement which it gives to regulated firms to challenge the decisions of regulators by way of litigation. At a practical level, to permit the Commercial Court to resolve a dispute of this type may be quite helpful. However, taking this course required the House of Lords to hold that the dispute to be essentially one of private law, and thus deny the patent public law background to the contract and determination, both of which owed their existence to the duties contained in regulatory legislation and licences.[88] Thus a radical public/private law divide effectively prevents the courts from fully recognising the hybrid nature of many contracts, not just in the utilities sectors, but in other areas such as public procurement.[89]

The second set of cases which are broadly wholesale in character is concerned with the rights of BT to cut off those service providers which it supplies with network facilities. Though the litigation has been contractual, the issues fell to be determined against a background of regulatory principles. In these case there emerged a juridical conception of the relationship between BT and the chatline firms which, although akin to a regular commercial contractual relationship, may also be subject to the specific regulatory requirements of the telecommunications sector and the more general requirements of contract law and competition law. It is of particular interest that firms have sought to rely on the duties contained in BT's licence, which, though enforceable by the DGT (via cumbersome enforcement processes noted above), were not originally conceived of in terms whereby they gave enforceable rights to customers.[90] In these cases the potential to draw public law duties into commercial contractual relationships, and thus the hybrid character of the relationships, was recognised.

The construction of a juridical conception of the relationship between BT and its commercial, service-providing customers was taken furthest in an interlocutory hearing. In *Timeload Ltd* v. *British Telecommunications Plc*[91] the Court of Appeal was asked to consider the relationship between statutory regulation and

---

[87] Director General of Telecommunications, Introductory Speech to ICAS Workshop, 28 Mar. 1994.

[88] The decision may have a wider application to the public/private divide in heralding "a new and yet more liberal test for deciding when an applicant can pursue a claim by way ordinary action than previously existed": Craig, n. 77 above, at 531.

[89] The term "hybrid" has been used to describe arrangements which consist of a mixture of market and hierarchical ordering. For example, Hutter and Teubner use the concept to explore "just-in-time organisations, franchising systems, money transfer networks and other networks in such sectors as energy, transportation and telecommunication": M. Hutter and G. Teubner, "The Parasitic Role of Hybrids" (1993) 149 *Journal of Institutional and Theoretical Economics* 706– 15. Thus the concept precisely captures the notion of relationships in the utilities sectors which are partly based on contractual notions of exchange and partly on the basis of administrative law notions of hierarchical decision making. For the hybridising implications of privatisation for law generally see G. Teubner, "After Privatisation? Invoking Discourse Rights in Private Governance Regimes" [1998] *Current Legal Problems* (forthcoming)

[90] See *Megaphone International Ltd* v. *British Telecommunications plc*, *Independent*, 1 Mar. 1989.

[91] [1995] EMLR 459. The discussion of the case draws on my fuller note: "Regulated Contracts in the Telecommunications Sector" (1994) 5 *Utilities Law Review* 12–13.

BT's contract terms. The case was an appeal from a decision that one of BT's commercial customers should be granted an interlocutory injunction to prevent withdrawal from that customer of the use of a particular 0800 (freephone) telephone number. Because, once more, the proceedings were interlocutory, rather than the full hearing of the case, the law was not fully argued. The Court of Appeal suggested that the presence of a statutory scheme of regulation might result in the incorporation of licence obligations placed on a service provider into service contracts as implied terms.

The plaintiff had set up an information service called Free Pages, consisting of a service where customers called the freephone number when looking for a particular type of service serving a particular locality. The service was provided free to the customer, but the businesses listed paid to be included. The service competed directly with BT's own Talking Pages service, offered on a 0345 number and therefore charged at the local call rate. By means which are uncertain (either due to a mistake at BT or due to a breach of duty by an employee) the plaintiff managed to obtain from BT the use of the number 0800 192192, and had with BT a standard contract for its use, and was thus able to exploit the public's knowledge of the 192 BT Directory Enquiries number. The plaintiff had operated the service since June 1993 and spent large amounts of money advertising and promoting the Free Pages service. BT alleged that the plaintiff's marketing campaign sought to associate the service with BT, which amounted to passing off, and wrote to the plaintiff asking Free Pages to cease advertising and to cease using the 0800 192192 number. Subsequently BT wrote to Free Pages informing it that the use of the 0800 192192 number would be terminated in one month from the date of the letter. Timeload, the owner of Free Pages, sought an injunction to restrain termination of the service until the dispute was resolved through litigation.

The judge granted an interlocutory injunction, applying the principles in *American Cyanamid* v. *Ethicon*[92] to the effect that there was a serious issue to be tried in relation to the construction and effect of clause 18(1) of BT's standard terms, and because of the possible application of section 3 of the Unfair Contract Terms Act 1977. Clause 18(1) reads:

> "Termination of service by notice. At any time after service has been provided this contract or the provision of any service or facility under it can be ended.
>   (1) by one month's notice by us; or
>   (2) by seven days' notice by you."

At first instance the judge had held that Clause 18(1) should be read with Clause 6 of the contract which permitted interruption of service for operational reasons, but with an obligation to restore service as soon as reasonably practical. He suggested that the terms of the two clauses were inconsistent.

Without deciding determinatively on the correct mode of interpreting a contract in a regulatory setting, in the Court of Appeal Sir Thomas Bingham MR

---

[92] [1975] AC 396.

suggested that in dealing with contracts issued by a regulated utility company a classical approach to the interpretation of clause 18(1) might not be appropriate. The Court of Appeal accordingly had regard to the conditions of BT's licence, and in particular Condition 1(1) which requires BT to provide telecommunications services to all who request it. The Master of the Rolls said:

> "I can see strong grounds for the view that in the circumstances of this contract BT should not be permitted to exercise a potentially drastic power of termination without demonstrable reason or cause for doing so."[93]

Furthermore he said that he shared the judge's view that Clauses 6 and 18(1) might be regarded as inconsistent and that the strict interpretation of Clause 18(1) suggested by BT seemed to fly in the face of what the plaintiff intended, the plaintiff being unlikely to have invested large sums in advertising a service if it believed that BT could suspend it at a month's notice without giving good reasons.

The Master of the Rolls indicated that he thought it unclear whether section 3(2) of the Unfair Contract Terms Act 1977 (UCTA) (noted above) should apply to a clause of a contract defining the service to be performed, rather than a right to deliver something less than provided for in the contract. But he added that:

> "It seems to me at least arguable that the common law could, if the letter of the statute does not apply, treat the clear intention of the legislature expressed in the statute as a platform for invalidating or restricting the operation of an oppressive clause in a situation of the present, very special, kind."[94]

A further issue arose in relation to the question whether the Director General of Telecommunications could be taken to have approved the contractual provision, thereby exempting it from the scope of UCTA, by virtue of section 29(2) of that Act. The Master of the Rolls said he doubted whether the fact the DGT had seen a provision could lead to the conclusion that he had approved it, especially as the DGT had no statutory jurisdiction or function in relation to approval of terms and conditions of such contracts. The Master of the Rolls concluded that there was a serious issue to be tried, and Hoffman and Henry LJJ concurred in this view. If, as the Court of Appeal suggested, the licence conditions take effect as generating implied terms which favour customers then BT's capacity to impose harsh terms on customers would be much reduced. Furthermore the Court of Appeal decision suggested that the courts will be extremely hostile to harsh terms in the contracts issued by regulated utility companies, and, if unable to use the Unfair Contract Terms Act 1977 to regulate such terms, they may be willing to extend common law regulation of harsh terms in the special conditions of contracts set against a background of statutory regulation.[95]

---

[93] At 467.

[94] At 468.

[95] In similar circumstances, but in relation to another company, BT itself issued legal proceedings against one of its own customers to restrain the customer from passing itself off as being part of BT directly and through its marketing strategy: *British Telecommunications plc* v. *Freephone Directory* (Ch.D, 1992), Lexis Transcript.

Nothwithstanding the fact of continued legal tussles, ultimately settled in 1996, the Freepages service, now trading as Scoot (which had at one time been owned by Timeload Communications), was by 1997 capitalised at £200 million on the basis of its continued usage of the very valuable 0800 192192 number.[96] The dicta of the Master of the Rolls effectively recognise the value in the "new property" in telephone numbers.

The approach of the Court of Appeal in *Timeload Communications* is reflected in the more recent Court of Appeal decision in an interlocutory action, *Zockoll Group Ltd* v. *Mercury Communications Ltd.*[97] Zockoll sought to exploit the possible development of alphanumeric telephone numbers, widely used in the United States, which allow customers to dial freephone numbers by remembering the letters corresponding to the numbers on the keypad. Anticipating the commercial possibilities arising out of the possible development of alphanumeric keypads in the UK, Zockoll contracted with Mercury Communications Limited (MCL) to use thousands of freephone numbers, most of which were not particularly memorable as numbers, but would be of great value should the alphanumeric keypad take off, because the letters were memorable. These numbers included 0500–PLUMBER and 0500–FLIGHTS. Zockoll was intending to franchise the use of these numbers at such time as they acquired value. MCL notified Zockoll that it intended to withdraw the 0500–FLIGHTS number from it, as it had another customer who would make more immediate use of it, and, following Zockoll's failure to secure an interlocutory injunction in the Chancery Division, did withdraw and reallocate the number. In the Court of Appeal Zockoll sought to have the number restored to it by grant of a mandatory injunction, pending a full hearing of its argument that any provision in the contract with MCL which permitted the withdrawal of the number was void by virtue of section 3 of the Unfair Contract Terms Act 1977 (noted above).

Clause 8.1 of the contract between MCL and Zockoll purported to permit MCL "to withdraw or change any telephone number used by the Customer on giving the Customer reasonable notice in writing" and provided that "[t]he Customer accepts that it shall acquire no rights whatsoever in any telephone number allocated by Mercury". Zockoll attempted to rely on the decision in the *Timeload* case in support of its argument for an injunction. At first instance the Vice-Chancellor had distinguished this case on the basis that the *Timeload* contract only involved one number, so "withdrawal of the number necessarily involved termination of the contract". In *Zockoll* the contractual right exercised by MCL was the withdrawal of one of 53 numbers which were the subject matter of the contract. He thought there was "no reasonably arguable basis for alleging that in this case there has been a breach of contract by Mercury in withdrawing the 0500 354448 number". Zockoll's appeal was made on the basis that

---

[96] N. Gilbert "The Great Telephone Fiasco", *Independent on Sunday*, 1 June 1997.

[97] CA, 27 Aug. 1997, unreported, Lexis transcript. It should be noted that the heading for this case on the Lexis database is incorrectly listed as "Zockoil" rather than the correct "Zockoll".

the Vice Chancellor had been wrong, as MCL knew the purposes for which the contract was made, and the withdrawal of the number would defeat that purpose. MCL responded by arguing, first, that the requirement of "reasonable notice" for the withdrawal of a number rendered the clause itself reasonable, as, depending on the circumstances, such reasonable notice might extend to a period as long as ten years and, second, that the withdrawal of one of 53 numbers did not render the contractual performance "substantially different" from what was reasonable expected, as required by section 3(2) of the Unfair Contract Terms Act 1977.

Phillips LJ rejected MCL's contention that the withdrawal of one number before it could reasonably have been expected to become profitable for Zockoll could not render the performance of the contract "substantially different", and said that Sir Thomas Bingham MR's arguments about "the potential operation of the common law" could not be ignored. Furthermore he thought it untenable for MCL to claim that the requirement of reasonable notice for the withdrawal of a number rendered Clause 8(1) of the contract reasonable when it had in fact only given 14 days' notice, in circumstances that would not allow Zockoll the anticipated benefit of the contract in respect of that number. Thus he held that Zockoll had an arguable case. Nevertheless, there being "substantial issues both of fact and law" to be resolved, a mandatory interlocutory injunction was not appropriate. On the facts Zockoll's position would not be improved by the grant of such a mandatory injunction, nor would justice be better served. From a commercial perspective Zockoll needed a speedy determination of the substantive issue, and Phillips LJ indicated that he was prepared to grant an order that the trial be expedited.

The wholesale contracts cases reveal the difficulties which the courts have in dealing with commercial relationships through the lens of contract law. In *Mercury* the logic of treating a regulatory relationship as a public law matter was denied. Conversely in the *Timeload* and *Zockoll* cases it was suggested that the interpretation of commercial agreements should not be blind to the regulatory framework within which they are made. Similar signs that the courts have difficulty in processing contractual relationships which have hybrid public and private law characteristics can be detected in the following discussion of retail relationships.

Retail Contracts

Disputes between customers in the retail market and their service providers do not appear ever to have been litigated in the telecommunications sector. The lack of litigation may in part be explained by doubts whether retail telecommunications services are supplied as a matter of statute or contract. It has recently been held that the pre-privatisation position has not been affected by the Electricity Act 1989, and that when electricity is supplied to retail customers under the statutory duty of the undertaker no contract exists.[98] The position of other utility sectors was not addressed by the Court. But there is a general assumption that, in relation to telecommunications, retail customers do have contracts with their service providers and BT recognises this.[99] Furthermore EC legislation now requires Member States to legislate to make it clear that customers have contracts with telecommunications providers.[100] However some of the factors in the *Dixon* case (a duty to supply, absence of bargaining between the parties) seem to apply at least to arrangements between BT and residential customers.

A second explanation for the absence of litigation in the telecommunications sector is that the regulator remains very active in overseeing conditions for customers in the market generally. Many matters about which customers might complain are effectively channelled through the regulator. Additionally, in the case of consumer contracts, the Office of Fair Trading has recently taken on new powers to regulate contract terms generally, and has been extremely active in seeking the rewriting of contracts in plain English and so as to avoid the use of unfair terms.[101] The absence of sectoral regulators and extensive regulatory obligations in most of the privatised New Zealand utilities sectors has led to much greater emphasis being placed on the potential of the common law to secure satisfactory service for customers.[102] In the UK litigation is only likely to spill out when the regulator declines to help or fails to provide the assistance sought.

One case in the electricity sector resulted in the apparent failure of the Director General of Electricity Supply to resolve the dispute. In *Gwenter* v. *Eastern Electricity*[103] the plaintiff was essentially asserting the right to service, under conditions where the electricity supplier alleged that the meter had been tampered with and had cut the customer off. The interlocutory action was for an order restoring supply pending the full trial. The judge made such an order, relying on section 16 of the Electricity Act 1989, which requires a statutory supplier to give supply, subject to exceptions which include the circumstances where the offence of tampering with a meter has been committed and the matter not remedied. The judge held that there was sufficient evidence for the plaintiff to have an arguable case that no offence had been committed and the balance of convenience lay very much in favour of requiring reconnection. She held that the delay by the plaintiff in making the application should not disqualify her,

---

[98] *Norweb* v. *Dixon* [1995] 3 All ER 952.

[99] I. Harden, *The Contracting State* (Open University Press, Milton Keynes, 1992), at 38–41.

[100] EC Directive 95/62/EC on application of ONP to Voice Telephony [1995] OJ L321/6, Art. 7.

[101] Unfair Terms in Consumer Contracts Regulations 1994, SI No 3159. See, e.g. the report from the Unfair Contract Terms Unit of the Office of Fair Trading on the extensive re-drafting which it required of the mobile phone contracts of Vodacall Limited, a subsidiary of Vodafone Group plc: Office of Fair Trading (1997) 3 *Unfair Contract Terms Bulletin* 45–50. This redrafting substantially altered the content of the contracts in favour of consumers.

[102] M. Taggart, "Public Utilities and Public Law" in P. Joseph (ed.), *Essays on the Constitution* (Brookers, Wellington, 1995).

[103] CA, 7 Feb. 1995, Lexis transcript.

specifically because during this time she had been attempting to find a resolution through the Office of Electricity Regulation (Offer). The Court of Appeal upheld this decision, Waite LJ holding that there was "an overwhelming case for interim restoration". In such cases the courts seem keen to adopt a "consumer-welfarist" approach, quite different from that adopted in relation to the PRS cases.

The somewhat arbitrary nature of the public/private divide in the utilities sectors is demonstrated by the fact that in subsequent litigation in a similar dispute the Northern Ireland High Court held that the monopoly private electricity supplier, Northern Ireland Electricity (NIE), was subject to judicial review.[104] Kerr J said in *Sherlock and Morris*[105] that he considered "the discharge of functions by NIE under the [Electricity (Northern Ireland) Order 1992 (SI 1992/231)] falls clearly within the field of public law". It was the public nature of the function, rather than the nature of the body supplying the service, which determined its amenability to judicial review. NIE was carrying out the same functions as a private company as it had as a public corporation prior to privatisation. A nationalised industry was clearly amenable to judicial review.[106] Furthermore he thought it would be anomalous to treat privatised utility companies as state authorities for purposes of European Community law,[107] but as wholly private entities for the purposes of judicial review. This aspect of the decision has been criticised on the basis that it is difficult to draw the line between privatised utility companies operating in competitive markets, to which it may not be appropriate to apply judicial review, and those retaining monopolies, which, on Kerr J's view are so amenable. Furthermore to treat companies in different ways for different purposes is defensible and need not be regarded as anomalous, where the purposes of treating privatised bodies as state bodies in Community law is to prevent governments evading responsibilities for failing to implement directives simply by changing the status of public bodies.[108] Perhaps the strongest criticism is to point to the anomaly of the Government attempting to free utility providers from the restrictions applying to public bodies while establishing "comprehensive regulatory regimes", only to have the courts reapply one of these restrictions, the availability of judicial review.[109]

In practice, Kerr LJ seemed to recognise the importance of channelling the dispute through the regulatory regime in preference to judicial review. Though

---

[104] A possibility argued for by Paul Craig in *Administrative Law* (3rd edn., Sweet and Maxwell, London, 1994), at 240. See also *Davies* v. *North West Water Ltd.* (CA, 17 Oct 1996), Lexis Transcript.

[105] QBD(NI), 29 Nov. 1996, noted by A. McHarg, (1997) 8 *Utilities Law Review* 123–5, 137.

[106] *Mercury Energy Ltd* v. *Electricity Corporation* [1994] 1 WLR 521 (PC). See also *Foster* v. *British Gas* [1990] ECR I–3313 (ECJ).

[107] Here he referred to the decision of Blackburne J to the effect that the privatised South West Water Services was to be regarded as a state authority for the purposes of the application of the EC Collective Redundancies Directive: *Griffin* v *South West Water Services Ltd* [1995] IRLR 15.

[108] A.McHarg, n. 105 above, 125, 137.

[109] *Ibid.*, 137.

NIE had failed to consider the representations of the applicants as to why their electricity supply should not be restored, the discretion of the court was exercised so as not to grant the applications. Effectively he was giving approval to the channelling of the applicants' dispute through the more appropriate mechanisms of (i) settlement of the matter between NIE and the applicants (ii) determinations on the individual disputes by the Director General and (iii) regulatory encouragement to changes in the policy for dealing with allegations of theft by NIE. NIE had offered on the hearing of the application of interim relief to install prepaid meters to both applicants' homes. Furthermore both applicants had applied to the regulator for review of the withdrawal of electricity supply, and a determination had been issued in one case. Finally a policy for dealing with allegations of theft of electricity between the regulator and NIE was being developed, and a statement issued by NIE substantially addressed the issue. Consequently Kerr J elected to refuse the applications for judicial review as an exercise of the Court's discretion.

FUTURE LITIGATION

Further litigation in the UK utilities sectors is likely in the future, with pressures for such change coming from a number of sources. First, the new Labour government's review of the utilities sectors is likely to lead to some measure of legislative reform, and ministers have already demonstrated a greater inclination to intervene in the utilities sectors than was evident with the previous government.[110] Secondly, EC utilities regulation, based in Treaty principles directed towards the creation of a single market, is more law-based in character than the traditional discretionary UK regimes.[111] Lawyers are already heavily involved both in lobbying on new legislation and working through the requirements of existing regulatory requirements.[112] British Telecom has used litigation aggressively as a means of enforcing the application of EC rules in other Member States so that it may secure access to their markets.[113] Thirdly, with liberalisation of the utilities sectors a comparatively late aspect of institutional reform, competition law is likely to take on a greater and central importance. As this occurs the juridical potential of the competition law regimes of both the UK

[110] McHarg notes, e.g., that in his first 6 months the new energy minister had "twice invoked a power to require reports on specific issues from the Director General of Electricity Supply (DGES) [footnote omitted], a provision used only once during the Conservative Party's whole term of office": A. McHarg, "Government Policy Towards the Electricty Industry under Labour" (1997) 8 *Utilities Law Review* 203–6, at 204.

[111] T. Prosser, *Law and the Regulators* (Oxford University Press, Oxford, 1997), 56.

[112] E. Tucker, "Lessons in Dealing with Brussels", *Financial Times,* 22 Aug. 1997, at 6.

[113] A. Cane, "BT Issues Legal Deadline for Telekom to Provide Figures", *Financial Times,* 15 Dec. 1997, at 18. The article notes continuing action against the German dominant operator, Deutsche Telekom, and legal action taken against Telecom Italia, France Telecom, Belgacom (Belgium) and KPN (Netherlands).

and the EC is likely to be tested.[114] Pressures for juridification may occur "in less obvious ways, for example freedom of information legislation and the incorporation of the European Convention on Human Rights into UK domestic law".[115]

There seem to be a number of different routes by which a process of juridification of competition policy in relation to the utilities sectors may occur as processes of liberalisation are worked out. The most obvious of these is via the activities of the MMC in reviewing licence modifications (noted above in the *Scottish Power* case). Other routes include the application of general competition law principles (provided for in the utilities statutes) and application of mergers principles. UK law is highly discretionary in this area and has not yet been highly juridified. The application of EC competition law in the UK is likely to be more juridical in form, as there is a considerable amount of jurisprudence and a well-developed practitioner community. This development is anticipated by the move of the Director General of Telecommunications to establish himself as a competition authority applying EC norms with an expert advisory committee and a new procedure for publishing details of investigations and precedents.[116] The Competition Bill, passing through Parliament at the time of writing, will significantly enhance the powers of all the utilities regulators to apply competition rules based on EC norms.[117] If the application of such competition principles becomes central to the work of the UK regulators we may expect that competition law will provide a major source of juridical activity in the utilities sectors, as it has done in New Zealand, which avoided completely an intermediate regulatory stage between public ownership and the application of general competition law in the utilities sectors.[118]

---

[114] One commentator has remarked that it is surprising that there has to date been little evidence of challenges to competition policy decisions and procedures generally in the courts, given that the firms or sectors reviewed do not have a continuing client relationship with the competition authorities, and consequently have little to lose by way of good relations in testing the boundaries and procedure of the competition jurisdiction: Craig, n. 104 above, at 219.

[115] C. Graham, "Judicial Review and the Regulators" (1997) 8 *Utilities Law Review* 107–8, at 108. This will depend in part on how the utilities sectors are treated by the legislation. The government has expressed a preference for treating utilities firms as part of the public sector for the purposes of freedom of information. In any case the application of freedom of information and human rights legislation to the regulatory offices is likely to have far-reaching consequences for their relations with firms they regulate and third parties.

[116] Oftel, *Procedural Notes of the Advisory Body on Fair Trading in Telecommunications* (Office of Telecommunications, London, 1997); Oftel, *Fair Trading Condition—Enforcement Procedure* (Office of Telecommunications, London, 1997).

[117] Oftel, *Dealing with Anti-Competitive Behaviour in Telecoms* (Office of Telecommunications, London, 1997), at para. 3.11.

[118] H. Janisch, "From Monopoly Towards Competition In Telecommunications: What Role for Competition Law" (1994) 23 *Canadian Business Law Journal* 239–78. See also the decision of the PC in *Clear Communications* v. *New Zealand Telecommunications Ltd* [1995] 1 NZLR 385, which provides a fairly clear warning about the risks of leaving the determination of rules for interconnection of telecommunications firms to the market subject only to the application of general competition rules prohibiting anti-competitive conduct.

In this chapter we have explored one set of indicators that the utilities sectors are becoming juridified—the pattern of litigation. This pattern reveals that certain issues and relationships have been more prone to litigation than others, and that there is evidence of increasing frequency. In this section we look at possible explanations for the increasing frequency in litigation and broader processes of juridification.

The simplest explanation for juridification in the utilities sectors is to link it to privatisation. However, privatisation in itself did not provide the conditions under which lawyers and legal values would be drawn into day-to-day relations. Though lawyers were heavily involved in the privatisation process, once this had occurred neither regulators nor regulated firms showed early inclinations to redefine relations in juridical terms. Though privatisation may have increased the expectation that utilities providers be held legally accountable, as are other private companies, for the quality of what they provide to wholesale and retail customers, this expectation was at least balanced by the duty and capacity of the new regulatory offices to resolve disputes and encourage the development of principles which would avoid further disputes. Thus, while the number of complaints against utilities companies has risen markedly since privatisation, these rarely spill over into litigation against the company involved. *Sherlock and Morris*[119] provides a rare example.

The separation of the regulatory functions in the utilities sectors from the service provision functions may also be thought to have created the conditions for juridification, in the sense that regulators and service providers may be expected to have divergent interests and a considerable stake in using law, among other instruments, to advance those interests. In fact the combination of the new legislative structures for regulation with market structures which substantially retained existing monopoly supply arrangements encouraged the regulators and service providers to negotiate their new relationships in a manner which was substantially consensual, and within which it was rare to resort to the legal framework or to lawyers to resolve disputes. The separation of functions between regulators and service providers has been important because it has required a fresh attempt to describe those relationships in legislation and other instruments such as licences. The new relationships and rules governing them have been a necessary prerequisite to juridification in the utilities sectors, as in other areas of public sector reform.[120] However these changes do not, in themselves, explain why the juridical potential of the new arrangements is being taken up. Where regulatory separation is seen as a factor in juridification is in a

---

[119] N. 105 above.

[120] See J. Broadbent and R. Laughlin, "Contracts, Competition and Accounting in Recent Legal Enactments for the Health and Education Sectors in the UK: An Example of Juridification at Work?" in S. Deakin and J. Michie (eds.)*Contracts, Co-Operation, and Competition* (Oxford University Press, Oxford, 1997).

quite distinct and small number of cases resulting from the perceived failure of a regulator to secure for customers a particular outcome in terms of the conditions of service provision (*Gwenter*,[121] *Smith*,[122] *Redrow Homes*,[123] *Maystart*[124]). This litigation by "outsiders" to the system does not necessarily reflect the ways of thinking of "insiders": regulators and licensees. Sporadic litigation by outsiders could leave day-to-day operation of the regime in a substantially non-juridified state.

The key change in the arrangements governing the utilities sectors which has led to a process of juridification is the development of policies of liberalisation. These policies have led to the potential or actual multiplication of service providers, often with complex new contractual arrangements between themselves or with the regulatory offices or both. Under conditions of liberalisation the incentive to maintain consensual relations between regulator and licensees is diminished, as the health of the sector is no longer so closely identified with the well-being of the dominant incumbent. To understand fully the way in which juridification is occurring we need to examine how these relationships are conducted on a day-to-day basis, to ask to what extent the interpretation of legal rules now guides behaviour which was previously governed by administrative or commercial values. Litigation provides only one indicator that a juridification process may be occurring because of liberalisation.

The key instances of litigation have occurred under circumstances where restrictions which had hitherto applied have been lifted or have been in the process of being lifted. Thus we have seen dominant incumbent firms seeking to improve the regulatory conditions as they face competition (the *BT*[125] and *Scottish Power*[126] cases), a dominant incumbent challenging the UK implementation of EC liberalisation measures (in relation to procurement and leased lines[127]), new entrants seeking to improve the conditions of entry (the *Mercury* case[128]), new entrants seeking to establish ground rules for the governance of valuable new commodities such as the right to use a particular telephone number (*Timeload*[129] and *Zockoll*[130]), and a pressure group challenging the relaxation of minimum service levels (*Save our Railways*[131]). The hypothesis that liberalisation provides the main pressure for juridification is supported by the observation that the greatest incidence of litigation has been in the telecommu-

---

[121] n. 103 above.
[122] n. 36 above.
[123] n. 41 above.
[124] n. 38 above.
[125] n. 49 above.
[126] *ibid.*
[127] nn. 54 and 55 above.
[128] n. 77 above.
[129] n. 91 above.
[130] n. 97 above.
[131] n. 64 above.

nications sector, where liberalisation is most advanced, and that there has been virtually no litigation in water, the least liberalised sector.[132]

Though liberalisation has been the main factor leading to juridification, other factors have, independently, made litigation a more attractive mechanism for resolving public law disputes. The more expansive attitude taken to judicial review generally by the Divisional Court since the 1960s has entered the consciousness of those whose activities are connected with public administration of one form or another.[133] This may make it more likely that those affected by administrative decisions conceive of those decisions in juridical terms instead of or as well as in administrative terms.

THE IMPACT OF JURIDIFICATION

The effects of drawing the legal framework into the regulatory relations within the utilities sectors can be examined in a number of different ways. Orthodox analyses point both to the advantages for decision-making of holding regulators to account in terms of the grounds of judicial review—illegality, unfairness, irrationality—and the risks associated with slowing decision making down,[134] interfering with expert decisions or the wishes of democratically elected government.[135] Such analyses have long recognised that any assessment of the precise impact of judicial intervention is problematic, particularly where looking for ripple effects within public administration generally from the comparatively small number of decisions which are judicially reviewed.[136] Any simple assumption that administrators, whether in regulatory offices or elsewhere, attempt to act legally, rationally and fairly and that such behaviour is the outcome of potential or actual judicial control is clearly questionable.

Part of the difficulty for the courts lies in the almost exclusive focus on public power and on the moments at which particular administrative decisions are

---

[132] But see *Davies* v. *North West Water Ltd.* (n. 104 above) and *R.* v. *Director General of Water Service, ex. p. Lancashire County Council, The Times,* 21 Feb. 1998.

[133] See G. Mezsaros, M. Sunkin and L. Bridges *Judicial Review In Perspective* (2nd edn., Cavendish Publishing, London, 1995).

[134] But it has been commented that judicial review actions and appeals can actually be disposed of remarkably quickly. See generally Loughlin, n. 2 above, at 401–2, and, in relation to the *TSW* case, n. 28 above, Prosser points out that the administrative process was not unduly delayed as the whole procedure from publication of the initial licence decision to the House of Lords handing down its decision in the judicial review action was less than 4 months: T. Prosser, "Regulation, Markets and Legitimacy" in D. Oliver and J. Jowell (eds.), *The Changing Constitution* (Oxford University Press, Oxford, 1994), 237–60, at 258.

[135] See, e.g., R. Baldwin and C. McCrudden (eds.), *Regulation and Public Law.* (Weidenfeld and Nicolson, London, 1987), at 59–61 ; A. Ogus, *Regulation: Legal Form and Economic Theory* (Oxford University Press, Oxford, 1994), at 115–17. A robust critique of the growth of judicial review is provided by R. Cranston, "Reviewing Judicial Review" in G. Richardson and H. Genn (eds.), *Administrative Law and Government Action* (Oxford University Press, Oxford, 1994), 45–80.

[136] G. Richardson, and M. Sunkin, "Judicial Review: Questions of Impact" [1996] *Public Law* 79–103.

made by regulatory agencies. But regulators do not possess a monopoly of power. Though independent, regulatory offices are constrained in their actions by powers retained by government ministers (both explicitly and implicitly), and held by licensees, both as part of the statutory framework and as a product of their virtual monopoly over commercial information needed by the regulator.[137] Thus, at a practical level the attentions of the legal system are not necessarily directed towards the actors who exercise the power. At a theoretical level the problem of the lack of capacity of regulatory law directly to control actions in the regulated sphere is as much a problem for regulators as it is for courts.[138]

Theoretical accounts question the capacity of the legal system to apply fully its values to other activities. The question of the relationship between law and other systems is one of the central themes of contemporary sociology of law. In some instances there is a reasonably good fit, for example between industrial organisation and exchange in the economic system, and company law and contracts respectively in the legal system.[139] The fit between the emerging law of public utilities and the provision of services is clearly not as strong. The question such an analysis raises for the relationship between the courts and utilities sectors is to what extent the involvement of legal values and courts can be supportive of activity in the utilities sectors, and under what conditions it might go beyond the capacities of the legal system. This problem of capacity applies equally to regulators as to courts. For both sets of state institutions, the capacity for direct control over the utilities sectors is limited. Indirect control may be possible to the extent that the signals sent out to utilities firms and others in the sector are suitable for recognition and adaptation to the new environment.

We can identify two sets of activities among utilities firms which might usefully be the subject matter of indirect intervention. The first is the drafting of contracts and the second is the drawing up and application of self-regulatory codes. A number of the regulators have been at their most effective when regulating indirectly, through encouraging firms to develop and publicise self-regulatory principles.[140] Such developments have allowed regulators to influence areas in which they have no formal statutory powers. Attention to the drafting and operation of contracts from the courts has done much to protect the investment of new firms seeking to offer innovative new services in the telecommunications sectors.

---

[137] Scott, Hall and Hood, n. 28 above.

[138] Teubner, n. 3 above, at 21.

[139] What is present here, in the language of systems theory, is a "structural coupling" between the economic and legal systems in the institutions of the company and the contract: Teubner, n. 3 above.

[140] Cf. *ibid.*, at 21. Some reservations have been expressed about the deployment of a model of "enforced self-regulation" in the UK utilities sectors. Prosser, notably, sees limits to the appropriate degree of delegation to firms "because of the existence of strong public interest elements in matters such as price control, and because of the existence of divergent interests on the part of different firms in relation to regulation for competition": T. Prosser *Law and the Regulators* (Oxford, Oxford University Press, 1997) 271.

Judicial control over the activities of regulators is likely to be most effective when it seeks to build upon existing features of regulatory regimes, promoting the use of existing extended procedures of consultation and public discussion of reasons for decisions and the exercise of dispute resolution functions.[141] Within such an approach "the official function of law, which is to decree changes in behavior recedes into the background, whereas its latent function, which is to regulate systems of negotiation becomes crucial".[142] Decisions exemplary of this approach include the judicial review applications of *Sherlock and Morris*,[143] which sought to channel the dispute into the most appropriate procedures, and the *BT* case,[144] in which the Divisional Court gave recognition to the organic development of the telecommunications regime through licence modification, and reinforced the general principles for such change which were implicitly being applied by the regulator. In each case the use of the court as a means to subvert the regulatory mechanisms provided in the legislation was effectively prevented.

Where the courts risk overstepping the capacities of the legal system is where they redefine regulatory activities in ways which are unfamiliar to those operating them, with the consequence that the courts apply unfamiliar or inappropriate procedures or values. The *Scottish Power* decision[145] provides an example of such difficulties. The court found it very difficult to determine whether to regard a licence modification as an instrument of general policy (which should properly be applied to all companies in similar positions) or an instrument of individuated decision-making (carrying with it protections of procedural, and perhaps substantive, fairness associated with such administrative decisions). The decision fully reflects such ambivalence, applying inappropriately rigorous standards of decision-making to the regulator over the particular event which was litigated, and permitting a licensee to subvert a statutory decision making procedure. This argument is not intended to provide a criticism of the judges, who we must recognise "are, to an extent, prisoners of the way the parties construct their arguments".[146] But it highlights the risks associated with inappropriate judicial control in upsetting the organic development of regulatory procedures.

Moreover, attempts by the court to impose an ideal-world decision-making model on a regulator do not necessarily mean that such a model is adopted. The first Director General of Telecommunications, Sir Bryan Carsberg, has admitted that the development of competition in the sector had been hampered by his refusal to provide reasons for his early decisions on interconnection. "As with all things, my inclination was to explain exactly what I had done and why I had

---

[141] T. Prosser, n. 111 above, 281–6. Prosser argues for a process of learning from US experience. By contrast my argument is for organic development of existing UK procedures.

[142] Teubner, n. 3 above, at 34.

[143] N. 105 above.

[144] N. 48 above.

[145] N .48 above.

[146] Graham, n. 50 above, 108.

done it."[147] But he had been advised that to give reasons would risk having them challenged in litigation, and that he should avoid this. Subsequently Oftel has developed a model of consultation and reason-giving which eschews fear of litigation, and which is widely recognised as a model, not just for other regulators, but for Whitehall more generally.[148] This did not happen directly through litigation or threat of litigation, but in spite of it.

CONCLUSIONS

This chapter has provided a discussion of one aspect of the process by which legal values are seeping into the provision and regulation of utilities services. A deeper investigation would encompass also a consideration of change in the day-to-day role of lawyers in bringing legal values to commercial and regulatory discussions within firms and regulatory offices. The activities of such legal actors are important in shaping organic changes in the way in which firms and regulators perceive their relationships, for example the increasing formality in enforcement relationships. The development of competition law principles in the utilities sectors is likely to increase the pressures for juridification associated with liberalisation. This is likely to occur as commercial decision-making is displaced to some degree by consideration of how to comply with competition rules, and administrative processes governing regulatory relations are increasingly shaped by the more formal and juridical processes of competition law.

Notwithstanding this limitation to the discussion, there is ample evidence of the greater incidence of litigation concerning regulatory relationships in the utilities sectors. I have offered the view that the main pressure encouraging greater use of litigation is the shift towards policies of liberalisation.

The central question raised by this chapter is what are the appropriate boundaries to the application of juridical values in the utilities sectors? The answers to this question lie in seeking to avoid having the legal system exceed its capacities to control activities outside the legal system, while, at the same time, seeking to exploit the capacity of the legal system to shape regulatory relations indirectly through fostering the values and practices which develop organically within the sectors themselves which most closely accord with legal values.[149] This may mean that different indirect interventions are appropriate in different sectors.

Just as regulation is most effective when responsive to organic developments in the regulated sector, so is legal intervention in regulation likely to work well

[147] Sir Bryan Carsberg,"Telecommunications Competition in the United Kingdom: A Regulatory Perspective" (1992) 37 *New York Law School Review* 285–99, 291.
[148] Details of this procedural model are set out in Oftel, *Improving Accountability: Oftel's Procedures and Processes* (Office of Telecommunications, London, 1997).
[149] See the discussion of the relationship between law and regulatory systems in W. Clune "Implementation as Autopoietic Interaction of Autopoietic Organisations" in G. Teubner and A. Febbrajo (eds.) *State, Law and Economy as Autopoietic Sytems* (1991/92 Yearbook in the Sociology of Law) (Giuffre, Varese, 1992), at 501–3.

when fostering such organic development.[150] For this reason the activities of lawyers in firms, regulatory offices and government departments may be as or more important for the development of legal values as the activities of the courts. With sensitivity it may be possible to avoid the twin problems that the legal system becomes too fragmented to maintain claims to universal legitimacy, on the one hand, and that it damages the regulated sectors through attempts to apply inappropriate universal norms of administrative, contract and competition law, on the other.

---

[150] See I. Ayres and J. Braithwaite, *Responsive Regulation—Transcending the Deregulation Debate* (Oxford University Press, Oxford, 1992).

3

Financial Services Regulation and Judicial Review: the fault lines

MARTYN HOPPER*

INTRODUCTION

On 20 May 1997 the Chancellor of the Exchequer announced the government's intention to embark on a fundamental and radical reform of the regulatory regime for financial services in the United Kingdom. The "two-tier" regime for the regulation of investment business in the UK, introduced by the Financial Services Act 1986 ("the 1986 Act") is to be abolished: from around Autumn 1999, the Financial Services Authority ("the FSA") (formerly known as the Securities and Investments Board ("the SIB"))[1] will be given direct statutory responsibility for the authorisation and regulation of all those conducting investment business in the UK, while the Self-Regulating Organisations ("SROs") currently recognised by the FSA under the 1986 Act will be "folded in" to the FSA. Prior to that, under the Bank of England Act 1998 the FSA has, from 1 June 1998, taken responsibility for the supervision of banks, listed money market institutions and related clearing houses, functions previously performed by the Bank of England. Under the later Financial Services Reform Bill, the FSA will also assume responsibility for the supervision of building societies (currently performed by the Building Societies Commission), friendly societies (currently the responsibility of the Friendly Societies Commission) and insurance companies (a regulatory function currently performed by HM Treasury).

This will result in a unified regulatory body exercising statutory powers and functions that will be responsible both to government and Parliament for the regulation of all investment business, deposit-taking business and insurance business conducted in the UK. In addition, it seems likely that the FSA will continue to perform a similar role in relation to the supervision of the financial markets (in the form of its supervision of investment exchanges and clearing houses)

* Enforcement and Legal Services Division, The Financial Services Authority. The views expressed in this paper are entirely personal and should not be attributed to the Authority. My thanks to Michael Blair QC, Loretta Minghella, Guy Sears, Jane Ridley and Shami Chakrabarti for their helpful comments on an earlier draft of this paper.

[1] The Securities and Investments Board changed its name to The Financial Services Authority on 28 Oct. 1997.

to that which the Authority currently performs under the 1986 Act. The new legislation, planned for introduction in the Parliamentary session commencing in
Autumn 1998, will therefore seek to create a regulatory authority exercising
statutory powers over a jurisdiction considerably wider than that of any comparable financial regulatory authority in the world.

To date, applications for judicial review of financial services regulators have
been relatively rare. In the ten years or so that have elapsed since the 1986 Act
came into force, the FSA, for example, has had to respond to only five such
applications. The reasons for this apparent reticence on the part of those
affected by the decisions of financial services regulators to call them to account
in the High Court would themselves provide an interesting subject for further
study. Possible explanations could include the quality of regulators' decision-
making processes, the fact that the legislation provides its own mechanisms for
adjudication of disputes and the supervision of regulators' activities, and the
possibility that the co-operation and participation of regulated firms in the regulatory process reduce the need to resort to the courts. It is also interesting to
speculate on whether the government's proposed reforms will lead to a increase
in the incidence of judicial review cases in this field. For present purposes it is
sufficient to note that the relative scarcity of case law makes it difficult to extrap-
olate general observations or principles concerning the courts' approach to
financial services regulation.

However, the scarcity of substantive judicial review applications does not
mean that judicial review does not, or will not, continue to play a very important role in financial services regulation. The difficulty lies in identifying the precise nature of that role. What ought the FSA, those who will be affected by its
decisions and activities, the government, Parliament and the public to expect
from the courts in the exercise of their supervisory jurisdiction? Do the decisions
of the courts in the cases that have been brought before them under the current
regulatory regime indicate that they are able to fulfil the role that should be
expected of them in the new regulatory world?

INSTITUTIONAL BACKGROUND

One cannot embark on an examination of the courts' role in this area without
an understanding of the delicately balanced institutional structure through
which the regulation of financial services[2] is currently delivered in the UK, and
of the changes to that structure which the government now proposes.

The 1986 Act envisaged a system of practitioner-based regulation within a
statutory framework. As such it represents a compromise between the advan-

---

[2] This paper concentrates primarily on investment business regulation as opposed to banking or
insurance regulation, although the government's proposals for reform involve conferring banking
and insurance regulation on the FSA and the term "financial services" must now be viewed in this
light.

tages claimed for self-regulation (such as enhanced expertise, flexibility and sensitivity) and the perceived need to inject a degree of public accountability and oversight in order to prevent the public interest being subverted to the interests of the regulated industry.[3]

At the foundation of the regulatory regime lies the statutory requirement that any person conducting "investment business"[4] in the UK must be either authorised or exempted from the requirement to be authorised.[5] Breach of that requirement is a criminal offence. The Act confers upon HM Treasury statutory powers to authorise investment businesses, and to make and enforce rules, regulations and "statements of principle" governing their conduct of investment business and imposing requirements as to their financial standing.

There, however, the constitutional orthodoxy ends. Most of the Treasury's statutory powers under the Act have been transferred to the FSA. The FSA is a company limited by guarantee whose Chairman and Board are appointed by the Chancellor of the Exchequer and the Governor of the Bank of England.[6] The composition of the Board must be such as to secure a proper balance between the interests of persons carrying on investment business and the interests of the public. In addition the FSA must continue to satisfy the requirements set out in Schedule 7 to the 1986 Act relating to arrangements for the discharge of its functions, taking account of the costs of compliance, monitoring and enforcement, investigation of complaints and the promotion and maintenance of high standards of integrity and fair dealing in the carrying on of investment business.

Further, statutory powers are delegated to enable the FSA to "recognise" other regulatory bodies. In particular, the FSA has power to recognise self-regulating organisations ("SROs") and professional bodies ("RPBs") for the purposes of their regulating the conduct of investment business by their members. Membership of an SRO or certification by an RPB confers the necessary authorisation to conduct investment business for the purposes of the Act. In addition, the FSA is responsible for the recognition and supervision under the Act of investment exchanges (including the London Stock Exchange and LIFFE[7]) and clearing houses.

Like the FSA, the SROs are companies limited by guarantee. However, their powers to regulate the activities of their members are derived not from statute but from the contract with their members, as set out in the organisations' rules. Although the FSA's statutory power to authorise and regulate investment firms

---

[3] See Gower Report, *Review of Investor Protection, report Part I*, Cmnd 9125 (HMSO, London, 1984) Part I; A. Page and R. Ferguson, *Investor Protection* (Weidenfeld and Nicolson, London, 1992), 82–4. For a summary of some more modern theories of self-regulation see A. Ogus, "Rethinking Self-Regulation" [1995] *OJLS* 97.

[4] The term "investment business" is extensively defined in Sched. 1 to the Act and includes dealing and arranging deals in investments, managing investments belonging to others, providing advice on the merits of buying or selling investments and establishing or operating a collective investment scheme.

[5] S. 3 of the 1986 Act

[6] See para. 1(1), Sched. 7 to the 1986 Act.

[7] The London International Financial Futures and Options Exchange.

remains, in 1993 the then Chairman of the SIB, Sir Andrew Large, made clear the SIB's intention to "pursue vigorously its policy of maximum withdrawal from direct regulation" of investment firms.[8] That objective has largely been achieved and the FSA is currently responsible for the direct regulation of only a handful of firms. Thus, under the 1986 regime, the front-line regulation of investment firms and investment markets is largely the responsibility not of the FSA, but of self-regulatory "recognised bodies".

In order to secure the autonomy of the SROs and other recognised bodies, the legal powers of the FSA to intervene in their activities are strictly limited. Under the statute the FSA has the nuclear deterrent of de-recognition[9] (thus depriving the SRO of the ability to confer authorisation by virtue of membership) and the power to seek compliance orders in the High Court where the FSA considers that a body no longer satisfies the requirements for recognition set out in the Act.[10] Similarly, HM Treasury's powers to control the activities of the FSA are limited. There is the nuclear deterrent of an order resuming the statutory functions transferred to the FSA,[11] but this requires the approval of both Houses of Parliament. The powers of the Treasury to issue directions to the FSA are strictly limited to circumstances where they are necessary to prevent restrictive practices[12] or to secure compliance with international obligations.[13]

THE PROBLEM OF ACCOUNTABILITY

One of the effects of this elaborate institutional structure is that, under the current regime, most of the day-to-day regulation of most investment business is conducted at two removes from government. It is immediately apparent that, while the legislation provides a clear mandate to the FSA, and the bodies recognised by it, to perform the task of regulating the financial services industry in the public interest, the institutional structure by which that mandate is to be fulfilled is not amenable to traditional concepts of ministerial responsibility and parliamentary accountability. The limitations on the legal controls which may be exercised by government over the FSA and by the FSA over the recognised bodies render the foundations of these regulatory bodies' *democratic* accountability particularly complex.

It is difficult to underestimate the importance of public accountability to any regulatory body. Public accountability is an essential element in securing the legitimacy of, and public confidence in, the exercise of regulatory power. Accountability is also vital to ensure that regulators use their powers faithfully

---

[8] Andrew Large, *Financial Services Regulation: Making the Two Tier System Work* (The Securities and Investments Board, London, May 1993).

[9] S. 11 of the 1986 Act.

[10] S. 12 of the Act.

[11] S. 115.

[12] S. 121.

[13] S. 192.

to pursue the public interest and the purposes envisaged by Parliament and to guard against the danger that the private interests of certain powerful groups (most notably the regulated industry itself) will take priority. In economic terms, public accountability assists in reducing the agency costs associated with the regulatory process by controlling the extent to which the regulator can depart from the interests of its principal(s) (government, Parliament and the public) in circumstances where those interests do not precisely tally with those of the regulator. In short, accountability is necessary to ensure that regulators do not act in their own interests rather than the interests which they are charged with promoting or protecting.[14]

The government's proposed reform of financial services regulation has clearly been influenced in part by concerns about accountability. The Chancellor's announcement of the reforms signalled the government's rejection of the traditional deference to self-regulation in financial markets and its concern that regulation of financial services in the UK should be placed on a fully statutory footing. Ministers have indicated that the financial regulatory reform bill will set out a framework designed to deliver the Government's aim of a regulator that is "clearly accountable to Government and to Parliament".[15] However, the FSA will retain its present position as an autonomous, non-governmental regulatory body performing statutory functions, and exercising considerable statutory power over a very wide constituency, at arms length from government.

I do not suggest that financial services regulators currently, or that the FSA will, operate in an accountability vacuum. Criticism of the orthodox theory of ministerial responsibility is well documented.[16] Some of the innovations of the 1986 financial services regulatory regime can be viewed as part of the incremental development of new and more effective instruments of accountability.[17] In addition to the laying of the FSA annual report before Parliament,[18] senior officers working within both the FSA and the recognised bodies have been happy to appear before Select Committees and (not being public officials) they have not considered themselves bound by the Osmotherly Rules and the Armstrong Memorandum.[19] Recently, advice given by the FSA to the Chancellor has been published following a period of public consultation, thus opening the policy-making process itself to public scrutiny and public participation.[20] It is

---

[14] See W. Bishop, "A Theory of Administrative Law" [1990] *Journal of Legal Studies* 489.

[15] See *Financial Services Authority: An Outline*, published by the FSA on 28 Oct. 1997, at para. 30.

[16] See D. Oliver, "Law, Politics and Public Accountability. The Search for a New Equilibrium" [1994] *Public Law* 238; N. Lewis and D. Longley, "Ministerial Responsibility: The Next Steps" [1996] *Public Law* 490.

[17] See further A. Page "Self-Regulation: The Constitutional Dimension"(1986) 49 *MLR* 141.

[18] As required by s. 117 of the 1986 Act.

[19] It will be recalled that these administrative fiats govern the appearance of civil servants before Select Committees so as to prevent officials giving evidence about advice given to Ministers and maintain the position that officials give evidence *on behalf* of their Ministers.

[20] See SIB Consultation Paper 97, *Maintaining Enhanced Market Liquidity* (SIB, London, May 1996); SIB Consultation Paper 100, *Stock Borrowing and Short Selling: Implications for the UK*

envisaged that such arrangements will continue, with certain enhancements, when the FSA assumes its wider responsibilities under the financial regulatory reform bill. In particular, the FSA will be required to report to the Chancellor of the Exchequer each year as to how well it has performed against specific objectives set out in the statute.[21]

However, the legal controls to secure financial services regulators' accountability to Parliament are limited. As Daintith has noted in his discussion of the independence of the Bank of England,[22] it is difficult for Parliament to operate *ex post* instruments of accountability whenever powers are vested in a non-Ministerial body such as the FSA. Although the FSA may be required to report to Government and/or Parliament and may be summoned by Select Committees, the chain of relations through which such accountability might be enforced passes through Ministers. If Ministers have no, or only very limited, control over the FSA, the foundations of the Authority's parliamentary accountability will continue to be constitutionally problematic. However, as Daintith observes, concerns that the constitutional foundations of *ex post* accountability to Parliament are not wholly secure can be met where "the functions of the relevant non-Ministerial body have been legislatively defined by Parliament with sufficient clarity for its performance to be monitored by reference to those legal standards, and to be subject to effective judicial control". Government has made clear its intention that the proposed financial regulatory reform legislation will place the regulation of investment business on a fully statutory footing, and the FSA will be required to perform its functions in accordance with objectives set down in statute. Thus the observation that "the task of meeting the challenge posed by the weakness of ministerial responsibility and filling a vacuum in accountability has been left to the judges",[23] ought to be of particular relevance to bodies such as the financial services regulators, whose activities are (for good reason) insulated from legal control by government.[24] To what extent then can we can look to the courts and administrative law to provide a suitable mechanism for securing the accountability of financial services regulators? How have the courts approached the range of bodies operating under the 1986 Act? Does their approach show that the courts are equipped

Equity Markets (SIB, London, Nov. 1996); *Stock Borrowing and Repo in UK Equities: Regulatory Recommendations* (SIB, London)—the Chancellor of the Exchequer indicated the Treasury's acceptance of the SIB's advice by way of a Parliamentary Written Answer on 7 Feb. 1997; and see the Chancellor of the Exchequer's published letter to Sir Andrew Large of 20 May 1997 (asking Sir Andrew to bring forward a plan to implement the Government's policy for reform of financial regulation), and the SIB's response in its report on *Reform of the Financial Regulatory System* (SIB, London, July 1997).

[21] This was confirmed in the Chancellor's speech on the occasion of the "launch" of the FSA on 28 Oct. 1997 at the QE2 Centre in London.
[22] T. Daintith, "Between Domestic Democracy and an Alien Rule of Law? Some Thoughts on the 'Independence' of the Bank of England" [1995] *Public Law* 118.
[23] Oliver, n. 16 above, at 246.
[24] As Lloyd LJ observed of the Take-over Panel in *R. v. Panel on Take-overs and Mergers, ex p.Datafin* [1987] 1 All ER 564 at 582d, the significant element of "self-regulation" in the regime "makes it not less but more appropriate that it should be subject to judicial review by the courts".

effectively to monitor the performance of the FSA and those other regulatory bodies who will remain after the Government's proposed reforms?

If the courts are to have an effective role in securing accountability they must stand ready to entertain worthwhile applications for judicial review against the various types of body responsible for the regulation of financial services in the UK. It is tempting to view as trite the proposition that the FSA and the recognised bodies are amenable to judicial review. However, it should be borne in mind that in many cases regulatory bodies operating under the 1986 Act have chosen not to resist applications for judicial review on the basis of arguments to the contrary. Consequently the jurisdictional point has not been the subject of detailed judicial analysis.

As regards the FSA, the source of its regulatory powers, duties and functions is the statute and the Orders transferring those functions from the Secretary of State and (more recently) the Treasury to the Authority. There can therefore be little doubt that the FSA is amenable to judicial review in relation to the performance of those functions, despite its formal status as a private company limited by guarantee. The position of the bodies recognised by the FSA under the 1986 Act is theoretically more problematic. The SROs derive their powers from the contract with their members, as (generally speaking) do the recognised investment exchanges[25] and the clearing houses.

The government's proposed reforms will go some way to dispensing with these problems: the SROs will cease to exercise their regulatory functions and their responsibilities will be performed by the FSA under statutory powers conferred by Parliament. However, even after the implementation of the reform legislation, a number of non-statutory bodies are likely to continue to remain responsible for the performance of certain regulatory functions. For example, it seems likely that recognised investment exchanges will continue to perform a regulatory role. Moreover, there are aspects of the regulatory regime that are based on non-statutory, consensual arrangements between financial services firms and their regulators which may survive reform: much conduct of business regulation (as opposed to prudential supervision) of banks and building societies is currently secured not by statutory regulatory control but by voluntary codes of practice;[26] and it is not yet clear precisely what will replace the various ombudsmen schemes which operate in the financial services field (some of which are voluntary schemes), or what the precise constitution or legal status of the replacement might be. Although the government's proposals represent a

---

[25] The exception is the London Stock Exchange's functions as UK competent authority for the official listing of securities, which are conferred by Part IV of the 1986 Act (see s. 142(6)).

[26] See, e.g., the UK *Code of Banking Practice* (2nd edn., British Bankers Association, Building Socities Association, Association for Payment Clearing Services, London, 1994).

significant shift away from "self-regulation", reliance on non-statutory forms of regulatory control seems likely to continue, albeit in a considerably more limited area.

The Court of Appeal's seminal decision in *Datafin* established that the absence of statutory or prerogative power was not a bar to judicial review. However, the precise basis on which bodies whose powers are not derived from statute should be considered amenable to the High Court's supervisory jurisdiction has remained unclear. The courts have experienced considerable difficulty in distinguishing between non-statutory public law bodies and bodies whose functions are to be regarded as purely domestic or private in nature, and therefore beyond the scope of judicial review.

Datafin and the cases which followed that decision reveal that the court is concerned with whether the body in question has not only significant *de facto* power in relation to matters which may be of public interest,[27] but also an element of government sponsorship in the exercise of the body's functions.[28] It is the fact that a body's activities are sponsored in some way by government which raises a presumption that those activities should be supervised by the courts according to public law principles.

Of course, state sponsorship alone is not sufficient. There are many activities undertaken by the state itself which may not be subject to the public law jurisdiction—engaging the services of employees or private contractors being obvious examples.[29] Regard must also be had to the nature of the functions being performed. The availability of judicial review will also depend on the extent to which the court believes that the task being performed by the body concerned "really partakes in some manner of 'governing' or 'public regulation' as opposed to private contracting".[30]

---

[27] "[T]he mere fact of power, even over a substantial area of economic activity, is not enough. In a mixed economy, power may be private as well as public. Private power may affect the private interest and the livelihoods of many individuals. But that does not subject it to the rules of public law" *per* Hoffmann LJ in *R. v. Disciplinary Committee of the Jockey Club, ex p. Aga Khan* [1993] 2 All ER 853.

[28] In *Datafin* Sir John Donaldson MR stressed that "[a]s an act of government it was decided that, in relation to take-overs, there should be a central self-regulatory body which would be supported and sustained by a periphery of statutory powers and penalties wherever non-statutory powers and penalties were insufficient or non-existent or where EEC requirements called for statutory provisions". See also *R. v. Disciplinary Committee of the Jockey Club, ex p. Aga Khan* [1993] 2 All ER 853 which suggests that a body whose birth and constitution owed nothing to the exercise of any governmental power may be subject to judicial review if it is woven into the fabric of public regulation or into a system of governmental control, or is integrated into a system of statutory regulation, or is a surrogate organ of government; *R. v. Football Association, ex p. Football League Ltd* [1993] 2 All ER 833, where it was held that the FA was not amenable to review because it lacked any "governmental underpinning"; *R. v. Governors of Haberdashers' Aske's, ex p. Tyrell* (*The Times*, 19 Oct. 1994)—city technology colleges held amenable to review.

[29] See *R. v. East Berks Health Authority, ex p.Walsh* [1985] QB 152; *R. v. Derbyshire County Council, ex p. Noble* [1990] ICR 808; *Home Office v. McLaren* [1990] ICR 824; *R. v. Lord Chancellor's Department, ex p. Hibbet & Saunders* [1993] COD 466.

[30] P. P. Craig, *Administrative Law* (Sweet & Maxwell, London, 1994), 568.

These limitations on the availability of judicial review reflect the fact that the jurisdiction has been fashioned to fulfil the courts' constitutional role of checking the abuse of public, governmental power, complementing as it does the role of ministerial responsibility and democratic accountability through Parliament. The functions of "government" and "public regulation" are probably incapable of precise definition. However, the scope of judicial review should reflect two important observations: first, the fact that the role of the modern state is not confined to matters such as foreign policy, the defence of realm, the policing of crime and the provision of public services but extends to the "regulation" of a wide variety of *private* activities in the "public interest"; secondly, the fact that the instruments used by the state to deliver public regulation are multifarious and increasingly novel.

Peculiar issues are raised by regimes which rely, as the 1986 Act regime did, on bodies constituted under private law that use powers derived from contract. The question here concerns the degree of governmental sponsorship and "interweaving" into a system of public regulation that will be required before a body or power can be considered amenable to judicial review. There is a difference between, on the one hand, conferring a statutory or governmental "seal of approval" on a private body in order to promote public confidence in that body's activities and, on the other, relying on a body to deliver an integral element in a system of public regulation. An easy example of the former is the authorisation of investment firms by the FSA or the SROs: few would suggest that authorisation renders the investment firm (no matter how powerful) a public body amenable to judicial review.

At the other end of the spectrum, few would seek to argue that the FSA or the SROs are not amenable to judicial review:[31] even though they are constituted under private law and, in the case of the SROs, depend on contractual powers, they are the bodies which are relied upon to deliver the regulation of financial services in the public interest and in accordance with the purposes of the Act. The SROs exist for the sole purpose of regulating their members' conduct of investment business. The "public interest" in the effective performance of that role is clear. Their activities are backed by the statutory framework contained in the 1986 Act. In particular, their *de facto* power is derived, in part, from the statutory restriction on the conduct of investment business.[32] In addition the Act

---

[31] See R. v. *Securities and Futures Authority, ex p. Panton* (unreported, 20 June 1994, CA): "I would certainly for my part wish to discountenance any . . . suggestion . . . that bodies such as the SIB and the self regulatory organisations which the Act established are immune from judicial review. It seems to me quite plain that they are bodies over whom the court can, in appropriate cases, and will, exercise a supervisory jurisdiction . . .": Sir Thomas Bingham MR; see also McCullough J in R. v. *Association of Futures Brokers and Dealers, ex p. Mordens Ltd (The Times,* 6 Sept. 1990).

[32] See Treasury and Civil Service Committee, Sixth Report, *The Regulation of Financial Services in the UK* (HMSO, London, Oct. 1995): the Committee concluded that the term "self regulation" was a misnomer and fails to reflect the SROs independence or the statutory basis of their authority—SFA told the Committee "in reality the "self-regulators" have become statutory regulators in all but name, drawing their power from the fact that it is illegal to operate without becoming subject to their authority" (paras. 24–5).

provides the FSA with a number of powers to assist in circumstances where the SROs contractual powers prove inadequate.[33] The public nature of the SROs functions is reinforced by the statutory requirements which they must satisfy in order to obtain and retain their recognition under the Act. The alternative remedies available to those aggrieved by their decisions are limited by a statutory immunity from damages[34] and by common law.[35] They do not have "monopoly" power in that firms conducting investment business have the option of seeking direct authorisation from the FSA. However, the SROs' *de facto* power over the industry is buttressed by the FSA's policy of withdrawal from direct regulation. The 1986 Act makes clear beyond doubt that the decision to rely on self-regulating organisations as the front-line regulators of the financial services industry was an "act of government", and the functions of the SROs fall squarely in the field of "public regulation". Thus, in *Governor and Company of the Bank of Scotland, Petitioners*[36] Lord Cullen considered the statutory and regulatory context of IMRO's[37] functions as an SRO and concluded that the supervisory jurisdiction of the Court of Session was competently invoked:

> "The close relationship between the objects of [IMRO] and the purpose and terms of the statute could be seen in [IMRO's] memorandum and articles of association. The public nature of the arrangements made by the Act was underlined by the provisions of s 62 under which a liability in an action for damages was attracted by a contravention both of the rules of a self-regulating organisation and the statutory rules. A study of the above showed that [IMRO] was performing public duties as an integral part of the system set up under the Act. For this purpose what mattered was the function of the respondent rather than its constitution or legal character. . . .
>
> . . . The objects and activities of [IMRO] are for the purpose of implementing the system of self-regulation which is laid down in the 1986 Act and under which the petitioner is authorised to carry on investment business."

However, difficulties arise in relation to bodies whose role is not clearly that of "regulator" or "regulated".

In *R. v. Insurance Ombudsman Bureau, ex p. Aegon Life*[38] the Divisional Court considered an application for judicial review against a body operating at the margins of the 1986 Act regime. The Insurance Ombudsman Bureau

---

[33] See, e.g., the FSA's statutory powers of investigation in s. 105 of the 1986 Act and the statutory power to bring civil proceedings for injunctions in s. 61 and to petition for the winding up of authorised firms under s. 72.

[34] See s. 187 of the 1986 Act. Note that the same immunity does *not* extend to the activities of the recognised investment exchanges and clearing houses; and it is of limited scope in relation to the activities of Recognised Professional Bodies.

[35] See *Yuen Kun Yeu v. Attorney General of Hong Kong* [1988] AC 175; Ferris J in *Tee v. LAUTRO* (unreported, 16 July 1996); and Lightman J in *Melton Medes v. SIB* [1995] 2 WLR 247 at 254–5.

[36] [1989] BCLC 700—the first application for judicial review of an SRO; it proceeded on the assumption that their decisions were amenable to judicial review, although the point was not conceded.

[37] Investment Management Regulatory Organisation.

[38] *The Times*, 7 Jan. 1994, CO/1609/93.

("IOB") was a body recognised under the rules of LAUTRO,[39] an SRO recognised by the SIB under the 1986 Act. The Act requires, as a condition of recognition, that an SRO must have "effective arrangements for the investigation of complaints against . . . its members". Those arrangements "may make provision for the whole or part of that function to be performed by and to be the responsibility of a body or person independent of the organisation".[40] Under LAUTRO's rules, SRO members were permitted to submit to the jurisdiction of the IOB and the IOB was recognised as performing LAUTRO's complaints investigation function for the purposes of the Act. The function of the IOB was (and, for the time being, remains) to provide an arbitration service for the investigation and determination of "complaints, disputes and claims made in connection with or arising out of (i) policies of insurance, (ii) contracts which constitute investment business as defined in the Financial Services Act 1986" effected with members of the IOB. LAUTRO encouraged its members to join the IOB, but it did not compel them to do so, and LAUTRO's rules provided for an alternative mechanism for the resolution of complaints against its members.

The applicant was a life assurance company and was a member of LAUTRO and the IOB. In March 1993 the Insurance Ombudsman made 23 awards of compensation against the applicants and it was these decisions which the company sought to challenge by way of judicial review.

The Divisional Court held that the IOB was not a body susceptible to judicial review on the grounds that the IOB's power over its members was solely derived from contract and it could not be said that the IOB was exercising "governmental functions". The case has been said to represent the culmination of the courts' retreat from the expansionist approach to judicial review heralded by *Datafin*. Of particular significance is Rose LJ's dictum that:

> " . . . even if it can be said that [the IOB] has now been woven into a governmental system, the source of the IOB's power is still contractual, its decisions are of an arbitrative nature in private law and those decisions are not, save very remotely, supported by any public law sanction."

It seems that, despite the suggestion in *Datafin* that the availability of public law remedies should be governed by the nature of the body's functions rather than solely by reference to the source of its powers, the Court in *Aegon Life* has reverted to a source-based test.[41] Rose LJ attached considerable weight to the statement made by Sir John Donaldson MR in *Datafin* that bodies whose sole source of power is consensual submission to their jurisdiction are not subject to judicial review. Having examined the history of the IOB as a body set up in 1981 by three insurance companies, Rose LJ went on to say:

> "The foundations of the IOB, initially, conspicuously lacked any trace of governmental underpinning. It was a free standing independent body whose jurisdiction was

[39] The Life Assurance and Unit Trust Regulatory Authority.
[40] See para. 6 of Sched. 2 to the 1986 Act.
[41] See R. Gordon and S. Grodzinski, "Insuring Against Judicial Review" [1994] *NLJ* 98.

dependent on the contractual consent of its members. It provided an alternative means of dispute resolution, outside the courts, for members of the public who chose to use it in relation to insurance companies who were members. I am unable to accept that the [1986 Act] directly or indirectly changed the character of the IOB's foundations or altered the source of its power. Furthermore, when Sir Thomas Bingham spoke of the Jockey Club not being 'woven into any system of governmental control'[42] I do not accept that he was thereby indicating that such interweaving was in itself determinative. On the contrary a substantial part of his judgement and that of Farquharson LJ is devoted to the negative implications as to judicial review if the body's power was derived from consent."

It therefore appears that the Court rejected Aegon Life's application on the basis that the *source* of the IOB's powers was consensual and the fact that the body could not be said to have been created by any act of government. The fact that the IOB was performing a function which had in the event become a part of the regulatory regime imposed by the 1986 Act was not sufficient.

The observation that implementation of the 1986 Act did not change the character of the IOB's foundations or the source of its powers is open to question. Although LAUTRO's rules[43] did not require its members to submit to the IOB's jurisdiction, where they chose to do so, the SRO's rules (as well as the member's contract with the IOB) required them to abide by the Ombudsman's decisions. Further, although membership of the IOB was optional under LAUTRO's rules, participation in a complaints arbitration scheme was not. If a member chose not to participate in such a scheme, LAUTRO would itself arrange for the investigation of complaints against that member. It is not therefore entirely accurate to suggest, as Rose LJ did, that it was open to members of LAUTRO to have such cases decided *solely* in the courts by reference to strictly legal principles. Although, as the court observed, the complainants had the option of suing LAUTRO members for breaches of LAUTRO's rules,[44] the intention evident from the Act is that investors should be provided with the added protection of a complaints investigation scheme operated or sponsored by the relevant regulatory body. As LAUTRO's own rules made clear, investors were to have the *right* to have their complaints investigated by a body independent of the firm against which they were made. Whether the investigation was conducted by LAUTRO or an independent complaints body such as the IOB was a matter for the firm concerned. Either way, the firm would be required to submit to decisions of an independent arbitrator, and would not be in a position to force aggrieved investors into costly and lengthy civil proceedings in order to secure redress. Such arrangements are and will remain an important regulatory tool for protecting the interests of investors.

---

[42] See *ex parte Aga Khan*.
[43] See LAUTRO rules, Part IX—Complaints.
[44] S. 62 of the 1986 Act confers private rights of action on investors in relation to breaches of FSA or SRO rules.

It is also difficult to see why the operation of such schemes should be subject to judicial review when undertaken by the FSA or the SROs themselves (as seems to have been accepted implicitly by the court), but not subject to the High Court's supervision where those same functions are performed by an independent body such as the IOB.

The *Aegon Life* decision and other more restrictive applications of *Datafin* principles,[45] raise wider questions over the extent to which other bodies operating under the umbrella of the 1986 Act, or the forthcoming reform legislation, will be amenable to judicial review. It is almost inevitable that where government seeks (as it did in the 1986 Act) to implement a regime of "self-regulation subject to governmental surveillance" the self-regulating bodies recognised for that purpose may pre-date the legislation. Although the SROs currently recognised under the 1986 Act were formally constituted for the purposes of becoming recognised bodies, the origins of some of these bodies may be traced back to organisations existing before the 1986 Act regime was established. Further, some of the investment exchanges (for example the London Stock Exchange and the London Metal Exchange) recognised under the FSA have a long history which certainly pre-dates *any* form of statutory regulatory intervention in the financial services arena.

The investment exchanges recognised by the FSA provide further examples of bodies whose function is not clearly that of "regulator" or "regulated". Unlike the SROs, these bodies are commercial enterprises whose activities are undertaken with a view to profit in an increasingly competitive global market. Persons wishing to deal in investments are not required to use the facilities of a recognised exchange to effect their transactions. Indeed it is perfectly possible for an investment exchange to operate without recognition from the FSA, provided that the entity conducting the investment business obtains authorisation from the FSA or one of the SROs. Recognition by the FSA in relation to these bodies might be viewed more as a "kite mark" aimed at ensuring public confidence in the integrity of the organised markets overseen by the exchanges. In return, the bodies are exempted from the statutory requirement to be authorised[46] and attract the benefits of the protections of Part VII Companies Act 1989 in relation to insolvency, winding up or default of market counterparties.

However, that exchanges no longer wield "monopoly" power in the sense alluded to in the case law[47] should not be allowed to obscure the fact that the

---

[45] See *R. v. Lloyds of London, ex p. Briggs* [1993] 1 Lloyd's Rep. 176 where it was held that there was no such public law element about the relationship between Lloyd's and Names as places it within the public domain and so renders it susceptible to judicial review—powers are exercised by Lloyds over its members solely by virtue of the contractual agreement of members of the Society to be bound by the decisions and directions of the Council and those acting on its behalf; *cf. R. v. Committee of Lloyd's, ex p. Posgate*, (*The Times*, 12 Jan. 1983) and *R. v. Chairman and Regulatory Board of Lloyd's, ex p. Macmillan* (*The Times*, 14 Dec. 1994); and see A. Lidbetter, "Judicial Review in the Company and Commercial Context" [1995] *BJIB&FL* 62 for further discussion of these cases.

[46] See ss. 36 and 38 of the 1986 Act.

[47] See *Datafin* where the court had regard to the fact that submission to the Takeover Panel's jurisdiction was not optional but was required of any person wishing to make take-over bids or

1986 Act clearly envisaged a *regulatory* role for the recognised investment exchange. The conditions for their recognition[48] include requirements that they must "ensure that business conducted by means of [their] facilities is conducted in an orderly manner and so as to afford proper protection to investors". An exchange must:

> "(a) limit dealings on the exchange to investments in which there is a proper market; and
>
> (b) where relevant, require issuers of investments dealt in on the exchange to comply with such obligations as will, so far as possible, afford to persons dealing in the investments proper information for determining their value."

It is significant that in the case of the London Stock Exchange this requirement is deemed to be satisfied by its compliance with Part IV of the 1986 Act which confers *statutory* powers, duties and functions on the Exchange as competent authority for the official listing of securities.

A recognised exchange is also required to have adequate arrangements for monitoring and enforcing compliance with its rules, and for the investigation of complaints in respect of business transacted by means of its facilities. Like the FSA and the SROs, it must be "able and willing to promote and maintain high standards of integrity and fair dealing in the carrying on of investment business and to co-operate, by the sharing of information and otherwise, with the Secretary of State and any other authority, body or person having responsibility for the regulation of investment business or other financial services".[49]

Like the SROs, the exchanges generally derive their powers from the contract with their members and with those issuers who wish their securities to be traded on the exchange. However, as with the SROs, those powers are supported by a periphery of statutory sanctions. Persons breaching the rules of a recognised exchange may be subject to discipline by the Exchange. However, if an exchange is unable to take effective action to enforce its rules regulating the conduct of investment business, the FSA has statutory power to bring proceedings for an injunction in the civil courts.[50] Breach of an Exchange's rules by an authorised investment firm may also result in disciplinary proceedings under the relevant SRO's rules.

The exchange may well have been constituted some considerable time before the 1986 Act was enacted and the formal source of its powers may (save in the case of the London Stock Exchange's listing function) remain unchanged. However, the Act envisaged that a recognised investment exchange should perform functions integral to the system of public regulation provided for in the

---

promote mergers in the UK. See also C.F. Forsyth, "Of Fig Leaves and Fairy Tales: The *Ultra Vires* Doctrine, the Sovereignty of Parliament and Judicial Review" [1996] *CLJ* 122. Modern systems of self-regulation may well promote *competition* between different regulatory bodies—see Ogus (1995) *supra* n.4.

[48] See Sched. 4 to the 1986 Act.
[49] See para. 5 of Sched. 4 to the 1986 Act.
[50] See s. 61 of the 1986 Act.

legislation. The fact that certain of the London Stock Exchange's functions as a recognised investment exchange are governed directly by statutory provisions conferring power on the competent authority for listing serves to illustrate that similar functions, when performed by other recognised investment exchanges, involve a significant element of public regulation.

It is reasonable to expect that the availability of judicial review expands in parallel with the expansion of the scope of governmental intervention in private activities. Where that intervention takes the form of recognising, empowering and enhancing existing systems of self-regulation, judicial review should not be denied on the ground that the constitution of the bodies entrusted with the task of regulating in the public interest pre-dates government action or that the formal, legal source of their powers is private law. Such a concern is evident from the judgment of Sir John Donaldson MR in *Datafin*, where he remarked that it would be disappointing if the courts "could not recognise the realities of executive power and allowed their vision to be clouded by the subtlety and sometimes complexity of the way in which it can be exerted".

It would indeed be disappointing if the courts refused to entertain applications for judicial review against bodies such as recognised investment exchanges on the grounds referred to in *Aegon Life*. Not only would this limit the ability of the courts to call such bodies to account for the performance of the regulatory functions entrusted to them under the legislation, it would also deprive the exchanges of the protections of the Order 53 procedure, which may be of particular importance in the context of financial services regulation. As Lloyd LJ said in *Datafin*, ". . . if the courts are to remain in the field, then it is clearly better, as a matter of policy, that legal proceedings should be in the realm of public law rather than private law, not only because they are quicker, but also because the requirement of leave under Order 53 will exclude claims which are clearly unmeritorious".[51]

Perhaps more importantly, to characterise the regulatory functions of such bodies as matters of private, contract law would place severe limitations on the ability of investors, whose interests the regulatory regime was designed to protect, to challenge the decisions of regulators with whom they have no contractual relationship. In *Aegon Life*, it was suggested that the applicants might have

---

[51] Although the effectiveness of the protections of Ord. 53 may, in any event, be under threat from the apparent acceptance of concurrent jurisdiction of the Ch. D. to entertain questions of fact and law relating to the exercise of contractual powers which might also be the subject of judicial review: see *R. v. Personal Investment Authority Ombudsman, ex p. The Burns-Anderson Independent Network plc* (CA, 21 Jan. 1997) where the court accepted that the Ch. D. had a concurrent jurisdiction: *SIB v. FIMBRA* [1991] 4 All ER 398 where the court allowed the case to proceed by way of originating summons because the parties consented and did not seek the protections of Ord. 53. In *Melton Medes v. SIB* the plaintiffs (unsuccessfully) brought an action for damages in relation to the SIB's disclosure of information allegedly in breach of s. 179 of the 1986 Act. Arguably, an alternative course for the plaintiffs would have been to challenge the decision to disclose by way of judicial review (*per* Lightman J at 255E–G). The fact that regulatory powers are derived from contract perhaps makes it easier to present disputes as private law claims, thereby circumventing the supposed procedural exclusivity of Ord. 53.

a remedy in an action for breach of contract. It is possible (though by no means clear) that the law of contract and the common law may be sufficiently flexible to impose obligations of similar effect to public law concepts of procedural fairness, illegality and irrationality.[52] However, it would be most unsatisfactory if such obligations were owed only to those in a contractual relationship with a body charged with functions of public regulation.[53]

It is important to bear in mind that what is at issue is whether judicial review is the appropriate way of controlling the particular institution or power in question. There is a strong argument that the court should not be bound by the legal form which the institution or power takes—regard must be had to the context in which the particular dispute arises.[54] In that light, the outcome in *Aegon Life* is not necessarily out of line with earlier authorities. There is no doubt that the IOB is a particularly problematic body. However, the basis on which it was concluded that the IOB was not amenable to judicial review seems unsatisfactory. It might be argued that an Ombudsman's functions in providing a forum for the informal arbitration of complaints may be such that it would be inappropriate to subject his decisions to judicial review. It might be feared that the supervision of the courts may introduce excessive legalism and formality into what is intended to be an informal process. However, the same arguments might apply to an Ombudsman scheme established and operated under statute as one established by contract. The source of the Ombudsman's power should not be the determining factor. Other decisions would suggest the use of several indicia in order to divine the nature of the Ombudsman's function, the extent to which it gives rise to the possibility of misuse of *governmental* power, and the suitability of judicial review as a method of checking such abuses.

These issues will be equally important when the courts come to consider the nature of their role in relation to any Ombudsman scheme which operates under the proposed reform legislation. Ministers have indicated that they see merit in some consolidation of the various Ombudsman and arbitration schemes which currently operate in the financial services arena and that the framework for handling complaints and resolving disputes between consumers and firms will be set

---

[52] As to which see Carnwath J's review of the cases concerning the use of the common law of restraint of trade to control the activities of domestic regulatory bodies in *Stevenage Football Club* v. *The Football League* (*The Times*, 1 Aug. 1996) and see Forsyth, n. 47 above, on the common law cases dealing with exercise of monopoly power.

[53] See *ex parte Aga Khan*, *per* Hoffmann LJ who expressed considerable doubt about the common law remedies available to persons with no contractual relationship with a private decision-making body such as the Jockey Club: "I do not think that one should try to patch up the remedies available against domestic bodies by pretending that they are organs of government".

[54] See A. McHarg, "Regulation as a Private Law Function?" [1995] *Public Law* 551; and see *R.* v. *London Commodity Exchange, ex p. Brealey* [1994] COD 145 where the applicant sought (unsuccessfully) to use the judicial review procedure to pursue a claim for damages against the Exchange in respect of costs incurred as a result of potatoes bought on the Exchange failing to meet the contract specification—the applicant alleged that the Exchange had failed to operate its compensation arrangements properly—Schiemann J held that the most appropriate forum for what was essentially a factual dispute on a claim for damages was the Commercial Court.

out in the legislation.[55] However, at the time of writing, it is not yet clear whether what is proposed is a compulsory Ombudsman scheme in which all regulated firms will be required to participate, or a voluntary scheme. Nor is it clear whether the determinations of any Ombudsman as to the liability of a firm to pay compensation will be legally binding on the firm. Such issues will be of vital importance in determining the nature of the court's supervisory function in relation to the Ombudsman, because they determine the nature of the Ombudsman's powers and functions. If all that is proposed is a form of voluntary, informal mediation then the court's supervisory role should be very different from that which it should perform in relation to an Ombudsman scheme which constitutes a forum in which legally binding determinations as to civil liability may be imposed on at least one of the parties. The decision in *Aegon Life* may hereafter need to be re-examined if the Ombudsman's jurisdiction and powers are to be set out in legislation. That should not *automatically* lead to the conclusion that the Ombudsman's decisions are amenable to judicial review, nor should it dictate the nature or intensity of review to which the Ombudsman should be subject—as noted above, the fact that a public body is excercising functions conferred by statute does not always result in the body's actions being amenable to review.[56] When considering the amenability to judicial review of the bodies that will operate within the purview of the new regulatory regime, the central question should be the extent to which the activities in question are concerned in the public regulation of financial services. The source of the bodies' powers is only one of several factors to be considered in addressing that issue.

STANDING

One of the consequences of the availability of public law remedies against a body is a relaxation of the principles on which litigants are given standing to challenge its actions. Recent case law on *locus standi* in judicial review shows a systematic broadening in the courts' interpretation of the "sufficient interest" test in Order 53, such that it is said that the courts ought not to decline jurisdiction on grounds of lack of standing to any responsible person or group seeking, on reasonable grounds, to challenge the validity of governmental action.[57] Again this reflects the court's constitutional role in supervising the activities of public bodies: the court is not solely concerned with vindicating the rights of individuals but has a wider role in ensuring that the powers exercised by public bodies are not abused.[58]

[55] *Financial Services Authority: An Outline*, n. 15 above, at para. 74.

[56] See S.A. De Smith, H. Woolf and J. Jowell, *Judicial Review of Administrative Action* (Sweet & Maxwell, London, 1995), at 3–037.

[57] See *ibid.*, 109–28; *R. v. Secretary of State for Employment, ex p. Equal Opportunities Commission* [1995] 1 AC 1; *R. v. Secretary of State for Foreign Affairs, ex p. World Development Movement Ltd.* [1995] 1 WLR 386.

[58] See Craig, n. 30 above, 29–31; W. Bishop, "A Theory of Administrative Law" [1990] *Journal of Legal Studies* 489.

The application of similar principles in the context of financial services regulation ought not to present problems. The demand for sensitivity to the needs of financial services regulators for speed and finality in their decision-making processes can adequately be reflected in the enforcement of the requirement that applications be made as soon as practical (and in any event within three months), in the grounds of review on which the courts will permit regulators decisions to be challenged successfully and in the use of the court's discretion to grant remedies.

Thus, the courts have entertained applications for judicial review against financial services regulators made by trade associations[59] and by individuals with no direct statutory or contractual relationship with the bodies concerned.[60] However, in *R. v. Stock Exchange, ex p. Else (1982) Ltd*[61] the court considered the standing of the minority shareholders of a company whose shares had been delisted by the Exchange , this decision being the subject of the challenge. One of the grounds relied upon by the applicants was the Exchange's failure to afford the shareholders an opportunity to make representations to the Committee on Quotations before the decision to delist was taken. In considering the question whether the applicants had sufficient interest for the purposes of Order 53, rule 3(7), Popplewell J said:

> "the general principles are not in doubt; their application to the variety of circumstances which arise in judicial review proceedings can cause difficulties; in the instant case I am quite satisfied that, if the investors have no right to be heard before the Committee, they equally have no right to be heard by the court."

That seems a surprising conclusion. It is difficult to see why the ability of the applicants to challenge the Committee's decision by way of judicial review should be dependent upon their success on their complaint of procedural impropriety. The two questions depend on different considerations.

On the issue of the shareholders' right to be heard by the Committee, the judge went on to decide that they had no such entitlement as a matter of common law. This conclusion appears to have been influenced by the Exchange's understandable and legitimate concern that affording such procedural rights to company shareholders would impose unacceptable delays on the Committee's proceedings and, due to the diverse views likely to be held by a constantly changing body of shareholders, would render the decision-making process unmanageable. However, weight also seems to have been attached to the argument that to permit the shareholders a right to make representations would in some way contravene the rule in *Foss* v. *Harbottle*.[62] The right to make representations

---

[59] *R v. SIB, ex p. Independent Financial Advisers Association* ("IFAA") [1995] 2 BCLC 76.

[60] *R v. LAUTRO, ex p. Ross* [1993] QB 17; *R. v. LAUTRO, ex p. Tee* (*The Times*, 30 May 1994).

[61] [1993] BCLC 834.

[62] (1843) 2 Hare 461, 67 ER 189: as a consequence of this rule, the circumstances in which shareholders are permitted to bring personal or derivative actions to enforce the rights of a company (e.g. against its directors) are extremely limited. This is viewed as a consequence of the fact that a corporation is a separate legal entity—see *Prudential Assurance* v. *Newman Industries* (*No 2*) [1982] 1

was viewed as that of the company's board of directors alone. While that con-clusion may be right as far as the shareholders' right to be heard before the Committee is concerned, it does not necessarily follow that the shareholders should have no standing to apply for judicial review of the Committee's decision on other grounds. To blur the distinction between these two issues risks con-fusing the purpose of the judicial review procedure in this context.

The purpose of a procedural right to make representations to a public body is to ensure that the body takes proper account of the views and interests of those affected by the decision. Such rights should not, however, be conferred where the nature of the decision makes such procedures impracticable or unduly burdensome or where the interests of the persons concerned are not of sufficient weight.[63] The purpose of the rules of standing is, however, quite different. They govern the circumstances in which the court's supervisory jurisdiction may be invoked. In accordance with the view that the courts have an important consti-tutional role in supervising the Exchange's performance of its regulatory func-tions, standing should not be denied simply on the ground that the applicant cannot establish a right to be heard by the body subject to review. Still less should standing be denied to shareholders on the basis of company law rules which are rooted in the principle of corporate personality and the courts' reluc-tance to become involved in a company's internal management. While it must be recognised that the merits of an application for judicial review may impact upon whether the court considers that the applicants have "sufficient inter-est",[64] it is difficult to justify tying the applicants' standing directly to their suc-cess or failure on only one of several grounds of judicial review which they may advance.

Happily, in *ex parte Else* Popplewell J was able to go on to consider the mer-its of the applicants' arguments that the Committee's decision should be set aside on the additional grounds of illegality and irrationality. This was because he felt it necessary to refer to the European Court of Justice the question whether the shareholders had a right to a hearing before the listing committee as a matter of EC law. On appeal[65] it was held that a reference to the ECJ was not necessary because the EC Directive on official listing plainly did not entitle

All ER 354 (but see also *Gerber Garment Technology Inc.* v. *Lectra Systems Limited* (CA, 18 Dec. 1996; *The Times*, 17 Jan. 1997).

[63] See *R.* v. *Monopolies and Mergers Commission, ex p. Argyll Group plc* [1986] 2 All ER 257. It is perhaps in the light of this "sufficient weight" criterion that Popplewell J's concern about the rela-tionship between a company and its shareholders is best understood.

[64] It is widely recognised that, since the decision of the House of Lords in *Inland Revenue Commissioners* v. *National Federation of Self-Employed and Small Businesses* [1982] AC 617, [1981] 2 All ER 93, the courts have been prepared to adopt a flexible approach to the test of "suffi-cient interest" in s. 31 of the Supreme Court Act 1981, such that questions of standing may well be dependent in part on the court's view of the merits of an application for judicial review and the importance of the issue involved. An example in the financial services field is *R.* v. *LAUTRO, ex p. Ross* (above) where the court glossed over the question of standing and concentrated on the sub-stantive merits of the applicants' procedural fairness challenge. See P. Cane, *An Introduction to Adminsitrative Law* (Clarendon Press, Oxford, 1992), ch. 3.

[65] [1993] QB 534, [1993] 1 All ER 420.

the shareholders to make representations about the committee's impending decision to de-list. Although the Court of Appeal declined to express a concluded view on the appeal against Popplewell J's decision on the applicant's standing, Sir Thomas Bingham MR said: "I would simply observe that the problems facing any shareholder seeking to mount such a challenge are formidable. In a highly sensitive and potentially fluid financial market, the factors listed in s 31(6) of the 1981 Act have a special significance. And the courts will not second-guess the informed judgment of responsible regulators steeped in knowledge of their particular market. But if, exceptionally, a shareholder were able to overcome these formidable problems, I question whether his claim to relief should fail for lack of sufficient interest." It is suggested that, in view of subsequent developments in the law of standing,[66] the *locus* of shareholders to bring applications for judicial review on such grounds should not be denied, save perhaps where the application is clearly without any merit.

GROUNDS AND INTENSITY OF JUDICIAL REVIEW

The question now arises of the principles which will be applied by the courts when they are asked to intervene in the activities and decision-making processes of financial services regulators amenable to the public law jurisdiction. It is assumed that the three grounds of review identified by Lord Diplock in the GCHQ case[67] are equally applicable to financial services regulators.[68] However, the way in which these general public law principles are applied in practice is necessarily influenced by the sometimes unique context in which financial services regulators are required to operate.

It is as well to remind ourselves of the well-known restraint on judicial intervention required by the basic principles of public law. Sir John Laws recently restated the position as follows:

> "The paradigm of a public law body subject to the public law jurisdiction is one whose power is conferred by statute. The statute is logically prior to it; and by the constitution it is for the courts to police the statute. But they do not act under the statute. They are altogether outside it. Their power is not derived from it; nor, ultimately, from any Act of Parliament. This state of affairs has two consequences. First, the judges have to see that the power given by the statute is not transgressed by its donee; secondly, they have no business themselves to exercise the powers conferred by it, precisely because they are not the donee. Hence the essence of the judicial review jurisdiction. It vindicates the rule of law not only by confining statutory powers within the four corners of the Act, but also by ensuring that the statute is not usurped by anyone—including the courts themselves."[69]

---

[66] See n. 58 above.
[67] *Council of Civil Service Unions* v. *Minister for the Civil Service* [1985] AC 374.
[68] See Sir John Donaldson MR in *Datafin*.
[69] Hon. Sir John Laws, "Law and Democracy" [1995] *Public Law* 72.

It is immediately apparent that the application of this statement of basic principle to the financial services regulators is problematic. While the FSA fits the paradigm, the recognised bodies do not. The Stock Exchange excepted, they are not the donees of any formal statutory powers under the 1986 Act. Nevertheless, the need for judicial restraint, so as to ensure that the courts do not usurp the decision-making functions of the regulators, remains.

In *R. v. Panel on Take-overs and Mergers, ex p. Guinness*[70] the Court of Appeal was acutely aware of this potential lack of "fit" between traditional public law concepts and the position of non-statutory regulators. Lord Donaldson said:

> "Illegality would certainly apply if the panel acted in breach of the general law, but it is more difficult to apply in the context of an alleged misinterpretation of its own rules by a body which under the scheme is both legislator and interpreter. Irrationality, at least in the sense of failing to take account of relevant factors or taking account of irrelevant factors, is a difficult concept in the context of a body which is itself charged with the duty of making a judgement on what is and what is not relevant, although clearly a theoretical scenario could be constructed in which the panel acted on the basis of considerations which on any view must have been irrelevant or ignored something which on any view must have been relevant. And similar problems arise with procedural impropriety in the narrow sense of failing to follow accepted procedures, given the nature of the panel and of its functions and the lack of any statutory or other guidance as to its procedures which are intended to be of its own devising. Similarly, in the broad sense of breach of the rules of natural justice, what is or is not fair may depend on the underlying value judgements by the panel as to the time scale which is appropriate for decision, the consequences of delay and matters of that kind."

He went on to suggest that acts and omissions of a body whose constitution, functions and powers are *sui generis* should perhaps be reviewed by the court "more in the round" and that the court, while basing its decision on familiar concepts, should eschew any formal categorisation. In *ex parte Guinness* the court therefore applied an "innominate ground" formed of the amalgam of Lord Diplock's own grounds with perhaps added elements, reflecting the unique nature of the panel and the environment in which it operates.

The difficulty is less acute in the case of the FSA and the bodies recognised under the 1986 Act. There the courts have the text of the Act from which to obtain guidance on the regulators' legislative mandate. However the purpose of the 1986 Act was to deliver a system whereby the decisions on the detail of the financial services regulation are arrived at through the process of self-regulation, subject to the FSA's (and ultimately the Treasury's) oversight. Although the financial services reform legislation will move away from the self-regulatory model, it will establish in its place a new regulatory process through which regulatory policy will be developed. It is important that the courts do not place undue limits on the freedom of the regulators if the fundamentals of the regulatory regime envisaged by Parliament are to be secured. The courts can also be

[70] [1990] 1 QB 146, [1989] 2 WLR 863, [1989] 1 All ER 509.

expected to remain acutely aware of the "special needs of the financial markets for speed on the part of decision-makers and for being able to rely on those decisions as a sure basis for dealing in the market" and that "such decisions affect a very wide public which will not be parties to the dispute and that their interests have to be taken into account as much as those of the immediate disputants".[71] As the courts have recognised, such considerations mean that they may not be the best forum for resolving complex issues of regulatory policy or for determining what regulatory action is appropriate in the public interest.

Thus, the case law is scattered with references to the need for particular judicial restraint in the field of financial services regulation. In *R. v. SFA, ex p. Panton*[72] Sir Thomas Bingham said of the FSA and the SROs:

> ". . . these bodies are amenable to judicial review but are, in anything other than very clear circumstances, to be left to get on with it. It is for them to decide on the facts whether it is, or is not, appropriate to proceed against a member as not being a fit and proper person and it is essentially a matter for their judgement as to the extent to which a complaint is investigated."

The need for the court to refrain from second-guessing the outcome of the regulatory process was recognised in *R. v. LAUTRO, ex p. Kendall*[73] where the applicant sought to attack LAUTRO's rules preventing the appointment of company representatives who were indebted to any member of the SRO. Latham J, noting that the provisions had been the subject of extensive consultation by LAUTRO, held that the rule was capable of being justified by reference to the SRO's function of securing, through the rules to which its members were subject, adequate protection for investors and, although it carried with it anomalies and potential injustice, the rule was not "unreasonable". Similarly, in *R. v. SIB and PIA, ex p. Sun Life Assurance Society plc*[74] Sedley J refused to strike down the SIB's scheme for financing the Investors Compensation Scheme on the basis that while the result might be harsh (because it required ex-LAUTRO members such as Sun Life to meet compensation claims arising out of the activities of ex-FIMBRA members), it was within the statutory power conferred on the SIB by section 54 of the FSA and the outcome was "a matter for the self-regulatory process and not for the court".

In *A v. B Bank (Bank of England Intervening)*[75] Hirst J concluded his judgement by saying:

> "I cannot stress too strongly the importance which should be attached to the Bank of England having, within the limits laid down by the 1987 [Banking] Act and the general law, unfettered and unimpeded scope for the exercise of their most important public

---

[71] *Per* Sir John Donaldson MR in *Datafin*; see also Lord Alexander of Weedon QC, "Judicial Review and the City Regulators" (1989) 52 *MLR* 640.
[72] Unreported, 20 June 1994, CA.
[73] [1994] COD 169.
[74] [1996] 2 BCLC 150.
[75] [1992] 1 All ER 778.

duties of regulation under the 1987 Act in the interests of the public, who are surely entitled to rely on the Bank of England to exercise those powers with integrity."

In other cases[76] the courts have paid particular attention to the expertise of regulatory bodies and the difficulties which the courts would have in embarking on an assessment of the substantive merits of their decisions save in cases of clear perversity. This is of particular relevance to the 1986 Act regime, where expertise and practitioner participation are two of the principal advantages claimed for the self-regulatory model.[77] It will continue to be of relevance under the proposed reform legislation: although the extent of reliance on overt forms of "self-regulation" will be more limited under the new regime, both government and the FSA place great emphasis on the importance of retaining high-calibre, expert regulatory staff in the new regulator and on the importance of practitioner involvement in the regulatory process.[78]

The cases make clear that, even though the legislative mandate given to financial services regulators may provide extensive guidance on the purposes for which their functions are to be exercised and (in the case of the FSA) the limits of their powers, the language of such provisions is often "open textured" and the courts must take great care not to substitute their own interpretation where to

---

[76] See, in particular, *R. v. Independent Television Commission, ex parte Virgin Television Ltd* [1997] EMLR 318, *per* Henry LJ: "we do not regard the Commission's judgement . . . as being in any sense 'readily reviewable' . . . Here, matters of judgement were entrusted to an expert body by Parliament. That body was also made responsible for finding the facts on which such judgement would be based, in circumstances where the level of the quality threshold was to be set by the Commission and no one else. Of its nature such an exercise is . . judgmental in character and, there-fore, one upon which opinions may readily differ. . . . It has to follow that a very heavy burden falls upon the party seeking to upset a qualitative judgement of the nature described and arrived at by the qualified and experienced body which is the Commission . . ."; see too *R. v. Independent Television Commission, ex p. TSW Ltd* [1997] EMLR 291.

[77] Although it is interesting to note that reliance on expertise as a rationale for securing regula-tors' legitimacy has been the subject of extensive academic criticism (particularly in the US)—see e.g., L. Bernstein, *Regulating Business by Independent Commission* (Princeton, NJ, 1955);, J.O. Freeman, *Crisis and Legitimacy* (Cambridge UP, Cambridge, 1978); T. McGarity, *Reinventing Rationality* (1991). The limitations of "expertise" were recognised implicitly by Andrew Large (1993) in his review of financial services regulation: "12.6 The matter of public interest directors is important to the perception of the nature of SIB as an organisation, and to the perception of its inde-pendence. . . . Leading financial services industry figures should be on the board with a clear man-date to uphold the public interest, not to act as representatives of the industry sector. The SIB's board's judgement needs to continue to be enhanced by including on the Board non-executive direc-tors with a background in the financial services industry. The experience and knowledge of such individuals has been of enormous value throughout. In my experience, both in my short time at SIB and elsewhere, such members in practice lay great emphasis on their public interest duties. The "public interest" aspect of the Board will be further reinforced if: (i) non-executive directors cur-rently active in the financial services industry did not form a majority of the non-executives; (ii) the majority of non-executives were drawn from a wide variety of distinguished backgrounds: this could in appropriate cases include those with experience of financial services but who are no longer actively involved in it.".

[78] See consultation papers issued by the FSA on 28 Oct. 1997 on *Consumer Involvement* and *Practitioner Involvement*. They make clear that the FSA is committed to consumer involvement in its work and sees a "key role" for practitioners in helping the new regulator to understand and be close to the regulated markets and the firms which operate in them.

do so would frustrate the intention that the issues in question should be resolved by the regulatory rather than the judicial process.

That said, it would be dangerous to rely solely on the regulatory process and the government's or Parliament's oversight—the ability of these processes to stop clear abuses of the power conferred on regulators may, as we have seen, be limited. The courts have an important role to play in ensuring that the regulators effectively implement the regulatory scheme set out in the legislation and do not abuse the powers put at their disposal.

Policing the Regulatory Process

The government has made clear its intention to introduce legislation which would result in a radical shift in financial services regulation, away from the 1986 Act emphasis on "self-regulation" and towards a more unified statutory regulatory body. In the meantime, however, the courts have a supervisory role in delivering the balance between statutory and non-statutory regulation which was struck in the 1986 Act. Thankfully the UK has not seen public legal battles between financial services regulators on the scale experienced in the US. However, the case law does provide pointers to the courts' role in enforcing the terms of the "contract" embodied in the legislation, with particular regard to the balance of power between the FSA and the recognised bodies.

So in *R. v. SIB, ex p. IFAA*[79] the Court was asked to consider the legality of the SIB's "guidance" on the action which the SIB expected the front-line regulators to take in order to ensure that authorised firms took remedial steps to address the widespread misselling of personal pensions between 1988 and 1994. The SIB's statement proposed a scheme which involved the self-assessment by the firms concerned of their compliance with regulatory requirements in relation to advice given on every relevant transaction, of any loss caused and of the appropriate redress. The Independent Financial Advisers Association, whose members were among the authorised persons expected to implement such a scheme, argued that the scheme was too onerous and sought to set aside the decision of the Board to publish the statement on the grounds, *inter alia*, that the statement was unlawful because the SIB had no power to direct members of an SRO or RPB to pay compensation to investors. The court accepted the SIB's case that it had not purported to give any direction to SRO or RPB members, but had merely issued guidance to recognised bodies (and to firms regulated directly by the SIB). However, in doing so the court, having reviewed the relevant provisions of the Act, confirmed that:

> "[T]he SIB have no power to enforce the provisions of the statement directly against [independent financial advisers] except perhaps against those few who are directly regulated by the SIB. The provisions of the statement are directly enforceable, if at all, by

[79] [1995] 2 BCLC 76.

SROs, and RPBs, whose powers are wholly derived from their constitution and membership. Where the necessary rules have been passed, they can be enforced against IFAs—unless struck down on judicial review . . .

. . . it is very much open to question whether the SIB could revoke recognition because a regulatory body failed to enforce a scheme for extracting compensation from its members. The SIB, as already mentioned, can apply to the court under section 61 for an order that money be provided by an authorised person for compensation. Can they achieve the same object without the aid of the court, by reason of their power to revoke if the regulatory body is obdurate?

We have thought it right to enter upon that topic because the extent of the SIB's powers is at the very heart of this application. Our answer is that the SIB have no direct power to enforce the Statement against IFAs, as is common ground; it is questionable whether there is any power over regulatory bodies that would enable the SIB to achieve its object indirectly; but that is not at present a live problem in this case, and may never be. What still has to be considered is whether the SIB, by the terms of the statement, were asserting powers which they did not have. Such a course, which might be described as a jactitation of power, should in our judgement be subject to the remedies of judicial review in an appropriate case."

Much of the above was obiter. However, it does reveal that the court was concerned to ensure that the SIB was not seeking to upset the delicate balance between its supervisory powers over the recognised bodies and those bodies' autonomy. In doing so the court was fulfilling its constitutional role of policing the regulatory settlement embodied in the 1986 Act and, in particular, requiring that changes to the rules affecting SRO members in the conduct of their affairs be effected through the appropriate channels envisaged in the Act and not by the back door.[80]

The Court accepted that the industry was "facing a problem of exceptional magnitude, and a proper solution was urgently required", and noted that the SIB's guidance was concerned with complex issues of regulatory policy. Nevertheless, it seems that the court would have felt able to intervene *if* it had considered that the SIB was seeking to abuse its position by asserting over authorised firms powers which it did not have.

A similar theme is evident from a Canadian decision relating to the Ontario Securities Commission's powers to issue guidance. In *Ainsley Financial Corporation and others* v. *Ontario Securities Commission*[81] the Ontario Court of Appeal held invalid a policy statement issued by the Commission relating to the sale of penny stocks. Examining the terms of the statement and the context in which it was issued, the court concluded that it was outwith the Commission's statutory powers because the statement contained mandatory provisions and constituted an attempt to impose a *de facto* legislative scheme, with detailed substantive requirements, for which the Commission lacked statutory authority.

---

[80] See Bishop, n.14 above.
[81] (1994) 77 OAC 155.

These cases serve to illustrate the importance of the courts' role in ensuring that the institutional arrangements and processes ordained and established by Parliament are followed. While the courts may be slow to upset the outcomes of the regulatory process, it is part of their role to ensure that regulators do not depart from it.

Reviewing the Substantive Outcomes of the Regulatory Process

The courts have a wider role in ensuring that the regulators remain within the "four corners" of their powers and do not exceed the terms of their powers or use them to further purposes not envisaged by the legislation. Again, however there is a need for judicial restraint. The need to ensure that the courts do not substitute their own view for that of the responsible regulator means that the courts should intervene only in cases of clear "illegality". As regards the FSA, its statutory powers are derived from, and limited by the terms of the 1986 Act.[82] Thus, the courts have entertained applications for judicial review in which complex arguments have been raised concerning the precise construction of certain of the FSA's statutory powers.[83] However, many of the FSA's powers and functions are framed in very broad terms and are less amenable to judicial definition. The FSA is also given wide discretion as to the use of its powers. In such a context the courts' role is necessarily limited. The courts are not well equipped to make decisions concerning, for example, the "fitness and properness" of persons to conduct investment business,[84] or whether a body meets the requirements for recognition as an investment exchange. As suggested by Julia Black's observations in Chapter 6 of this work, there is a case for affording the regulators a "margin of appreciation" in the application of statutory provisions (or the interpretation of their own rules), the breadth of which will vary according to the nature of the function being performed and the terms of the statute. The courts need to guard against the danger that, by characterising issues presented to them as issues of law, they may increasingly impinge on territory which is properly the domain of the regulatory body. Here the courts' intervention should be limited to cases where a regulator seeks to use its power for a purpose clearly not within the purposes envisaged by the Act, or there is procedural impropriety or *Wednesbury* unreasonableness in the narrow sense.

---

[82] Although the FSA is a company limited by guarantee, its regulatory powers are limited to those provided in the statute (*per* Staughton LJ in *R. v. SIB, ex p. IFAA*).

[83] See, e.g., cases concerning the construction of the FSA's power to make compensation rules (s. 54 of the 1986 Act)—*SIB v. FIMBRA* [1991] 4 All ER 398; *R. v. SIB and PIA, ex p. Sun Life*; and (on the interpretation of the SIB's rules) *R. v. Investors Compensation Scheme, ex parte Bowden* [1995] 3 All ER 605 (HL). See also *R. v. SIB, ex p. Interdata UK Ltd* (13 Sept. 1996) which concerned the construction of the SIB's statutory investigation powers in s. 105 of the Act.

[84] *R v. SFA, ex parte Panton, per* Sir Thomas Bingham MR: "[i]t is for SFA to decide, on consideration of the appropriate facts, whether or not to proceed against a member on the grounds that the member is not a fit and proper person".

The position of the recognised bodies is more problematic: as their powers are derived from contract, they are not necessarily limited by the terms of the 1986 Act,[85] albeit that they must meet the requirements set out in the Act in order to retain their recognition. It may not therefore be sufficient to show that, for example, a recognised investment exchange has acted for purposes outside the four corners of the legislation. The exchange has an existence independent of the statute and can, subject to the usual limitations of company law, do as it chooses. Indeed, it is implicit in the 1986 legislation that the recognised bodies will take to themselves powers which are not available to the FSA as the statutory regulator. Most notably, SRO and RIE rules provide for the power to fine their members—a power not currently available to the FSA (although it is anticipated that the reform legislation will remedy this problem). How then are the four corners of the recognised bodies' powers to be defined for the purposes of public law? Where statute provides for regulatory functions to be performed by recognised bodies using instruments of private law (such as contract) to determine the powers which those bodies take over their members (subject to the FSA's oversight and to the parameters set out in the legislation), considerable latitude should be given to those recognised bodies to make full use of the flexibility provided by private law. However, in keeping with their responsibilities as bodies charged with public regulation they should not seek to act in a way which is clearly in conflict with the purposes and objectives of the Act. Whether such a ground of judicial review should be viewed as a form of "illegality" or "irrationality" is not clear. In *ex parte Kendall* the court seems to have proceeded on the assumption that it was necessary to be satisfied that LAUTRO's rules regarding the indebtedness of appointed representatives could reasonably (in the *Wednesbury* sense) be related to the legislative purpose at which they were aimed, namely ensuring, as is required by the statutory qualifications of an SRO, that members of LAUTRO were "fit and proper" to conduct investment business and that LAUTRO's rules provided adequate protection for investors. Thus, although a recognised body's rules are an outcome of the self-regulatory process and are founded in private contract law between the body and its members, it seems that the courts will draw on the periphery of statutory provisions which underpin the recognised body's status in determining whether those rules are reasonable or seek to pursue an improper purpose.

In *ex parte IFAA*, while the court upheld the SIB's statement it concluded that:

> "In our judgement the statement ought to say that notwithstanding paras 41 and 42, IFAs are not to be required to take any step which will invalidate their insurance cover

[85] Although the *vires* of recognised bodies will be limited by the terms of their Memorandum and Articles of Association, this does not prevent the members from changing the objects and powers of the organisation. In July 1996, for example, the Personal Investment Authority announced its intention to call a special meeting of its members to extend the SRO's scope to enable it to regulate the marketing and sale of long-term care insurance products by PIA members. Such products are outside the definition of "investment" in Sched. 1 of the 1986 Act. In the event, the PIA's plans were superseded by the Treasury's announcement that it would seek to amend the Act so as make such business an authorisable activity.

without their insurers' consent. To the extent that it does not say that, the statement is wholly irrational."

Of course, the SIB agreed to amend the statement accordingly, and the application was dismissed. It is not clear how it could have been said that the statement issued by the SIB was, owing to the suggested omission, a statement which no reasonable SIB could have made.[86] But behind this rare suggestion of irrationality on the part of a financial regulator lies the court's concern that, without this qualification, the purpose at which the SIB's statement was aimed, namely the compensation of investors, and therefore the purposes of the Act, might be frustrated. As Staughton LJ had earlier concluded, in the case of many small IFAs their professional indemnity insurers remain "the one source of funding which could be relied upon to provide compensation for investors". Although the court was there concerned with the actions of the SIB, it is submitted that the same considerations should apply to the actions of recognised bodies, despite the differing sources of their powers.

Procedural Fairness

Perhaps the issue most frequently considered by the courts in relation to financial services regulation is that of procedural fairness. Such issues often arise in the context of disciplinary proceedings before regulatory bodies. Because such proceedings generally take the form of trial-type processes, it is to be expected that the courts will feel more competent to opine on their fairness. However, it is also the case that the consequences of such proceedings for the persons subject to them are significant. Determinations made by regulators as to whether a person should be or should remain authorised, or should be disqualified from being employed by authorised firms may well result in depriving the individuals involved of their livelihood. Allegations of misconduct proved against regulated persons may have severe ramifications for the reputation and business of the firms concerned or for the employability of individuals. It is therefore to be expected that the intensity of judicial review of such processes will be greater.[87] At the same time, the regulatory system is designed to promote speedy and effective action to discipline misconduct and, where appropriate, secure redress for investors. While the regulators' procedures should be "fair and reasonable and include adequate provision for appeals" the processes used are designed to be efficient and flexible.

The cases show that the courts have been sensitive to the special needs of the regulatory bodies in this regard. The courts have provided valuable guidance on the regulators' duty to act fairly in relation to third parties who may be

[86] See Paul Walker in ch. 7 of this book for an examination of "irrationality" as ground for judicial review of commercial regulators.
[87] See *R. v. LAUTRO, ex p. Ross* [1993] QB 17, *per* Glidewell LJ at 50G. On "intensity" of judicial review more generally, see De Smith, Woolf & Jowell, n. 56 above, 586–93.

adversely affected by their determinations (even though they may not be in any contractual relationship with the regulator).[88] However they have also resisted attempts to introduce excessive legalism into regulatory processes[89] and sought to preserve regulators' ability to take speedy and effective action where the public interest so requires. Thus in *ex parte Ross* Glidewell LJ said:

> "I accept that very frequently a decision made which directly affects one person or body will also affect, indirectly, a number of other persons or bodies, and that the law does not require the decision-making body to give an opportunity to every person who may be affected however remotely by its decision to make representations before the decision is reached. Such a principle would be unworkable in practice. On the other hand, it is my opinion that when a decision-making body is called upon to reach a decision which arises out of the relationship between two persons or firms, one of whom is directly under the control of the decision-making body, and it is apparent that the decision will be likely to affect the second person adversely, then as a general proposition the decision-making body will owe some duty of fairness to that second person, which, in appropriate circumstances, may well include a duty to allow him to make representations before reaching the decision. This will particularly be the case when the adverse effect is upon the livelihood or the ability to earn of the second person or body."

However, he went on to endorse Mann LJ's reasoning that the purpose of the powers of intervention which LAUTRO had exercised was the protection of investors and that the achievement of that objective would sometimes require urgent action. That urgency may be incompatible with a duty to hear representations *before* the making of the decision to issue an intervention notice. Drawing again from the similar *statutory* powers conferred on the SIB, it was said that LAUTRO's rules reflected the intention in the Act that such powers should be exercisable immediately pending further enquiries and investigations and without affording those affected a right to make representations first. Persons affected (not just the authorised firm concerned) ought, however, to be allowed to make an immediate application to the regulatory body to set aside the intervention notice. In this way the court sought to balance the need for fairness in the treatment of those affected by regulatory power against the need to allow regulatory bodies sufficient freedom to enable them to take the action they consider necessary in the interests of investors.

The difficult balance between regulatory effectiveness and the requirements of due process is also relevant to the operation of Ombudsmen schemes in financial services regulation. The prospect that the new financial regulatory reform legislation may seek to place on a statutory footing the operation of the various different Ombudsman schemes operating within the purview of the 1986 Act

[88] *Ex p. Ross; ex p. Tee*, n. 60 above.

[89] See, e.g., *R. v. Association of Futures Brokers and Dealers, ex p. Mordens Ltd*, (*The Times*, 6 Sept. 1990), where the court refused to overturn the SRO's Appeal Commissioner's decision that it was for AFBD and its advisers to decide what evidence to adduce to support their case and that he could not order discovery of documents sought by the appellants.

raises important questions about the fairness of the procedures to be used. As noted above in the context of the *Aegon Life* case, the fact that the Ombudsman system may be placed on a firm statutory footing, and therefore become more obviously amenable to judicial review, does not remove the inherent tension between seeking to provide an informal, speedy arbitration service for investor complaints and providing a process which meets both domestic and international standards of due process. Clearly the court will have a role in ensuring that Ombudsmen comply with any procedural requirements set out in the legislation. However, as has been made clear in recent cases concerning the procedures followed by the Pensions Ombudsman, quite apart from any statutory provisions, it is the function of the court to ensure that fair procedures are adopted, paying due regard to the particular jurisdiction in issue. While an Ombudsman procedure is intended to be quick, inexpensive and informal, the courts have (taking into account the serious consequences of the Ombudsman's decisions for the parties) required compliance with certain minimum standards of natural justice, including requirements that the parties be informed of the nature of the allegations made against them, along with all potentially relevant information obtained by the Ombudsman, and then must be given a "fair crack of the whip" and a fair opportunity to provide any answer they may have.[90]

Parallel Proceedings

Similar considerations apply in other contexts: the issues of "double jeopardy" which may arise in regulatory proceedings can be particularly difficult. The complexity of the current institutional structure of financial services regulation, and the interrelationship with other areas such as criminal law enforcement and private civil liability, mean that peculiar issues of procedural fairness are presented. The difficulties encountered by those having to deal with overlapping parallel enquiries by different regulatory bodies and law enforcement agencies have been considered in a number of cases. The principles on which the court would intervene were set out by the Court of Appeal in *R. v. Panel on Takeovers and Mergers, ex p. Fayed.*[91] There it was suggested that the Court had power to intervene to prevent injustice where the continuation of one set of proceedings may prejudice the fairness of the trial of other proceedings. That power is not, it appears, limited to where the regulatory body's refusal to stay its proceedings is irrational—what was fair was a matter for the court.[92] However, the power had to be exercised with great care and only where there is a "real risk of serious prejudice which may lead to injustice". Moreover, the courts will give

---

[90] See *Duffield v. Pensions Ombudsman* (unreported, Carnwath J, 2 Apr. 1996) and *Seifert v. Pensions Ombudsman* [1997] 1 All ER 214.

[91] [1992] BCC 524.

[92] See *ex p. Guinness; R. v. Monopolies and Mergers Commission, ex p. Stagecoach Holdings plc* (*The Times*, 19 July 1996).

considerable weight to the regulatory tribunal's view of what is fair—the initial decision to grant or deny an adjournment being at the tribunal's discretion.

In R. v. *Institute of Chartered Accountants in England & Wales, ex p. Brindle*[93] the Court of Appeal appeared to suggest that the court's role was more akin to a "balancing exercise" in which the importance and urgency of the regulatory process is weighed against the risk of prejudice to the individual. Nolan LJ indicated that his primary concern was with whether the continuation of the regulatory proceedings would prejudice the appellants in the conduct of their defence in civil proceedings to an extent which could not be justified in the public interest. Hirst LJ went further and suggested that "it was inherently unfair that two tribunals should contemporaneously be considering the same issue". If that dictum had been taken as a principle of general application, it would have presented severe difficulties to financial services regulators. Those difficulties were addressed by the court in R. v. *Chance, ex p. Smith*.[94] There Henry LJ accepted that the court was required to conduct a balancing exercise of weighing the public interest in the prompt and efficient operation of the regulatory process against the risk of serious prejudice to the fairness of the trial of other proceedings. However, in doing so, the court would give great weight to the views of those responsible for the regulatory proceedings as to the public interest in pursuing those proceedings with all speed consistent with justice. Henry LJ went on to stress the importance of the public function performed by regulatory bodies in taking effective disciplinary action against regulated firms and individuals. He explained the importance of the Joint Disciplinary Schemes proceedings in meeting public concern about the conduct of the auditors in the Maxwell affair and continued:

> "where there is such public concern, there is an obvious need for that concern to be met with all speed consistent with justice. If the disciplinary proceedings designed to address that concern are stayed pending resolution of the civil proceedings, we are doubtful whether that public concern will often be met when it has to await the prior resolution of these civil proceedings. Even where the civil proceedings are focused on the area covered by the regulatory functions, the remedies of fine and disqualification that may be required to meet the public concern are not available in those proceedings. Often the civil actions will settle without pronouncement by the court and that is likely to happen a long time after the events that initially caused the concern. By then it may be too late for the disciplinary proceedings to play their allotted role in meeting that concern."

In dismissing the accountants' application for review of the Disciplinary Scheme's decision not to stay its proceedings pending the outcome of the civil claims against the auditors, the court took into account a number of factors, including the risk of inconsistent decisions, possible prejudice from the applicants having to fight battles on "two fronts", prejudice from the documents

---

[93] *The Times*, 12 Jan. 1994; for comment see M. Beloff and C. Lewis, "Bringing Accountants to Book: Statutory Regulation and Civil Litigation" [1994] *Public Law* 164.

[94] [1995] BCC 1095.

which may be created during the course of the disciplinary proceedings and the
urgency and importance of the disciplinary proceedings. In doing so the court
rejected the argument that Hirst LJ's dictum in *Brindle* was intended as a principle of general application. For the reasons indicated by Henry LJ, such a principle would not give adequate weight to the strong public interest in speedy and
effective regulatory action being taken in such cases.

CONCLUSIONS

The innovative mix of statutory and non-statutory regulation placed the 1986
Act regime squarely on the San Andreas fault that lies beneath the overlapping
systems of public law and private law. As a result, the traditional public law
principles applied by the courts in judicial review have sometimes faltered in the
face of bodies which do not comply with the paradigm of the public law body
whose power is conferred by statute. The language of private law, including
notions of consensual submission, privity of contract and corporate personality,
has on occasions been utilised to deflect the courts' from their constitutional
role.

Nevertheless, as the above survey of some of the case law illustrates, the
underlying themes are familiar: the need to ensure that regulators act in accordance with the purposes which can distilled from the legislation; the need to
promote principles of good public administration in regulatory decision-
making; and the need to ensure that the courts do not usurp the role of the regulators or impose legalistic principles and procedures which will unduly hamper
them in the performance of their public functions.

The government is now committed to the introduction of legislation which
will place primary responsibility for the regulation of financial services firmly in
the hands of a unified statutory regulator. The new legislation will therefore
adopt what has become an almost orthodox method for achieving Parliament's
objectives in the field of public regulation—reliance upon a non-governmental
body exercising powers and performing functions conferred upon it by primary
legislation. However, while the source of the new FSA's powers will be statutory, thereby reducing uncertainty as to the precise scope of judicial review in
this area, this will not resolve the fundamental issues with which the courts must
grapple when faced with a challenge to a regulator's actions. The legislation will
present a new constitutional "contract" in the financial services arena, the terms
of which it is (in part) the courts' responsibility to police. There will be a significant reduction in reliance upon "self-regulating" bodies to achieve the objectives of the legislation. The legislation will ordain a new regulatory process in
which regulated firms, consumers, the public, government and Parliament, as
well as the regulators, will continue to have a role. The courts will have a limited but vital role to play in ensuring that that process is operated in accordance
with the terms and purposes of the legislation and the requirements of proce-

dural fairness. They will need to be prepared to intervene to remedy clear abuses of regulatory power. At the same time, the courts must be careful not to usurp the regulatory process ordained by Parliament. They should continue to be slow to upset the outcomes of that process, save in cases of clear error, and they should be conscious of their own role in providing an environment in which those outcomes can effectively be achieved.

The fault lines which have emerged in the courts' approach to financial services regulation under the 1986 Act regime arguably reveal an occasional unwillingness to identify and grapple with these familiar and important issues. The use that has been made in some of the cases of arguments based on legal form to obscure the true nature of the regulatory process has meant that the courts have, on occasion, allowed themselves to side-step fundamental questions concerning their role in financial services regulation—questions which they will have to address head-on in the context of the more statutory system now promised by the government.

4

Court Procedures and Remedies in the Context of Commercial Regulation

MICHAEL SWAINSTON*

INTRODUCTION

In this paper I address four matters: the current law concerning the appropriate venue and procedure for cases which raise both public and private law issues ("mixed cases"); the differences in procedure and remedies according to where a mixed case is pursued; whether such differences are justified in cases concerned with commercial regulation, and particularly self-regulation; and how procedural law should evolve to cope with mixed cases in this context. The thesis is that the current procedural bifurcation between administrative law cases in the Divisional Court and general High Court litigation is unjustified. Administrative law remedies should be available outside the Divisional Court.

PROCEDURAL TREATMENT OF MIXED CASES

The root of the procedural problems concerning mixed cases is the House of Lords decision in 1983 in *O'Reilly v Mackman*[1] where prisoners failed in their attempt to challenge disciplinary decisions of prison visitors by means of claims for declarations by writ and originating summons in the Queen's Bench Division and Chancery Division. The House of Lords held that following the introduction of the new RSC Order 53, any challenge to the validity of an administrative act had to be undertaken by way of an application for judicial review in the Divisional Court, subject to the limitations on such applications and the protections for respondents there set out. According to Lord Diplock:

> "The position of applicants for judicial review has been drastically ameliorated by the new Ord. 53. It has removed all those disadvantages, particularly in relation to discovery, that were manifestly unfair to them and had, in many cases, made applications

* Brick Court Chambers.
[1] [1983] 2 A.C.237.

for prerogative orders an inadequate remedy if justice was to be done. . . Now that those disadvantages to applicants have been removed and all remedies for infringements of rights protected by public law can be obtained on an application for judicial review, as can also remedies for infringements of rights under private law if such infringements should also be involved, it would in my view as a general rule be contrary to public policy, and as such an abuse of the process of the court, to permit a person seeking to establish that a decision of a public authority infringed rights to which he was entitled to protection under public law to proceed by way of an ordinary action and by this means to evade the provisions of Ord. 53 for the protection of such authorities. My Lords, I have described this as a general rule; for, although it may normally be appropriate to apply it by the summary process of striking out the action, there may be exceptions, particularly where the invalidity of the decision arises as a collateral issue in a claim for infringement of a right of the plaintiff arising under private law, or where none of the parties objects to the adoption of the procedure by writ or originating summons. Whether there should be other exceptions should, in my view, at this stage in the development of procedural public law, be left to be decided on a case to case basis. . ... "

The corollary was quickly established that an applicant could not proceed under RSC Order 53 unless he had a "public law" claim. There have been two damaging consequences of the public/private divide established in this way. First, it has necessitated difficult attempts to categorise cases with mixed public and private law elements as *either* public *or* private and there are severe penalties for error. Ordinary civil law proceedings may fail or be stayed because the proper forum for the public law element of the case was the Divisional Court, and alternative proceedings in the Divisional Court may by that stage be time-barred because of the three month time limit on applications for judicial review.[2] Secondly, as developed below, the Courts have been inhibited in their substantive development of judicial review to supervise public regulation by private contract. This is a serious problem, given the modern emphasis on private contract as a tool of government.

MITIGATION OF THE O'REILLY DOCTRINE IN CASE-LAW

There has been some mitigation of the procedural aspect of the problem by two case law initiatives which broaden the jurisdiction of the ordinary civil Courts to deal with public law issues.

---

[2] The Crown is skilled in extracting tactical advantage from this confusion. For example, in public employment cases it has resisted applications for judicial review on the ground that civil servants had contracts of employment so that the claims were if anything private law claims: e.g. *R. v Lord Chancellor's Department ex p. Nangle* [1992] 1 QB 897. At the same time it has resisted writs issued by civil servants on the grounds that they did not have contracts so that the claims were if anything public law claims: *McClaren v Home Office* [1989] ICR 550.

The Private Rights Test

The first is a series of cases beginning with *Roy v Kensington & Chelsea Family Practitioner Committee*[3] holding that where private rights are at stake, they can be asserted and vindicated in an ordinary civil action notwithstanding that the facts also raise public law issues. So in *Roy*, a doctor was enabled to bring a private law claim for the balance of his "basic practice allowance" which the health authority had withheld on the ground that he had not been devoting a substantial amount of his time to his NHS practice. Under the relevant regulations, he was only entitled to the full amount if in the opinion of the Committee he was so devoting a substantial amount of his time. Dr Roy issued a writ claiming, *inter alia*, payment of the balance and asserting that he had sufficiently devoted himself to his practice. The Committee applied to strike out his claim on the basis that he should have sued by way of an application for judicial review under RSC Order 53.

The House of Lords ruled that because the doctor had an accrued right to the money, he could sue for it without first bringing Divisional Court proceedings to challenge the decision of the health authority that he did not qualify for the funds.

Lord Lowry decided the case on the basis of the doctor's private right to the money, either in contract or under the relevant legislation. In the course of his speech, he considered the extent of the procedural exclusivity of RSC Order 53 dictated by *O'Reilly v Mackman*. He accepted Counsel's submission that two interpretations were possible: a broad approach, under which Order 53 would only be mandatory if private rights were not in issue and a narrow approach, according to which applicants must proceed by way of judicial review in all proceedings which challenge administrative acts or decisions. He decided the case in terms of the narrow approach, holding that the only issue in the case was whether the claimant had an accrued private right, but made clear that he favoured the broad approach, and the balance of subsequent case law and academic comment has agreed with him.[4]

According to the broad approach, the viability of a writ action depends on whether the plaintiff has a private law right in addition to any public law complaint. This rather formalistic test has the virtue of neutralising the rather formalistic problems posed by *O'Reilly v Mackman* in most cases with mixed public and private law elements. Indeed, it creates an exception which more or less swallows the *O'Reilly v Mackman* rule in the mixed public and private law cases where *O'Reilly v Mackman* is relevant. However, traps remain for the unwary over the issue of whether a private right exists, particularly where the claimant does not have the benefit of a contract with the public authority.

---

[3] [1992] AC 624.
[4] Law Com No. 226: *Administrative Law: Judicial Review and Statutory Appeals* section 3.11.

For example, in *British Steel plc v Customs and Excise Commissioners*,[5] British Steel failed at first instance to recover duties which it alleged it was never obliged to pay because the Commissioners had wrongly refused to give it dispensation under the applicable revenue regime. Laws J held that it had no private law claim because it had not first challenged in Divisional Court proceedings the refusal of the Commissioners to grant the dispensation. He distinguished *Roy* because the doctor had an accrued private law right without any public law intervention. He distinguished the claim for repayment of tax wrongly demanded in *Woolwich Equitable Building Society v IRC*[6] because there, the unlawfulness of the tax demand was admitted, so that again, there was no need for public law intervention to perfect the private law restitutionary claim for repayment of tax.

The Court of Appeal in an unreported judgment reversed Laws J. But the analysis is rather obscure and focuses on the question whether there was a private right. Sir Richard Scott VC decided that British Steel had a private right to recover the money, relying in particular on Lord Brown-Wilkinson's analogy of money paid for no consideration in the *Woolwich Equitable* case. Millet LJ also considered that there was a private law right, though without analysis of the juridical basis for it.

It is submitted that determination of the case in terms of whether there was a private right was somewhat arbitrary. It involved no consideration at any stage of the factors which ought to have been relevant to the propriety or otherwise of "ordinary" civil proceedings as opposed to dedicated judicial review in the Divisional Court. For example, it would seem sensible to take into account the nature of the particular case, the appropriateness of applying to the plaintiff's claim the fetters on public law applications inherent in RSC Order 53, and whether the central issues call for the specialist expertise of the Divisional Court in judicial review, or specialist expertise in some other discipline somewhere else. Tax in the Chancery Division comes to mind.

An Abuse of Process Test

These problems are to some extent addressed by a new test propounded in *Mercury Communications Ltd v Director General of Telecommunications*.[7] The principal dispute was between Mercury and British Telecom, both of whom had licences to run telecommunications systems under section 7 of the Telecommunications Act 1984. In 1986 they entered into an agreement for Mercury to have access to BT's lines pursuant to condition 13 of BT's licence. The agreement provided for renegotiation of its terms after 5 years if either party considered that there had been a fundamental change in circumstances

---

[5] [1996] All ER 1002.
[6] [1993] 1 AC 70.
[7] [1996] 1 WLR 48.

during that time, and for differences which could not be resolved to be referred to the Director General of Telecommunications. The parties referred the matter of pricing to the DGT in 1992. Mercury subsequently sought to challenge his decision on the basis that the Director General had misinterpreted the scope of costs which were to be taken into account. The procedure adopted was an originating summons seeking a declaration as to the true construction of the relevant provisions in condition 13 of BT's licence. BT objected on the basis that any such challenge would have to be brought in the Divisional Court.

Lord Slynn delivered the principal speech in favour of Mercury and the other Law Lords agreed. He noted that the basis for the *O'Reilly v Mackman* rule was a perception that to proceed outside Order 53 might amount to an abuse of process. But he noted that Lord Diplock had envisaged exceptions to the procedural exclusivity of Order 53, and considered that exceptions were a small price to pay "to avoid the over-rigid demarcation between procedures reminiscent of earlier disputes as to the forms of action, and of disputes as to the competence of jurisdictions apparently encountered in civil law countries where a distinction between public and private law has been recognised". He went on to observe that it was of particular importance to retain flexibility "as the precise limits of what is called "public law" and what is called "private law" are by no means worked out". Then he identified the "overriding question" as "whether the proceedings constitute an abuse of the process of the court . . .". It was not an abuse to proceed by originating summons in the commercial court given that the dispute was primarily contractual, and given the suitability of the commercial court to resolve the central issues. He met the problem of circumvention of the procedural fetters in Order 53 by suggesting that the court hearing the action may have regard to Order 53 and seemingly apply its limitations by analogy.[8]

On the other hand, the abuse of procedure test has its own difficulties. In particular, it is a highly subjective criterion whose application by the court is difficult to predict.[9] Substantial well-advised plaintiffs like British Steel plc may still take the wrong course, with disastrous consequences. In practice this means that in any case of doubt, practitioners are effectively compelled to advise complainants to start proceedings in the Divisional Court first (because the Divisional Court procedure includes a facility for converting a judicial review application into an action by writ whereas a writ action cannot be converted the other way) or to combine an application for judicial review with a parallel writ.[10] Further, the abuse test has the limitation that it is a procedural device to solve a procedural problem. It only goes so far in addressing the fundamental problems which arise from the bifurcation of public and private law procedures.

---

[8] At p 58B.

[9] Generally, where one manner of proceeding is considered by the Court to be more appropriate than another, it is an abuse of process to adopt the other: see the decision of the Court of Appeal in *Buckland v Palmer* [1984] 1 WLR 1109. Judges can easily have different views on which procedure is most appropriate for a particular point. Laws J had the *Mercury* case cited to him in British Steel.

[10] See Richard Gordon Q.C., *Judicial Review Law and Procedure* (2nd Ed., London, 1996) p. 111.

Procedural Differences

Applications under Order 53 in the Divisional Court are subject to a short three month time limit, special requirements of standing and a threshold test of arguability at the leave stage. None of these requirements affects mixed cases which are brought in the ordinary courts. Whilst Lord Slynn has suggested that other courts may consider and apply the Order 53 limitations by analogy, it is not easy to see how that can be done without procedural changes.[11] There is no obvious power to bar a writ action after 3 months.

Attitude

Notwithstanding the changes wrought by the new Order 53 which caused Lord Diplock to consider it would be an abuse to litigate public law issues outside the Order 53 procedure, real differences persist in the form and flavour of proceedings in the Divisional Court and the ordinary courts. For example, despite the nominal power of the Divisional Court to resolve disputed issues of fact with witness evidence, it does not happen often.[12] Despite lofty endorsement of the power of the Divisional Court to issue advisory declarations to decide key points in cases even where there has been no formal decision to attract the prerogative remedies,[13] it is difficult to get one.[14] The indications are that complainants who need to resolve issues of fact are better off elsewhere.[15]

---

[11] Lord Slynn may have had in mind that the power of the ordinary courts to make declarations of right is discretionary. But the claim may be for relief which would not be discretionary, like the return of money (cf *British Steel plc v Customs and Excise Commissioners* [1996] 1 All ER 1002).

[12] See Lord Diplock in *O'Reilly v Mackman* [1983] AC 237:

"... it will only be on rare occasions that the interests of justice will require that leave be given for cross-examination of deponents on their affidavits in applications for judicial review. This is because of the nature of the issues that normally arise upon judicial review."

The exceptions are indeed exceptional, and ordinarily the Court proceeds on affidavit: see the descriptions in Richard Gordon Q.C., *Judicial Review: Law & Procedure* (2nd Ed. 1966) at 162 and Clayton & Tomlinson, *Judicial Review Procedure* at 165.

[13] *R. v Secretary of State for Employment Ex p. Equal Opportunities Commission* [1995] 1 AC 1

[14] The reluctance of the Divisional Court to enter into disputed facts and to grant advisory declarations at an interlocutory stage are both illustrated by *R. v PIA Ombudsman and another ex p. The Burns Anderson Independent Network* Transcript 21st January 1997.

[15] Lord Lowry recognised the existence of potential disputes of fact as a reason for private right cases to be resolved in the ordinary courts in *Roy v Kensington & Chelsea Family Practitioner Committee* [1992] 1 AC at 650E.

Substantive Differences

There are some suggestions that the choice of forum will also carry substantive advantages. For example, in *Roy*, Lord Lowry thought that it would not be possible to recover money in proceedings by way of judicial review.[16]

ARE DIFFERENCES JUSTIFIED?

(a) Tactical Manoeuvring

As long as procedural or substantive differences exist and apply fortuitously according to the forum in which a mixed case is brought, much energy of litigators will be expended on procedural manoeuvring to bring the case in the forum with the best tactical advantages.

(b) The Defence Anomaly

This seems particularly sterile when the procedural constraints of RSC Order 53 are regularly avoided simply by the expedient of waiting to be sued as opposed to taking positive steps as applicant. So in *Wandsworth LBC v Winder*,[17] the defendant was able to dispute arrears of rent on the ground that certain resolutions and notices of increase were ultra vires for unreasonableness, long before development of the private rights exception for plaintiffs in *Roy v Kensington & Chelsea Family Practitioner Committee*.[18] In *British Steel plc v Customs and Excise Commissioners*[19] (reversed on different grounds, see above) Laws J said with equanimity that his decision might have been different if, instead of paying under protest and claiming back the tax paid, British Steel had waited to be sued by the Commissioners.[20]

---

[16] [1992] 1 AC at 654B. See also Peter Cane, *Self Regulation and Judicial Review*, (1987) 6 *CJQ* 324 at 339.

[17] [1985] AC 461.

[18] [1992] AC 624.

[19] [1996] 1 All ER 1002

[20] See *British Steel v Customs & Excise Commissioners* [1996] 1 All ER at 1013C:

"... Where a defendant to a private law suit has a defence which consists in arguments against his plaintiff based on public law, he will not be non-suited for being in the wrong court: see *Wandsworth London BC v Winder* ... This principle has been criticised extra-judicially by Lord Woolf, in 'Public Law-Private law: Why the Divide? A Personal View' [1986] *PL* 220 at 233–234 and his 1989 Hamlyn Lectures *'Protection of the Public – A New Challenge'* (London, Sweet & Maxwell, 1990) pp29–30, but it is hard to see how it can be an abuse of process or contrary to public policy for a defendant to assert any defence which legally arises when someone else takes him to court. However the position of a defendant seeking to raise a public law issue does not of course arise in the present case, and accordingly no argument upon it was addressed to me; I refer to it only because it gives extra emphasis to the juridical basis of the *O'Reilly* rule, the avoidance of abuse of process."

It is unfortunate that the defence anomaly did not feature in argument. It is respectfully submitted that it makes no sense for British Steel's position to be different according to whether they had paid or not.

(c) Negative Impact on the Substantive Development of Judicial Review

Procedural problems would be more tolerable if they were only procedural problems. But another negative feature of procedural bifurcation is the encouragement which separate public and private law procedures give to the idea that private rights and public law are distinct and mutually exclusive, and to an automatic equation of contract with private rights. This has led the Divisional Court to refuse public law remedies in circumstances where a commercial regulator has acted pursuant to a contractual power.[21]

This tendency is well illustrated by *R. v The Independent Broadcasting Authority ex parte the Rank Organisation plc*.[22] Rank was in the process of a takeover bid for Granada plc, which held a broadcasting licence from the IBA. The IBA vetoed Rank's entitlement to vote more than 5% of Granada plc's shares without hearing any representations from Rank as to its proposals for programming etc. The Court of Appeal refused review because the IBA had acted pursuant to private contractual rights under the Articles of Association of Granada plc, albeit that the relevant provisions giving it a veto were inserted through the pressure of its statutory powers under the Broadcasting Act.[23]

The result of this reluctance to interfere in contract cases is particularly unjust in cases like *Rank* where the party aggrieved by the exercise of contractual power is not even a party to the contract, and has no prospect of private law redress because of contractual privity.[24]

Where the complainant is a party to a contract with the regulator, public law review has often been excluded *a fortiori*. The principal cases involve sport: *Law v National Greyhound Racing Club*;[25] *R. v Disciplinary Committee of the Jockey Club ex p. Aga Khan*.[26] But the equation of contract with private rights has produced similar results in commercial cases: *R. v Lloyd's of London, ex p. Briggs and others*.[27]

---

[21] The fact that prerogative orders have not been applied to powers derived from contract has led to the extrapolation that Order 53 cannot apply to such powers. But the remedies under Order 53 include declarations and injunctions which lay against domestic tribunals before creation of the Order 53 procedure. See e.g. Denning LJ as he then was in *Lee v The Showmen's Guild of Great Britain* [1952] 2 QB 329 at 346:

"The remedy by certiorari does not lie to domestic tribunals, but the remedy by declaration and injunction does lie, and it can be as effective as, if not more effective than, certiorari. . ."

[22] Court of Appeal (Civil Division) (Transcript: Association) 26 March 1986.

[23] In *R v The Lord Chancellor ex parte Hibbit and Sanders (A Firm) and Another* Times 12th March 1993 Rose LJ endorsed *Rank* as authority that:

"The public importance of the work done does not make the matter one of public law (see *McClaren v Home Office* per Dillon LJ at 832 H). The exercise of a private law function, even when pursuant to a statutory power is not susceptible to judicial review (see *R. v IBA, ex parte Rank*, The Times 14 March 1986 (a transcript of 13th March 1986))".

[24] This is quite apart from the terms of the contract, which are invariably hostile.

[25] [1973] 1 WLR 1302.

[26] [1993] 2 All ER 853.

[27] [1993] 1 Lloyd's Rep 176.

This approach ignores the reality that where government uses contract to achieve regulation, either directly or indirectly by threatening more formal regulatory structures unless self-regulation is put in place, the relevant contracts are not voluntary and consensual.[28] Freedom of contract is not a justification for leaving the parties to their contractual rights.

It is appropriate to acknowledge that there has been a more interventionist approach in the context of contractual regulation of financial services. Under the Financial Services Act 1986, a firm must be authorised to do "investment business" and authorisation is principally by membership of self-regulatory organisations ("SROs") which control their members by contractual enforcement of their rules. The Financial Services Authority (FSA), on behalf of the Treasury, lays down certain mandatory inclusions in the rules and vets their rule books for compliance. Applying *Datafin* criteria,[29] acts of certain of the SROs have been held susceptible to review.[30]

On the other hand, the position is unclear regarding ombudsmen established by the SROs to rule on informal[31] compensation claims by customers. In *R. v Insurance Ombudsman Bureau ex p Aegon Life Assurance Ltd*[32] the Divisional Court refused review in the case of the Insurance Ombudsman, on the basis that submission to his jurisdiction was the product of a consensual submission of the industry prior to statutory regulation rather than statutory pressure. There is more "statutory underpinning" for the SRO ombudsmen's decisions in the sense that the SRO ombudsmen are clearly the creatures of the SROs which owe their existence to the Financial Services Act 1986. However, it is not clear that development of ombudsman procedures was a mandatory inclusion in their rules.[33]

---

[28] See S. Fredman and F. Morris, *The Cost of Exclusivity: Public and Private Re-examined* [1994] *PL* 69 at 74.

[29] *R. v Panel on Take-overs and Mergers ex p. Datafin* [1987] QB 815

[30] See *R. v Financial Intermediaries Managers and Brokers Regulatory Association ex p. Cochrane* Times, 23rd June 1989, [1990] COD 33; *R. v Life Assurance and Unit Trust Regulatory Organisation ex p. Ross* [1993] 1 QB 17; *R. v LAUTRO ex p. Kendall* [1994] COD 169.

[31] For example, the PIA Ombudsman's terms of reference say that he is not bound by any legal rule of evidence and that he can decide according to "general principles, rules, codes, guidance and standards" in preference to enactments, rules of law and judicial authority where the latter would be less favourable to the complainant.

[32] Times 7th January 1994

[33] An SRO must have "effective arrangements for the investigation of complaints against . . . its members". But these seem not to necessitate ombudsman procedures, or provision in ombudsmen's terms of reference that they can depart from the strict law: the SIB Core Conduct of Business Rules simply require an adequate complaints procedure. The SIB Guidance Release No 3/95 on Standards of Regulation for SROs, says (at para 5) that:

"An SRO should establish and maintain policies and procedures which aim to achieve the following:
– thorough and prompt investigation of complaints received from investors against firms which cannot be resolved between the firm itself and the investor, and referral of any relevant matters to those responsible for enforcement and discipline;
– reparation, where appropriate, for investors who are found to have suffered loss arising *from breaches of rules*;
– an independent means (eg a Complaints Commissioner) for assessing *whether a complaint has been properly handled within the mechanism set up by the SRO*;
– thorough and prompt investigation of complaints received against the SRO itself, by a person or persons who are not the subject of the complaint." (emphasis added).

cont/

It is perhaps unfortunate that the Courts have been so absorbed with the classification of mixed cases in the field of commercial regulation that they have not gone further and addressed the application of public law remedies to private contract cases where, because of the one-sided nature of the contracts, private law offers scant protection. The scale of potential abuse is illustrated by some of the Pensions Ombudsman statutory appeals.[34] There are no such statutory appeals in relation to the SRO ombudsmen's decisions.

(d) Particular Factors Re Commercial Regulation

In the field of commercial regulation the emphasis on the form and venue of proceedings is particularly unfortunate. Mixed cases concerning commercial regulation very often involve particular facts. Usually, the commercial party is affected by a very specific decision of the regulator. They are not cases where subordinate legislation is sought to be struck down with massive ramifications for the orderly conduct of public administration. In these circumstances the protections for respondents within the RSC Order 53 procedure seem particularly inappropriate.[35]

IV. SOLUTIONS

The Law Commission has proposed overcoming the difficulties caused by the public/private divide by building on the restrictive approach to the exclusivity principle taken in *Roy* and greater procedural facility for the transfer of cases in and out of the Divisional Court.[36] It is submitted that this is not a satisfactory approach, because it fails to address the point that separate procedures inhibit the development of effective judicial review of regulation by contract. Paradoxically, the emphasis on the private law aspect of mixed cases in *Roy* may exacerbate this substantive problem.

It would be odd if investor compensation schemes should be subject to judicial review when undertaken by the SIB or the SROs themselves but not where those same functions are performed by an independent body such as the IOB. But, if the *Aegon* analysis stands, that may be the result if the ombudsmen procedures are seen as consensual as opposed to dictated by the FSA and SIB.

[34] See for example the appalling cases of *Duffield v Pensions Ombudsman* [1996] Pensions LR 286 and *Seifert v Pensions Ombudsman* Tran. 30th July 1996. Aside from finding serious breaches of natural justice in both cases, Lightman J challenged the Ombudsman's determination in the latter case of his own motion on the ground of "unintelligibility". He summarised his conclusion "that the Ombudsman has gone seriously astray, not merely in the contents of the Determination, but also in the way his investigation was handled and the decision reached and expressed".

[35] In a case on specific facts, there seems little need for a three month time limit to promote general certainty. Standing will rarely be a problem in mixed cases because the private law aspect will general entail a sufficient degree of interest in the proceedings on the part of the plaintiff. This is especially so in commerce where vexatious litigants are relatively few. If a case would not pass the threshold arguability test on a leave application, it might very well be struck out.

[36] Law Com. No. 226 para 3.7.

The ideal solution would be procedural reform to allow public and private law remedies to be claimed in the same proceedings in the ordinary courts. If it were thought necessary to accord special protection to the sort of respondents who were the intended beneficiaries of the Order 53 fetters on judicial review applications, it could be done by specific rules dealing with the particular cases where a threat to orderly administration exists, such as attempts to strike down subordinate legislation.[37]

It may be said that such an approach would carry the disadvantage of loss of specialisation of the Divisional Court judges in relation to public law cases. However, it has the advantage that public law or mixed cases could be assigned to judges with specialist expertise in the substantive law relevant to the administrative decision in issue, such as tax or financial services. Moreover, public law has now developed sufficiently that its principles are increasingly familiar outside the Divisional Court, and that trend is set to continue in the light of the *Roy* and *Mercury* decisions. It may be strengthened by broader judicial input, and raised to the level of a subject like tort which all judges are expected to know. It may also be strengthened by more direct confrontation with contract, where the new abuses of power are emerging.

---

[37] Lord Slynn has attempted to achieve a similar focus by preserving Order 53 exclusivity in this kind of case, notwithstanding his otherwise liberal abuse of process test. See *Mercury Communications Ltd v Director General of Telecommunications and Another* [1996] 1 WLR 48 at 58A:

> ". . . it cannot be said here . . . that the procedures under Order 53 are so peculiarly suited to this dispute (as they would be in a claim to set aside subordinate legislation or to prohibit a government department from acting) that it would be a misuse of the court's process to allow the originating summons to continue."

5

The Need for Wholesale Reform on Vires Issues in Public and Private Law

CHRISTOPHER CLARKE QC and CATHARINE OTTON-GOULDER*

INTRODUCTION

There is an acute need for wholesale reform on the fundamental issues of *vires* of public bodies, both in public and in private law. This paper adumbrates and analyses these issues and the bizarre and unacceptable consequences of the orthodox treatment of them. It also proposes some solutions. Those fundamental issues are: first, the distinction between want of capacity and abuse of power and the effect of an act purportedly done by a body which either wholly lacks the capacity to do that act or acts in abuse of a power which it does possess; secondly, the use of the words and phrases "void", "voidable" and "nullity"; and, thirdly, the relationship between public and private law in the context of want of capacity and abuse of power.

THE DISTINCTION BETWEEN WANT OF CAPACITY AND ABUSE OF POWER

Upon an orthodox analysis of decisions and acts of public bodies, if a public body makes a decision in which it takes into account irrelevant or ignores relevant considerations, or in which it behaves irrationally, or with actual or apparent bias (i.e. commits a public law error), its decision is void and of no effect, and any contract concluded purportedly pursuant to that decision is unenforceable. The purported counterparty is left to such remedies as he may have in quasi-contract. No distinction is to be drawn between decisions of a type which the body can never take and decisions of a type which could have been taken lawfully but in respect of which the decision-making process has gone awry. The contract concluded as a result of a decision which might have been legitimate is treated in the same way as one which could never have been legitimate: both are nullities. Once it is established in judicial review proceedings that the

*Brick Court Chambers. This paper was prepared for the Seminar Series, "Commercial Regulation and Judicial Review".

body has committed a public law error, the decision is shown to have been void for all purposes.

Plainly there must be some way of seeking to ensure that bodies do not purport to exercise powers which they do not have and do not vitiate the exercise of those powers which they do possess by taking into account irrelevant matters or disregarding relevant matters. But that end is not satisfactorily achieved by eliding two distinct categories of decision, namely those where there is no capacity to make the decision in question and those where there is an abuse of a power in making that particular decision. Moreover, the elision of those distinct categories leads to absurdity.

First, as a matter of common sense, there is a difference in kind between the act of a body which purports to do something which it simply has no power to do (no matter what the circumstances) and the act of a body which does have the requisite powers but misuses those powers, when purporting to exercise them. The various ways in which a public body may act unlawfully cannot satisfactorily be accommodated under one heading of excess of jurisdiction or excess of power. In many instances there is simply an abuse of power or procedural irregularity or unfairness in the exercise of the power.

Secondly, it is possible by objective means available to all to ascertain the powers of a body, and hence for a third party to assess the risk it is running in concluding a contract with that body. One can look at a company's memorandum and articles of association: one can consider the relevant statutes, rules and regulations and form a view of the powers of a public body. A third party has no comparable right to discover the motives for a decision and the processes employed whereby that decision has been reached. There is, therefore, some rationale for fixing third parties with knowledge of the powers of a public body and the consequences of those powers. The same considerations justify a refusal automatically to ascribe to those third parties knowledge of those motives or processes, or to burden them with the consequences of impropriety in those motives or processes.

The present position is that a counterparty to a contract with a public body will find that the contract is unenforceable if the public body has acted *Wednesbury* unreasonably in matters internal to itself of which the counterparty knows nothing, even if it could not have known of those matters. As long ago as 1904, Buckley J pointed out how great were the risks for a lender to a corporation for this very reason, since the contract might be vitiated by the presence or absence of some motive:

> "A corporation, every time it wants to borrow, cannot be called upon by the lender to expose all its affairs, so that the lender can say, 'Before I lend you anything I must investigate how you carry on your business, and I must know why you want the money, and how you apply it, and when you do have it I must see you apply it in the right way.' It is perfectly impossible to work out such a principle".[1]

---

[1] *In Re David Payne & Co. Ltd* [1904] 2 Ch. 608.

For precisely that reason, in 1972, Parliament provided protection for those lending to a local authority:

> "A person lending money to a local authority shall not be bound to enquire whether the borrowing of the money is legal or regular or whether the money raised was properly applied and shall not be prejudiced by an illegality or irregularity, or by the misapplication or non-application of any of that money."[2]

and, again, in 1989:

> "A person lending money to a local authority shall not be bound to ensure whether the authority have power to borrow the money and shall not be prejudiced by the absence of any such power."[3]

For the same reason, the courts and, later, Parliament provided protection for those dealing with companies. By virtue of section 35 of the Companies Act 1989, any transaction which is entered into by the company shall not be called into question by reason of any limitation in the company's constitution. Directors remain personally liable to the company unless that personal liability is removed by special resolution.

No such protection is afforded to counterparties to contracts with public bodies which are not companies. Nor is any such protection afforded in relation to contracts with local authorities which are not loans. Every such contract carries a risk of unenforceability as a result of an improper motive on the part of the public body. Even if the counterparty does not know of the impropriety and has no reason to suspect it and even if the public body carries on with the contract while convenient and accepts benefits provided under it, the public body is free, at some later date of its choosing (when, perhaps, the contract has become disadvantageous to it) to disown it. (Conversely, the unenforceability of a contract may be to the advantage of the counterparty.)

The aspects of the principle which are particularly objectionable are that the public body may disown the contract by asserting its own impropriety and wrongful conduct, whenever it chooses; and, nonetheless, may retain the benefits supplied purportedly pursuant to that invalid contract. It has long been settled law that a personal claim, or claim in quasi-contract, based on an *ultra vires* loan contract cannot succeed because success would amount to the enforcement of an *ultra vires* contract (*Sinclair* v. *Brougham*[4]). Those who provide services or goods may well be in no better a position than a lender. They may not be able recover compensation on a *quantum meruit* or otherwise in quasi-contract because there could be no implied promise for any reasonable compensation (see *Re Jon Beauforte (London) Ltd*[5] and *Guinness Plc* v. *Saunders*[6]). Thus, it may well be said that a public body's contract is only valid at its option.

---

[2] Local Government Act 1972, Sched. 12, para. 20.
[3] Local Government and Housing Act 1989, s.44(6).
[4] [1914] AC 398.
[5] [1953] Ch. 131.
[6] [1990] 2 AC 663.

Take the interest-rate swap contracts. The local authorities substantially performed those contracts until compelled to stop. Most local authorities (Hammersmith included) were net recipients of payments in the early years (the mid to late 1980s) when interest rates were relatively low. By early 1989, interest rates had risen and, if the contracts had been valid, the Hammersmith losses would have totalled several hundred million pounds. It was not possible at that date to calculate its exposure accurately but, roughly speaking, Hammersmith was likely to lose a further £100 million for every 1 per cent rise in interest rates. As was anticipated in 1989, interest rates continued to rise during the remaining life of most swap contracts.

In the ensuing litigation,[7] Hammersmith asserted that it had no power to conclude the contracts and that, if such power had been vested in it, it had abused its power, as a consequence of which the contracts were void and unenforceable. The House of Lords held that local authorities wholly lacked the necessary capacity; but, if Hammersmith had possessed that power, Hammersmith abused it in concluding those contracts, whether or not the banks knew of the abuse. Some might think that Hammersmith was cynically taking advantage of its own wrong in disowning its obligations under the swap contracts. In the event *Hazell* decided that Hammersmith entirely lacked the requisite capacity, so there was no question of Hammersmith's relying on its own abuse of its powers.

The effect of the *Allerdale*[8] decision is that the result would be no different if local authorities had possessed that power: public bodies may avoid liability under contracts concluded in abuse of powers possessed by them even if the counterparty to the purported contract were unaware of that abuse. In that case, Allerdale Borough Council wanted to provide a swimming pool for its area. Allerdale did not want to borrow the money itself, because the effect of doing so would have been to exceed its permitted borrowing limits. To achieve this end, therefore, in purported exercise of its powers under section 111 of the Local Government Act 1972, Allerdale acquired a company to develop a site by building a leisure pool and time-share units, the sale of which was intended to meet the cost of the pool; the bank lent the company £4.5 million by way of principal and £1.5 million by way of interest; and Allerdale gave the bank a guarantee of £6 million in respect of the company's obligations to the bank. The company went into liquidation and the bank called on the guarantee.

The Court of Appeal affirmed the decision at first instance, holding that Allerdale had no power to build time-share units and that the establishment of the company and the giving of the guarantee were part of a scheme designed to circumvent the controls on local authority borrowing and fell outside both the express and the implied powers of the council. Those acts were therefore *ultra vires*. Since the decision to adopt the scheme could not be treated as being made

[7] *Hazell* v. *Hammersmith and Fulham London Borough Council* [1992] AC 1.
[8] *Crédit Suisse* v. *Allerdale Borough Council* [1997] AC 306.

for a proper purpose or within the discretionary powers of the council, the decision was void and the guarantee wholly unenforceable. The company could not pay; Allerdale was relieved of any liability to pay under the guarantee; and Allerdale kept the swimming pool and the time-share units which had been built with the bank's money.

The Court of Appeal specifically held that the fact that Allerdale had an improper purpose was fatal, even if Allerdale had otherwise had the capacity to make the decision in question. Since the claim was a private law claim, albeit one against a public body, the consequences of Allerdale's decision to give the guarantee were the same as those which flowed where one of the parties to the contract lacked capacity; there was no effective distinction in this context between want of capacity and abuse of power.

Two of the judges in *Allerdale* thought that the absence of any effective distinction between these two categories was unsatisfactory. Peter Gibson LJ thought this area so difficult that he preferred not to express any view on the effect of invalidity because of abuse of power,[9] in particular, when the public body is relying on its own improper conduct to escape liability:

> "Where a governmental body wishes to escape an ultra vires contract with a citizen, two of the main aims of the doctrine of ultra vires might appear to be in conflict, i.e. the aim to protect citizens against illegal actions by government and the aim to protect the public and the public purse from the effects of illegal conduct by government. As a matter of policy, there is much to be said for the view that a citizen who contracts in good faith with a governmental body should not have to bear the risk that the contract may be beyond the legal powers of that body".[10]

Neill LJ also thought that the present law was unsatisfactory, but believed that it was not open to the Court of Appeal (in view of *Anisminic Ltd* v. *Foreign Compensation Commission*[11] and *Wandsworth LBC* v. *Winder*,[12] particularly) to classify the *ultra vires* decisions of local authorities into categories of invalidity.[13]

It is ironic that public law should have elided these two distinct categories while it has maintained a false dichotomy between "void" and "voidable", especially since the dichotomy between the latter pair of concepts has its historical roots in the distinction between that which was outside the power of the public body in question and that which was an error in the exercise of that power.

"VOID"/"VOIDABLE"/"NULLITY"

Orthodoxy also maintains the use of the categories "void" and "voidable". The distinction between those categories corresponds to the historical distinction

---

[9] At 437E.
[10] At 344 E.
[11] [1969] 2 AC 147.
[12] [1985] AC 461.
[13] At 344B.

between jurisdictional and non-jurisdictional error. Historically, the court intervened (and could with constitutional propriety intervene) if the body in question exceeded its jurisdiction. If the body's decision was within its jurisdiction, there were no grounds for intervention. To this rule the jurisdiction to intervene for error of law upon the face of the record was an exception. In that case the error was within jurisdiction and the decision was not void but voidable. The distinction between jurisdictional error and non-jurisdictional error of law on the face of the record has been swept away by *Anisminic*.[14] Now all errors of law, whether jurisdictional or non-jurisdictional, are reviewable. The distinction between jurisdictional and non-jurisdictional errors of law is for most practical purposes extinct.

The concepts "void", "voidable" and "nullity" have long outlived their usefulness and the orthodox analysis should be abandoned. A truly void act or decision is a nullity: a state of nothingness. It gives rise to no rights or obligations, is without legal effect, and may be ignored. Following that logic, some courts in some decisions have refused to entertain or decline to allow appeals against decisions classified as void.[15] But the fallacy of treating a decision reached contrary to natural justice as entirely void and therefore unappealable was exposed by the Privy Council in *Calvin* v. *Carr*.[16]

In any event, to treat such acts as completely ineffective does not accord with reality. So-called "void" acts or decisions are—as the law recognises—highly effective and have both factual and legal consequences in a number of situations.

First, until a court has determined the act or decision to be invalid in proceedings properly constituted for that purpose by a person with *locus standi* to bring them, it is entirely effective. Injunctive relief may be granted to enforce it and must be obeyed.[17] As Lord Radcliffe said in *Smith* v. *East Elloe RDC*:[18]

> "An order, even if not made in good faith, is still an act capable of legal consequences. It bears no brand of invalidity upon its forehead. Unless the necessary proceedings are taken at law to establish the cause of invalidity and to get it quashed or otherwise upset, it will remain as effective for its ostensible purpose as the most impeccable of orders."

Secondly, if no steps are taken to impugn the decision in question it will become as impregnable as if it had been entirely valid in the first place, as with orders of the court.[19]

---

[14] *Anisminic Ltd* v. *Foreign Compensation Commission* [1969] 2 AC 147.

[15] *R.* v. *Jones (Gwyn)* [1969] 2 QB 33 (an appeal to the CA was the wrong route where committal to the magistrates was invalid); *Metropolitan Properties (F.G.C.) Limited* v. *Lannon* [1969] 1 QB 577 (certiorari rather than appeal was the correct route where a breach of rules of natural justice was involved).

[16] [1980] AC 574, 589G–591C.

[17] *Hoffmann-La Roche (F) & Co. AG* v. *Secretary of State for Trade and Industry* [1975] AC 295, 367.

[18] [1956] AC 736, 759–70.

[19] *Gale* v. *Gale* [1966] Ch. 236, 242 and 247; *Isaacs* v. *Robertson* [1985] AC 97, 103.

Thirdly, even if the act or decision is successfully challenged (in the sense of being shown to be vitiated by error) the court may refuse to strike it down, in which case it will be as valid as the most regular of decisions. The court is particularly likely to refuse relief if third parties have relied upon the validity of the decision. Thus in *R. v. Secretary of State for Social Services, ex p. AMA*,[20] the court declared certain regulations to be *ultra vires* (for want of compliance with mandatory consultation requirements imposed by statute) but refused to quash them. Similarly in *Ex p. Cotton*,[21] Mann J held an instrument to be *ultra vires* but refused to declare it so to be. The effect of such decision is that the impugned instrument remains in full force and legal effect. In *R. v. Monopolies Commission, ex p. Argyll Group Plc*[22] the majority view of the court was that the Chairman of the Commission had no power to decide alone that the "proposal to make arrangements such as are mentioned in the reference" had been abandoned and to apply to the Secretary of State for his consent to lay aside the reference; but refused to grant relief. In *R. v. Panel on Takeovers and Mergers, ex p. Datafin Plc*[23] it was held that the courts should allow the decisions of the Takeover Panel to take their course (even if wrong).

Fourthly, the courts may uphold orders in part, as an alternative. Thus in *Agricultural Horticultural, Forestry Industry Training Board v. Aylesbury Mushrooms Limited*[24] the Minister had failed to consult the Mushroom Growers' Association before making an order establishing a training board for the agricultural, horticultural and forestry industry. The court held that the order should take effect subject to a rider that it did not apply to the growers of mushrooms (i.e. should only have partial effect).

Fifthly, the courts have even been known to convert a decision made where there was simply no power to make it into an effectively valid decision by the expedient of refusing to grant relief. In *R. v. Monopolies Commission, ex p. Argyll Group Plc*,[25] the court refused to quash a decision of the Chairman of the Commission, notwithstanding his lack of power to make it.

These decisions show that the use of the term "void" in this context is meaningless in any absolute sense. If the "void" decision of a public body is valid for all purposes until actually set aside, then "void" acts do not differ from voidable acts. Both are valid until quashed.

The distinction between void and voidable acts has given rise to unjust results. In *DPP v. Head*[26] the majority of the House of Lords held that a conviction of a man for carnal knowledge of a detained mental defective was wrong, because the Home Secretary's detention order was invalid, not being supported by the two medical certificates required by statute. Lord Denning dissented. The

[20] [1986] 1 WLR 1.
[21] *The Times*, 5 Aug. 1985.
[22] [1986] 1 WLR 763.
[23] [1987] 1 QB 815, 842.
[24] [1972] 1 WLR 190, 194 and 196.
[25] [1986] 1 WLR 763.
[26] [1959] AC 83.

error was—he held—a mere error on the face of the record and within jurisdiction so that the detention order was voidable only and valid and effective at the time of the offence, so justifying the conviction. To make the question of conviction or not turn on whether the order of detention is void or voidable is wholly unsatisfactory, as Lord Somervell observed.[27] The question should simply be whether or not the defendant had intercourse with an apparent mental defective.

In contrast note the case of *Chief Constable of the North Wales Police* v. *Evans*.[28] This was a case of breach of the rules of natural justice in relation to the dismissal of a probationary constable four years before. According to the conventional analysis the decision was void *ab initio* and the constable was entitled to continue as such. But the House simply refused to pronounce the decision void (which the Court of Appeal had done), being unclear what consequences would flow from such a declaration. Instead it merely declared that the constable was entitled to the same remedies, not including reinstatement, as he would have had if the Chief Constable had unlawfully dispensed with his services.

Both Sedley and Laws JJ have gone so far as to suggest that these orthodox views must be abandoned. Stephen Sedley QC (as he then was) contended in an article[29] that, faced by an invalid administrative act which in conventional phraseology might be termed a nullity, the court should rewrite the legal relationship between the parties in order to give workable effect to both law and fact. This may have the undesirable effect of reintroducing the Lord Chancellor's foot as a measure of justice, but it is a pointer in the right direction. In an illuminating chapter,[30] Laws J pointed out that the orthodox analysis failed to resolve crucial problems both in judicial review cases and in private proceedings or criminal prosecutions.

THE PUBLIC LAW/PRIVATE LAW DIVIDE

It is also necessary to reform the present interrelations between public and private law. Thus far, courts have assumed that some relief is available in one court which is not available in another. If a public body has acted *Wednesbury* unreasonably in reaching a decision to enter a contract which it could legitimately have made, the court may, on an application for judicial review of that decision, quash it as a nullity, or it may in the exercise of its discretion refuse relief. No such discretion is available to a private law court. This difference may give rise to injustice. An applicant for judicial review may fail to have the decision

---

[27] At 104.
[28] [1982] 1 WLR 1155.
[29] S. Sedley QC, *The Good, the Bad and The Voidable*, Justice Review II.
[30] Laws J, 'Illegality: The Problem with Jurisdiction' in M. Supperstone and J. Goudie (eds.), *Judicial Review* (Butterworths, London, 1992).

quashed, as a result of which the contract concluded because of that decision will be as valid and enforceable as if there had been no *Wednesbury* unreasonabless: but he may succeed on the same facts as a defence and for the purpose of obtaining a declaration by way of counterclaim. This was the situation in *Wandsworth LBC v. Winder*.[31]

Conversely, a plaintiff may be met by the defence of a public body by which it asserts its own *Wednesbury* unreasonableness and contends that the contract purportedly concluded as a result of that irrational decision is void and of no effect. The private law court has no choice but to treat the contract as void and unenforceable, even if that same public body would have failed to have its own decision quashed on a judicial review, upon the hypothesis that the court would have exercised its discretion against the public body. That was the situation in *Allerdale*. (The Court of Appeal decided that, even if there had been the requisite capacity, and the defect had been one of abuse of power only, the court would have been just as much obliged to treat the contract as void. Since it refused to transpose public law discretion to its (private law) court, the court did not decide how it would have exercised its discretion.)

Further, it is not possible to prevent the same issues being litigated both by way of judicial review and also by ordinary action, with the undesirable possible consequence of conflicting results. An applicant may obtain leave to review a body's decision judicially but the outcome will not give rise to *res judicata* or issue estoppel in an ordinary action. Conversely, an applicant may be refused leave for judicial review and yet be compelled to meet the point as defendant in an ordinary action without the benefit of the substantive discretion of the court to decide whether to quash the decision. Can it really be right that Crédit Suisse could only have obtained the benefit of that discretion if Allerdale had applied for leave for judicial review and sought a declaration in that application that the guarantee was *intra vires Allerdale*? Such a consequence is grotesque. Allerdale had no interest in seeking a judicial review: and Crédit Suisse probably had no power to seek a declaration by way of judicial review proceedings that the guarantee was *intra vires*. It might well be said that Crédit Suisse lacked the necessary *locus*, or that the use of judicial review for a declaration that the guarantee was *intra vires* for the purposes of enforcing that guarantee was not permissible. Furthermore, there must be many cases where the counterparty to the public body has no intimation that the public body intends to rely upon its own wrong as an *ultra vires* defence to the claim, until after the expiry of the relevant time limit within which judicial review must be sought.

Moreover, it is not possible to choose the forum to suit the interest of the applicant. If the complaint is solely of a right protected by public law, to begin proceedings by writ or originating summons is an abuse of the process, and the action will be struck out.[32] Conversely, it is only possible to enforce a contract

---

[31] [1985] AC 461.
[32] *O'Reilly v. Mackman* [1983] 2 AC 237.

in private law courts; an application for judicial review can only be made by leave of the court, whereas in an ordinary action a plaintiff may proceed, and a defendant defend, as of right.

It is true that the courts have increasingly recognised some of the problems caused by this false dichotomy and have tried to resolve them. In *Mercury Communications Ltd* v. *Director General of Telecommunications*[33] the House of Lords held that it was important to retain flexibility in the distinction between public and private law and that Mercury's procedure by way of originating summons was at least as well suited to the determination of the issues (of construction of the licence) as judicial review would be.

But this only dealt with one type of application, namely, that where there is a discretion vested in the ordinary court in dispensing private law. Such a court retains a discretion whether to grant or refuse a declaration even where it would be open to the court to grant one. That discretion cannot differ significantly from the discretion vested in a court dispensing public law in deciding whether or not to quash a decision. Yet, even here, on the present state of the law, the outcome is affected by the procedure chosen. The grant of a declaration that a particular decision is *ultra vires* leaves open the status of acts done and contracts concluded as a result of that decision, whereas everything following a quashed decision is simply a nullity (on an orthodox analysis).

When a court is dispensing private law, it has a discretion whether or not to grant certain relief, e.g. injunctions, rescission, rectification, specific performance, declarations. In such cases, the outcome is not much affected by the fact that the claim proceeds by way of ordinary action in private law. There remain, however, significant anomalies, whose impact is the more startling when one considers the plaintiff seeking to enforce contractual or tortious rights against a public body. These anomalies arise in relation to claims where the court dispensing private law has no discretion vested in it to withhold or grant relief by way of damages or an order for payment of the price or under a guarantee, irrespective of any abuse of power by that public body.

Lord Woolf has expressed deep concern about these anomalies. In the first of the 1989 Hamlyn Lectures[34] he states:

> "I am, however, appalled that a situation should be able to arise where Mr. Winder would not succeed on an application for judicial review because the Court would not exercise discretion in his favour but he could still succeed on the same facts as a defence and for the purpose of obtaining a declaration by way of counterclaim. It appears that for no good reason we now have as a result of the *Winder* case not only an exception to the *O'Reilly* v. *Mackman* principle but also have accepted that different standards will apply where the invalidity of a council decision is relied on as a defence from those which will apply when it is relied on as the grounds for an application for judicial review. . . . The problem may be related to the fact that the Courts have yet to establish clearly the effect of a decision being void . . ."

[33] [1996] 1 WLR 48.
[34] At 30–1.

The particular situations where injustice seems likely to result from these anomalies are those where the public body wishes to escape liability under a contract by relying on its own abuse of power and those where the counterparty to that contract was unaware of the abuse of power on the part of the public body. The case must be *a fortiori* where there is a combination of those situations.

PROPOSED REFORMS

What is necessary is to permit—indeed, to require—a private law court, when deciding issues of public law which have arisen in the action, to approach and decide the issues of public law as if those issues were before it on an application for judicial review, or as if there were a claim for a declaration (namely that the relevant decision were void (or voidable)), exercising its discretion in the manner in which it would have done in deciding whether to quash the decision or to grant a declaration that the decision was void.

In addition to the import of a substantive discretion whether to enforce a contract, it would also be necessary to make procedural reforms in order to align the procedure of an ordinary action with judicial review. The chief points are the requirement for leave and the time limit. There is much to be said for requiring a plaintiff who wishes to raise points of public law as part of his claim to be bound by the same restrictions as bind those applying for judicial review. If Allerdale had sought a declaration that the guarantee was *ultra vires* there would be no good reason for its being permitted to avoid the requirement for leave or the time limit.

On the other hand, a defendant does not choose to have proceedings brought against him, nor when they are brought. He should have the freedom to raise issues of public law as of right by way of defence. But that freedom should be made subject to the court's discretion (applicable in all public law cases) whether or not to grant a remedy. The effect in *Allerdale* would have been that the court would have had the freedom to choose whether or not to enforce the guarantee. The asymmetry between the positions of the plaintiff and defendant admittedly remains and must remain, unless one were to abolish the requirement for leave and the time limit for judicial review applications. To abolish that requirement and limit for judicial review would be impracticable, but the vice of the asymmetry is much diminished by the importing of the substantive discretion when a person (whether plaintiff or defendant) raises a point of public law.

There remains the problem of decisions taken by a public body which it never had power to make and the contracts made as a result. It would be possible to treat such decisions and contracts as being of no effect whatever. In consequence, those dealing with public bodies would still be obliged to beware transactions into which the public body had no power whatever to enter. There does not seem to be any injustice in this result.

On the other hand, the criticisms of the concepts of "void" or "nullity" logically have the same force as those of the concept "voidable". This suggests that a private law court should have a discretion whether or not to treat as quashed a decision which the public body had no power to make, just as a public law court has such a discretion. If the courts are to have a discretion to treat as void purported contracts purportedly made by a public body which had no capacity to conclude such contracts, the counterparty would be worse off than he would now be if he were contracting with a company, because the court would have a discretion, which would not be the case if he had contracted with a company. There is justification for such a distinction. A local authority is not in the same position as a company, and those who are compelled to fund the expenditure of local authorities arguably need greater protection than is needed for shareholders. That greater protection is afforded by the discretion. An alternative resolution of this conceptual problem would be the guidance than it would only be in very exceptional circumstances that a court would exercise its discretion in favour of a decision which there was no capacity to make.

Nonetheless, whatever the analysis when there is simply no capacity to conclude a particular contract, the reforms we propose would at least achieve justice where there has been abuse of power. Public bodies would not be able, by relying on their own abuse of power, to pocket a loan without ever having to repay it or dishonour a guarantee given to a counterparty who knew nothing of the abuse of power involved or keep goods or the benefit of services supplied without having to pay for them. Difficulties are not resolved by the use of the chamaeleonic "*ultra vires*" or "void", contrary to the views espoused by orthodoxy.

It has been suggested[35] that local authorities should have a "power of general competence" and that, in particular, improper purposes should be defined so that they will not include "setting out, in what is perceived to be the public interest, to achieve a laudable social objective by a lawful, even if ingenious, mechanism that seeks to order the authority's affairs so as to deploy the financial resources available to it to best advantage". The proposal of a general competence has rightly been criticised[36] as amounting to the offer of a blank cheque to a local authority. It is essential that the law should reflect the special position of council-tax payers and the special need for their protection. Moreover, this proposal fails to distinguish between capacity and abuse of power. It is important to maintain that distinction because a third party may well be in a much better position to ascertain whether the local authority has capacity or not than it may be to discover whether the local authority is acting in abuse of its powers. The suggestions we have made would meet these difficulties.

[35] By James Goudie QC, 'Judicial Review' in *Law Reform for All* (Blackstone Press, London, 1996), at 134.
[36] By the Financial Panel (Colin Bamford Chief Executive FLP) in *The Private Finance Initiative: Legal Powers of Local Authorities* (31 Oct. 1995) approved by Carnwath J in 'The Reasonable Limits of Local Authority Powers' [1996] *Public Law* 244 at 263.

It may be said that there is unacceptable uncertainty in the vesting of a discretion in the court to decide whether the decision is to be treated as binding. The response must be that the courts have developed guidance for the exercise of other discretions vested in the courts which removes noxious arbitrariness; and there is no reason such guidance could not be developed in this context also. In the last resort, the loss of complete certainty is a price worth paying for justice.

It may also be thought that these problems have all been resolved by the Local Government (Contracts) Act 1997 (which became law on 27 November 1997). That would be a misapprehension of both the intended and the actual effect of that Act. Most importantly, it does not deal (or purport to deal) at all with abuse of power, which is the cause of the most acute concern.

Moreover, the Act is limited to contracts concluded by local authorities for the provision or making available of assets or services (or both) for the purposes of, or in connection with, the discharge by the local authority of any of its functions.[37] Subsection 1(2) confers power on a local authority to enter into a contract with the financier where the local authority has power to make the provision contract but the finance is supplied to the counterparty to the provision contract, as opposed to the local authority itself. It is difficult to see how this would work in practice. It would not have helped in *Crédit Suisse*, because there the authority was not itself providing anything. There was the problem of impermissible delegation. In short, the Act tries to deal with this problem in a piecemeal way, which is inappropriate.

In addition, the mechanism of the operation of the Act is profoundly unsatisfactory. If contracts are capable of falling within the Act, protection is afforded only if the stipulated certification procedure has been followed. In principle, it is wrong that whether a contract is enforceable should depend upon certification procedures. In practice, it is not difficult to foresee litigation concerning compliance with that procedure, and injustice resulting.

CONCLUSION

Some fundamental changes in the conceptual framework of public law are necessary.

First, it must be recognised that the purported decision of a body which has no power to make those decisions (ever) has an essentially different character from that of a decision made in abuse of a power.

Secondly, it must also be accepted that the words "void", "voidable" and "nullity" have no absolute meaning, and they have no useful part to play in describing or analysing decisions of public bodies. Their continued use should be deprecated.

---

[37] S.1(1).

Thirdly, the view should be adopted that there is no inevitable correlation between the characterisation of a defect (i.e. whether there is no power or the power has been abused) and whether any particular remedy is available. Whether or not the body had the power to make the decision in question or misused that power, the court should have or be given a discretion whether or not to quash the decision.

Fourthly and finally, the courts should make it plain that the function of judicial review is to control the making of decisions by public bodies, and not to decide the merits of any particular decision. In consequence, judicial review (and not appeal) remains the appropriate means of controlling public bodies' decisions, whether the issue is absence of power or abuse of power.

6

Reviewing Regulatory Rules: Responding to Hybridisation

INTRODUCTION

Why look at the review of regulatory rules? The position is surely quite clear: if a regulatory body issues a rule and a dispute arises as to its interpretation, the court will simply interpret the rule and leave it for the regulator to apply. If its validity is questioned, then the court will look to the primary statute to determine whether the body had the power to make it. Review of regulatory rules, or perhaps more accurately regulatory instruments, raises a number of issues, however, both in terms of what the judicial approach is, and what it should be. The focus of this chapter is accordingly on the court's approach in cases which concern the validity, adherence to or interpretation of regulatory instruments. The chapter has two main themes: the first is to explore the nature and significance of judicial control of the interpretation of regulatory instruments, and the second is to use the review of such instruments as a context in which to explore the courts' response to a wider phenomenon, viz. the increasing complexity and hybridity of the "regulatory state".

In interpreting regulatory instruments, be they clothed in statute or in statute based rules, then the post-*Anisminic*[1] and *Page*[2] position is that it lies to the court to determine the meaning of such an instrument, and to the regulator to apply that meaning to the fact situation before it. There is only one "correct" interpretation, and it is for the court to determine it. The subordinate body is not allowed to err in any way. In orthodox terminology, all errors go to jurisdiction. It is argued that this approach, and the language in which it is cloaked, is flawed on a number of grounds. First, it is rooted in a particular theory of interpretation which is both implicit and contestable. Secondly, it is tied to a particular, unitary, conception of the constitution and legal system which

* Law Dept., London School of Economics. My thanks go to the participants in the seminars on Commercial Regulation and Judicial Review held at the LSE in Apr. 1997 for their comments; views, errors and ommissions remain my own.

[1] *Anisminic* v. *Foreign Compensation Commission* [1969] 2 AC 147.
[2] *Page* v. *Hull University Visitor* [1993] 1 All ER 97.

is in need of revision. Thirdly, that it has implications for the way in which regulatory bodies perform their functions, including the nature of rules which they can form. Fourthly, that it has the potential to threaten the integrity of the review function itself, turning it in effect into a process not of review but of appeal.

The "correctness" approach to interpretation is not only flawed in itself, but has been outpaced by the *Datafin* expansion of judicial review to regulatory bodies and instruments which are not rooted in statute. The development of the regulatory state is characterised by techniques, and instruments of regulation have been used which do not conform to the constitutionally familiar format, and the complexity which characterises the forms that regulatory instruments may take is echoed by the variety of institutional frameworks in which they operate. Both differ markedly from the "plain vanilla" system of statutory regulation, in which a department or statutory body either makes or implements decisions according to criteria set out in primary legislation, or under a grant of statutory power issues rules which are to govern a particular sector of industry or activity. Indeed the character of the current regulatory state is such that the classic categorisation of primary and delegated legislation issued by government departments or statutory agencies operating under more or less general statutory mandates, or indeed prerogative powers, falls far short of encompassing the types of regulatory instruments and institutional structures which exist.

In falling outside this classic constitutional structure, the variety of forms which such structures and instruments can take poses problems for the operation of judicial review. Difficulties arise not so much because of their complexity and variety *per se*, but because of their hybridity. What particularly characterises these instruments and structures is that in them the elements of "public" and "private" are commingled. Thus instruments and structures such as contracts and companies, which are familiar in one context, that of business and commerce, are being used in a significantly different one: that of regulation. Moreover, the exact role of the state in such structures is often obscure. To take the phenomenon of self-regulation as an example, it is possible to identify four broad forms, defined according to the nature of state involvement: mandated self-regulation, in which a collective group (for example an industry or profession) is formally or informally required or designated by the government to formulate and enforce norms within a framework defined by the government, usually in broad terms; sanctioned self-regulation, in which the collective group itself formulates the regulation, which is then subjected to government approval; coerced self-regulation, in which the industry itself formulates and imposes regulation but in response to threats by the government that if it does not the government will impose statutory regulation; and voluntary self-regulation, where there is no active state involvement, direct or indirect, in promoting or mandating self-regulation. Such hybrid bodies and instruments render the issue of determining their "public" or "private" status for the purposes both of the application and operation of judicial review remarkably complex.[3] It is not proposed to consider all aspects of the courts' response to the development of this hybrid form of regulation, simply the issues of interpretive control and of the validity of regulatory rules.

In order to explore these issues it is convenient to consider the court's response to three questions. These are first, to what extent should the court control the interpretation of regulatory rules; secondly, on what basis will rules be struck down; and thirdly, to what extent does the answer to these questions depend on the public/private nature of the rules, the body issuing them or the body making a decision in accordance with them? The chapter will consider these issues in two broad contexts in which they have arisen. The first is that of disputes arising as to the interpretation, validity and application of rules or other forms of regulatory instrument issued by a range of regulatory bodies, including the more specific issue of the review of those exercising a dispute-resolution function within that regulatory system. The dominance of the doctrine of parliamentary sovereignty means that within this first context three different situations need to be distinguished, varying with the statutory pedigree of the regulator and/or the rules: public and statutory regulators, public but non-statutory regulators and non-public regulators. The first and second parts consider the courts' response in the most straightforward, statutory context, and argue that in order to understand the significance of these reseponses we need to understand the implicit approaches being adopted to interpretation and to the relationship of courts and regulators. Such approaches become apparent when the court is confronted with hybrid regulators interpreting non-legal rules, the focus of the third part. Here it becomes clear that, deprived of its normal justifications for intervention, the judicial approach flounders.

The second broad context is that of regulatory and contractual "networks". The fourth part considers the nature of the impact of regulatory rules or instruments on the legal relationships entered into by those operating in the regulated field. In examining how the courts have answered the questions posed above in these two contexts, it becomes clear that little explicit attention has been given to which particular approach should be adopted, and what its implications may be. Nonetheless, there are some signs that the courts may be responding by developing principles in both private and public law which reflect the hybridity of the institutional structure of the regulation.

QUESTIONS OF INTERPRETATION AND VALIDITY: THE CURRENT POSITION

The central issues which arise in the review of the interpretation and validity of regulatory rules are in essence those of control and autonomy which pervade judicial review more generally. As discussed in the Introduction to this volume, in considering the role and nature of judicial review in this area, there are

---

[3] See further J. Black, "Constitutionalising Self Regulation" (1996) 59 *MLR* 24.

tensions between arguments for the control and supervision of the exercise of power, particularly governmental power, in accordance with principles of parliamentary sovereignty, and/or (depending on the theory adopted) societal norms and values, and on the other, arguments for the political and legal autonomy of regulators, based alternatively in recognition of their expertise, their need for operational autonomy, the call for legal pluralism and/or the need to guard against excessive legalism: juridification.

These tensions are as apparent in the context of the interpretation of regulatory rules as they are in other areas of judicial review. The more the court insists on a particular interpretation of the rules, then clearly the more the regulator's legal and interpretive autonomy is curtailed. The assertion by the court of its supremacy in interpreting regulatory instruments is one which requires closer examination, however, for it has a particular dimension not shared with the other grounds of review. The doctrine of correctness of interpretation, that "all errors go to jurisdiction" is rooted in a particular theory of interpretation which is contestable, and in a constitutional theory which although orthodox, is open to challenge.

Before we consider this in more depth, it is necessary to set out briefly what the current position is concerning the interpretation of primary legislation, secondary and tertiary rules.

Primary Legislation and "Freedom to Err"

The legal position relating to the regulator's intepretation of primary legislation lies firmly in the orthodox doctrines of judicial review: the primacy of the principle of parliamentary sovereignty and the assertion of the courts as the sole determinators of legal meaning.[4] Although its death was slow and frequently painful,[5] the distinction between jurisdictional and non-jurisdictional errors of law was finally killed by *Page*,[6] completing the job begun by *Anisminic*.[7] It is for the court, not for inferior courts or subordinate tribunals, to decide on the meaning of the statutory provisions which those bodies apply and which govern their activities. The justification for such a position was placed firmly on the principle of *ultra vires*, itself asserted as the fundamental principle underlying judicial review. Lord Browne-Wilkinson stated:

---

[4] For a recent restatement of this orthodoxy see Lord Irvine of Lairg, "Judges and Decision Makers" [1996] *Public Law* 59.

[5] As witnessed by *Pearlman* v. *Governors of Harrow School* [1979] QB 56; *In Re Racal Communications Ltd* [1981] AC 374; *O'Reilly* v. *Mackman* [1983] 2 AC 237; *R.* v. *Greater Manchester Coroner ex p. Tal* [1985] QB 67. See J. Beatson, "The Scope of Judicial Review for Error of Law" (1984) 4 *OJLS* 22; C. Emery and C. Smythe, "Error of Law in Adminsitrative Law" (1984) 100 *LQR* 612; P. Craig, *Administrative Law* (3rd edn., Sweet & Maxwell, London, 1994), ch. 10; P. Cane, *Introduction to Administrative Law* (3rd edn., Clarendon Press, Oxford, 1996), ch. 6.

[6] *Page* v. *Hull University Visitor* [1993] 1 All ER 97.

[7] *Anisminic* v. *Foreign Compensation Commission* [1969] 2 AC 147.

"In all cases, save possibly one, this intervention by way of prohibition or certiorari is based on the proposition that such powers have been conferred on the decision maker on the underlying assumption that the powers are to be exercised only within the jurisdiction conferred, in accordance with fair procedures, and in a *Wednesbury* sense . . ., reasonably. If the decision maker exercises his powers outside the jurisdiction conferred, in a manner which is procedurally irregular or is *Wednesbury* unreasonable, he is acting *ultra vires* his powers and therefore unlawfully."[8]

The position is thus that when applying statutory provisions or subordinate legislation, any error made as to the meaning of those provisions is an error which goes to jurisdiction: there is no room for the decision-maker to take a wrong, but reasonable, interpretation. This is so even with respect to statutory terms which are inherently vague, such as "substantial", the interpretation of which may fairly be a matter of judgement. In such circumstances, as Lord Mustill made clear in *South Yorkshire Transport*, the interpretation of statute should not always be seen as a "hard-edged" question; it may be that the terms used were so broad that they could not, and should not, be given a "spurious degree of precision".[9] Nevertheless, in that instance, it was still for the court to guide the body as to the criteria. It may be that the criteria established are so vague that in applying them to the facts of the case different decision-makers might reasonably reach different conclusions, but it is only at this second stage, that of application of criteria to the facts, that the test becomes that of rationality, not of correctness.[10] Thus it is envisaged that the interpretation of the law and its application to the facts is a two-stage process, with the court having primacy in the first stage, the regulator in the second.[11]

Although the distinction between jurisdictional and non-jurisdictional errors was never a happy one, its abolition does not come without criticism,[12] nor without some uncertainty as to its capacity for an after-life.[13] Criticisms will be considered in more depth below, but it is worth noting here that in order to adopt this position the courts also have to maintain that there is a distinction between the interpretation of a statutory provision, which is a matter for the courts, and its application, which is a matter for the regulator. The distinction between interpretation and application is one which is to a large extent

---

[8] Lord Browne-Wilkinson, at 107A–C. The exception referred to was the power of the court to quash a decision taken within jurisdiction where there was an error of law on the face of the record, but since removed by the extension of the ultra vires principle in *Anisminic* (107C–E).

[9] *South Yorkshire Transport and another* v. *Monopolies and Mergers Commission* [1993] 1 All ER 289 (HL), 298A–F; see further 295C.

[10] At 298.

[11] See Lord Mustill in *South Yorkshire Transport Ltd* v. *Monopolies and Mergers Commission* [1993] 1 All ER 289 (HL) at 294J.

[12] See e.g. Craig, n. 5 above, 372–83.

[13] E.g. Craig has suggested that it may be that a distinction still exists as to the scope of review for error of law between tribunals and inferior courts: *ibid.*, 361. Moreover, it is not clear which bodies the courts will recognise as applying not the "general law of the land, but a peculiar, domestic law" ([1993] 1 All ER 97 at 108D, *per* Lord Browne-Wilkinson), and so outside the operation of the jurisdictional principle. On this latter point, see further below.

artificial.[14] Moreover, it is not particularly honest. Lord Mustill's judgment in the *South Yorkshire* case itself indicates how the interpretation given to the statutory provision can be determined more by considerations of how much discretion a body should have in making its decision rather than the exact meaning of the legal provision, which itself may be extremely broadly and vaguely framed.

Review of Delegated Legislation

The same broad grounds of judicial review are exercised with respect to delegated legislation as they are to other exercises of discretionary power, but delegated legislation and rule-making are still regarded as distinctive activites. So although all heads of review are applicable to delegated legislation, they apply in a slightly different form.[15]

Subordinate legislation clearly has to be within the powers and purposes of the primary statute. On the issue of interpretation, while all errors of interpretation may go to jurisdiction (if the rules are found to have legal status), the courts have recognised that such rules may not be drafted with the same precision and so the standards of interpretation applied may not be so strict as for primary statutes.[16] Further, the content of subordinate legislation can be challenged on the ground that it is being used for improper purposes, is partial or unequal, manifestly unjust, discloses bad faith, involves such oppressive or gratuitous interference with rights as could find no justification in the minds of reasonable men,[17] is too vague,[18] or because it abrogates fundamental rights without such abrogation being expressly sanctioned in the primary legislation.[19] However, the review of delegated legislation on the grounds of rationality is generally seen to be less intensive than with respect to other types of administrative decisions.[20]

---

[14] And indeed, in relation to decisions by a court on questions of mixed law, fact, and degree, was described by Lord Diplock in *Re Racal* to be one that only a "scholiast" would attempt to draw: [1981] AC 374 at 383H–384A.

[15] See generally, Craig, n. 5 above, 262–6. See generally R. Baldwin, *Rules and Government* (Oxford, OUP, 1995) especially 82–104; R. Baldwin and J. Houghton, "Circular Arguments: The Status and Legitimacy of Administrative Rules" [1986] *PL* 239; G. Ganz, *Quasi-Legislation* (Sweet & Maxwell, London, 1987).

[16] *R. v. Criminal Injuries Compensation Board, ex p. Schofield* [1971] 2 All ER 1011; *R. v. ICS, ex p. Bowden* [1995] 3 All ER 605 (HL).

[17] *Kruse* v. *Johnson* (1898) 2 QB 91, although if the instrument has been approved by Parliament, and is concerned with highly sensitive political issues, the courts have indicated that a very high threshold of unreasonableness will be applied: *Nottinghamshire CC* v. *Secretary of State for the Environment* [1986] AC 240.

[18] *McEldowney* v. *Forde* [1971] AC 632; *Bugg* v. *DPP* [1993] 2 All ER 815.

[19] *Attorney General* v. *Wilts United Dairies Ltd* (1921) 39 TLR 781; *R. v. Secretary of State for the Home Dept., ex p. Leech* [1993] 4 All ER 539; *R. v. Lord Chancellor's Department, ex p. Witham, The Times*, 13 Mar. 1997.

[20] Craig, n. 5 above, 264.

It is also worth noting that the principles of procedural fairness also differ with respect to the formation of delegated legislation as opposed to other types of administrative action, and that failure to comply with natural justice does not invalidate the delegated legislation.[21] In the absence of any statutory duty or a representation giving rise to a legitimate expectation,[22] there is no general duty to consult, although the court may imply one.[23] Where such a statutory duty is imposed, consultation must provide adequate information about what it is intended to do, and sufficient time for consultees to respond.[24] Finally, even where a ground for review has been established, the discretion to refuse a remedy might be more readily used.[25]

Particular difficulties arise when the legal status of the rules is not prescribed by statute and is therefore unclear.[26] In determining the rules' status, and in particular whether a decision-maker is bound by the rule or whether non-compliance with it means the decision-maker has acted unlawfully, the courts have paid attention to the legislative mandate and precision of the rule itself.[27] Alternatively, a rule or statement may be binding through the operation of the doctrine of legitimate expectations,[28] and expectations can also arise with respect to rulings given on an individualised basis if the applicant makes full disclosure of the relevant circumstances, and the ruling is sought from and given by the appropriate person within the administrative or regulatory body,[29] or from a course of conduct in which strict compliance with the rule has been repeatedly waived.[30]

[21] *Bates v. Lord Hailsham* [1972] 1 WLR 1373.
[22] *R. v. Liverpool Corporation, ex p. Liverpool Taxi Fleet Operators' Association* [1972] 2 QB 299.
[23] *Bates v. Lord Hailsham* [1972] 1 WLR 1373. Where a regulation affects only one particular body, that body may however be entitled to see the information which led to the formation of the rule: *R. v. Secretary of State for Health, ex p. United States Tobacco Inc.* [1992] 1 All ER 212, and see *R. v. Devon CC, ex p. Baker* [1995] 1 All ER 73, but *cf. R. v. North Yorkshire Family Health Services Authority, ex p. Wilson, The Times,* 28 June 1996. On the duty to consult see further Cane, n. 5 above 193–9; M. Supperstone and J. Goudie, *Judicial Review* (Butterworths, London, 1997, 2nd ed), ch 7.
[24] *R. v. Devon CC, ex p. Baker* [1995] 1 All ER 73. Leave for review of an amendment to Lautro's rules on the basis that there had been insufficient consultation was refused, as Lautro had in fact issued a series of consultation papers, it was simply that the applicant had not seen them: *R. v. Lautro, ex p. Kendall,* 14 Apr. 1992, Lexis.
[25] *R. v. Secretary of State for Social Services, ex p. Association of Metropolitan Authorities* [1986] 1 WLR 1; although *cf. Agricultural, Horticultural and Forestry Industry Training Board v. Aylesbury Mushrooms Ltd* [1972] 1 All ER 280.
[26] See the confusion over the status of the Immigration Rules: *R. v. Chief Immigration Officer, ex p. Bibi* [1976] 1 WLR 979; *R. v. Secretary of State for Home Affairs, ex p. Hosenball* [1977] 1 WLR 766; *R. v. Secretary of State for the Home Department, ex p. Ram* [1979] 1 WLR 148; *R. v. Chief Immigration Officer, ex p. Kharazzi* [1980] 1 WLR 1396.
[27] Baldwin, n. 15 above, 86–91.
[28] *R. v. Secretary of State for the Home Department, ex p. Khan* [1985] 1 All ER 40; *R. v. Liverpool Corporation, ex p. Liverpool Taxi Fleet Operators* [1970] 2 QB 299; *HTV v. Price Commission* [1976] ICR 170. See further Baldwin, *ibid.,* 82–106.
[29] *R. v. IRC, ex p. MFK Underwriting Agents Ltd* [1990] 1 WLR 1545; *R. v. IRC, ex p. Matrix Securities Ltd, The Times,* 19 Feb. 1994 (published notice had been given of the appropriate part of the IRC to which to apply for ruling).
[30] *R. v. IRC, ex p. Unilever plc* [1994] STC 841.

Guidance and Directions

The interpretation of guidance and directions poses the courts with particular problems. Rule-making by departments and regulators can take a wide range of forms, ranging from published instruments issued under specific grants of legislative power to internal guidance and circulars.[31] Rules may be directed at those outside government, or simply be internal to a department; alternatively they may be issued by one part of government and addressed to another. Instruments in the latter category are effectively instruments of intra-governmental regulation, and their validity and interpretation in specific areas of commercial regulation have been the recent subject of review. Their nature and status have however caused some slight confusion.

The distinction between guidance and direction was set out in *Laker Airways*; it must be in the issuer's powers to give such guidance or direction and where the body has the power to give guidance only, that must not amount in effect to a direction.[32] The difficulties arise when the court is called upon to review the interpretation of such instruments. In *ex p. Save Our Railways* the court held that in interpreting the guidance issued by the Secretary of State it was not construing a statute or even subordinate legislation.[33] The document had to be read in a practical, down-to-earth way, as a communication by a Secretary of State to a public official, and the language used was not to be invested with more precision than it would naturally bear; individual paragraphs had to be read in the context of the whole document and of the Act. That said, a relatively restricted interpretation of the terms used in the guidance (that minimum service levels had to be "based on" existing ones) was given: the court held that the phrase meant that changes had to be marginal, not significant or substantial.

There was however some indication that the courts are unsure of how to respond to such guidance: in the Divisional Court Macpherson J stated that the document was an internal one and wondered whether the issue of its meaning was appropriately a matter for the court, notwithstanding the fact that it was made under statute.[34] In contrast, in considering guidance given by SIB[35] to the SROs[36] and RPBs[37] as to how they may require their members to conduct a review of past pensions business, which it has only implicit statutory power to provide, the court exhibited no such doubts or reticence on the issue of its interpretation. It also further held that the same tests for rationality applied to the

---

[31] See further Baldwin, n. 15 above.
[32] *Laker Airways Ltd v. Department of Trade* [1977] QB 643.
[33] *R. v. Director of Passenger Rail Franchising, ex p. Save Our Railways and others*, The Times, 18 Dec. 1995 (CA).
[34] *R. v. Secretary of State for Transport, ex p. Save our Railways*, The Times, 12 Dec. 1995 (DC).
[35] Securities and Investments Board.
[36] Self-regulatory organisations.
[37] Recognised Professional Bodies.

guidance as to subordinate legislation, and found that the guidance was in fact irrational in one respect.[38]

CHALLENGING THE "CORRECTNESS" APPROACH

The approach which the court takes to the issue of the interpretation of primary legislation and indeed to other administrative rules illustrates the interconnection in this area of judicial review of a particular theory of interpretation and an orthodox theory of constitutional law. Moreover, the language in which it is cloaked makes the correctness approach difficult to challenge. Who would seriously allow bodies to "err" in making decisions; when could errors ever be justified?

If we take away the idea of correctness, however, and argue instead that there is no inherently "correct" interpretation, rather that there is, for example, simply a series of community-constructed meanings, then interpretation becomes inherently contestable and the notion of error falls away. The argument which we then have to have is why it is the court's interpretation rather than the regulatory body's which should prevail.

It is suggested here that we need to explore more closely the assumptions underlying the current judicial approach in this area, and that drawing on that analysis argue that rather than insisting on there being one correct interpretation, the court should recognise that there may be a range of interpretations that rules, particularly vague rules, may have. In using rationality rather than correctness as the basis for review of interpretation, the court would also preserve the integrity of judicial review, and allow it to operate on a much clearer basis in an area where it currently flounders, *viz.*, with respect to those bodies which are not rooted in statute and whose rules are not legal instruments.

In order to appreciate the significance of the issue of interpretation, we need to step back and consider the nature of rules in a more abstract sense. Rules are linguistic structures which when endowed with legal status are distinctive, authoritative forms of communication. As linguistic structures, they require interpretation and application, as Hart long ago observed.[39] In asserting that rules have one "correct" meaning, the courts are implicitly adopting a particular theory of interpretation. That is, that language has an intrinsic, objective meaning: that "meaning resides 'in' language somewhat the way furniture resides 'in' a room".[40] The task of the court is simply to determine what that meaning is. This interpretive theory in turn provides legitimacy for the court's

---

[38] R. v. *SIB, ex p. IFAA, The Times*, 18 May 1995. See further Martyn Hopper's contribution in this volume.

[39] H.L.A. Hart, *The Concept of Law* (Clarendon Press, Oxford, 1961), 123.

[40] G. Graff, "'Keep off the Grass', 'Drop Dead', and Other Indeterminacies: A Response to Stanford Levinson" (1982) 60 *Texas LR* 405 at 405.

function. There is necessarily a correct interpretation: the court is not con-
structing meaning, but divining it.[41]

This interpretive approach is contested by those arguing from a number of
quarters, but who may be broadly divided into two camps: the nihilists and the
conventionalists. The nihilists argue that all language and its interpretation is
simply subjective, dependent on the reader alone.[42] Those who adopt the nihilist
position often then move to contest the legitimacy of adjudication: if their meaning is simply subjectively constructed by the reader, why should we agree to
adopt the court's interpretation over anybody else's?[43] The conventionalists in
contrast argue that the objective/subjective distinction is inappropriate: rather
meaning is constituted by interpretation, which is in turn a function of varying
combinations of shared understandings, knowledge of language, conventions
and context.[44] The implications of this approach for the role of the court are
more complex: the meaning of a rule is that which is accorded it by a particular
interpretive community. The issue then is which community's understanding is
that which the court should recognise. Should the court always assert that
within the legal system terms have a meaning which is distinct from that which
would be attributed to it by those outside that system (e.g. "consideration" in
contract law does not mean kindness), or should the court rather recognise the
understanding that other interpretive communities have of a particular term or
rule, and not seek to impose a different, legal, construction?

Theories of interpretation in the jurisprudential context thus tend to become
inexorably intertwined with theories of adjudication. This is not the place to
enter wholesale into that debate. It is rather to draw out its implications for the

[41] The degree to which the position of objectivity is held varies considerably from those who
argue that words have a "natural" meaning: M. Moore, "A Natural Law Theory of Interpretation"
(1985) 58 *S Calif LR* 277, and "The Interpretive Turn in Modern Theory: A Turn for the Worse?"
(1989) 41 *Stanford LR* 871; D. Brink, "Legal Theory, Legal Interpretation, and Judicial Review"
(1988) 17 *Phi. & Pub. Aff.* 105 and "Semantics and Legal Interpretation (Further Thoughts)" (1989)
2 *Canadian Journal of Law and Jurisprudence* 181–91, to those who try in less extreme ways to
assert the possibility of objective meaning, see, e.g., O. M. Fiss, "Objectivity and Interpretation"
(1982) 34 *Stanford LR* 739. For a discussion of objectivity see A. Marmor, "Three Concepts of
Objectivity" in A. Marmor (ed.), *Law and Interpretation* (Clarendon Press, Oxford, 1995).

[42] For critical legal theorists who expound the thesis of radical indeterminacy, see, e.g., references cited at n. 43. This view is also held by those who, with a certain amount of dismay, see it as
the logical consequence of the rejection of the objectivity thesis: see, e.g., S. Levinson, "Law as
Literature" (1982) 60 *Texas LR* 373.

[43] For expressions of the indeterminacy thesis and the link with legitimacy see, e.g., J. Singer,
"The Player and the Cards: Nihilism and Legal Theory" (1984) 94 *Yale LJ*; 1, A. Altman, "Legal
Realism, Critical Legal Studies, and Dworkin" (1986) 15 *Phi. & Pub. Aff.* 205; D. Kennedy, "Legal
Formality" (1973) 2 *J Leg. Stud.* 351 and "Form and Substance". For a consideration (and refuta-
tion) of this part of the indeterminacy thesis see K. Kress, "Legal Indeterminacy" (1989) 88 *Calif LR*
283; J.L. Coleman and B. Leiter, "Determinacy, Objectivity and Authority" in A. Marmor, n. 41
above.

[44] The "middle way" is found by a range of writers through various routes. One of the most tren-
chant rejectors of the objective/subjective dichotomy, however, is Stanley Fish: S. Fish, *Is There a
Text in This Class?* (Harvard University Press, Cambridge, Mass., 1980) and *Doing What Comes
Naturally* (OUP, Oxford, 1989). This approach has also recently been expounded by Hutchinson:
A. Hutchinson, "Taking Rules Sceptically" (1995) 58 *MLR* 701.

role of the courts in the particular context of judicial review. As noted above, in asserting that statutes or rules have one particular meaning, the courts are implicitly adopting an objectivist approach. In the judicial review context, this is in turn rooted in orthodox Diceyan constitutional theory and in a unitary notion of the legal system. That is that the High Court is the guardian of the law and the determinator of what the law does provide,[45] and that all are subject to the "ordinary law of the land" applied by the "ordinary courts".[46]

Adopting a conventionalist approach, in contrast, would not lead so inexorably to such a conclusion. Rather, the courts would be required to recognise that meaning is a function of a community's understanding: the same terms may mean different things to different interpretive communities. This does not mean that conventionalism cannot reside alongside a unitary conception of the legal system, however, in which it is for the courts to determine what that meaning should be for that system. There is still another step in the argument which has to be taken, *viz.* that the court should recognise and permit the interpretations of other communities. Although it does not of itself take that step, nevertheless what the conventionalist approach does highlight is that the assertion by the court that there is one, correct, interpretation, has to be independently justified in the way that the objectivist approach does not so clearly require.

That justification presently comes, as noted, under orthodox constitutional theory. It is contended here that that orthodoxy should be revised, for two reasons: first, because it has implications for the effectiveness of those bodies implementing statutory systems of regulation and forming regulatory rules and other instruments, and for the operation of that regulatory system; secondly (and a reason which should resonate more loudly for the holders of such a theory), because it threatens the integrity of the review function itself.

The most frequently noted implication of the control by the courts of the interpretation of regulatory instruments is that it can lead to the courts imposing interpretations which do not make sense in the regulatory context in which they have to apply, and which either ignore the purposes of the legislation or rules, or are based on inaccurate or inconsistent ideas of them; further, the purposes may themselves be impossible to divine.[47] Moreover, it fails to recognise the expertise of such bodies and their experience of the operation of the regulation. Commentators such as Craig and Cane thus suggest that the courts should subject all questions of law decided by administrative agencies to review according to a standard of reasonableness.[48]

---

[45] In *Page* the non-reviewability of the visitor's interpretation of the university statutes was justified in part on the ground that the issues in question were not really part of the "general law" at all, and so do not threaten this centralised application of ordinary law: [1993] 1 All ER 97 at 108D.

[46] A.V. Dicey, *The Law and the Constitution* (10th edn., Macmillan, London, 1959) (edited by E.C.S. Wade), 203; on the unitary conception of law see further, H.W. Arthurs, "Rethinking Administrative Law: A Slightly Dicey Business" (1979) 17 *Osgoode Hall LR* 1.

[47] See, e.g., Aidan Robertson's commentary on the South Yorkshire Transport case: A. Robertson, "Substantial: What's in a Word?" [1993] 5 *ECLR* 217.

[48] Craig, n. 5 above, at 375 ff.; Cane, n. 5 above, at 127. Contrast Irvine, n. 4 above.

These criticisms are here supported; moreover the analysis of interpretation and a recognition of the decisions involved in rule-making suggest further implications of the correctness approach for the operation of the regulatory system. There is first the issue of certainty. In the demand for certainty what is being sought is the assurance that my interpretation of the rule will accord with others'; most notably that of the body which has the ultimate authority to determine the application of the rule. Drawing on the conventionalist analysis of interpretation outlined above, what is necessary is that rule-maker, regulated and adjudicator have a shared understanding of the rule's meaning. Close judicial involvement in the rule application process could in practice be a source of uncertainty if the judicial interpretation is not one which the regulator and regulated would share.[49] The regulator could try to pre-empt, or at least guide, judicial interpretation by issuing rules or guidance which are more precise, and in which there is less room for differences of understanding and so interpretation. However, the issuing of precise rules has a number of potential implications for the regulatory system. Precise rules can increase complexity, and ultimately have the paradoxical effect of decreasing certainty. Precise rules, particularly when coupled with judicial recognition of a formalist approach to interpretation, facilitate creative compliance: the deliberate and tactical use of literal or formal interpretations of rules to circumvent their purpose; compliance with the "letter" rather than the "spirit".[50]

Finally, judicial control over interpretation, as manifested in the correctness approach, serves to exacerbate the juridification of the regulatory system. Juridification, the introduction of legal norms and values into non-legal systems, is a phenomenon increasingly noted by public lawyers.[51] In imposing its own understanding of legislative or other regulatory instruments, and its own canons of interpretation, the court is directly introducing legal values into that regulatory system. It is the desire to protect regulation from such judicial intervention that leads to the demand for non-legal forms of regulation: voluntary codes of practice or systems of self regulation, or the deliberate withdrawal of private rights of enforcement with respect to the breach of particular regulatory rules.[52]

---

[49] See further J. Black *Rules and Regulators* (OUP, Oxford, 1997), ch. 1.

[50] D. McBarnet and C. Whelan, "The Elusive Spirit of the Law: Formalism and the Struggle for Legal Control" (1991) 54 *MLR* 848 and "Beyond Control: Law, Management and Corporate Governance" in J. McCaherty, S. Picciotto and C. Scott (eds.), *Corporate Control and Accountability* (OUP, Oxford, 1993), D. McBarnet, "It's Not What You Do, But the Way that You Do It: Tax Evasion, Tax Avoidance and the Boundaries of Deviance" in D. Downes (ed.), *Unravelling Criminal Justice* (McMillan, London, 1991).

[51] See, e.g., Colin Scott's ch. in this volume; M. Loughlin, *Legality and Locality—The Role of Law in Central-Local Government Relations* (OUP, Oxford, 1996); C. Harlow and R. Rawlings, *Law and Administration* (2nd edn., Butterworths, London, 1998).

[52] Breach of the principles made by the Securities and Investments Board (now the Financial Services Authority) under s.48A FSA was deliberately excluded from the operation of s.62 FSA (the right of a private investor to bring a civil action for damages against an authorised firm for breach of the rules) simply to enable the principles to be written using vague and general language: see further Black n. 49 above, ch 3.

The correctness approach does not just have implications for the regulatory system, however. It is suggested that in adopting this approach the courts are in danger of threatening the integrity of the review process itself. In asserting that all legal rules have a correct interpretation, and that it lies to the court to determine that interpretation, the court is in effect allowing appeal on a point of law to those aggrieved by a regulator's decision on the application of a rule. As the scope of the regulatory state expands, and as commercial firms find that their business operations are increasingly affected by the interpretations which regulators give to regulatory instruments, the more the courts will find themselves called upon to review that regulatory decision. In adhering to the correctness approach, the courts are opening the judicial doors to such applicants, effectively allowing for each an avenue for appeal where statute may not in fact provide one.

But, as noted above, the argument that a particular interpretive approach should be adopted does not of itself resolve the constitutional argument of why the courts should refrain from imposing their own intepretation. However, support for such restraint can in fact be found even in a fairly conservative form of constitutional theory. It is that the court should recognise that the use of vague and general terms represents an implicit delegation of power to an agency to determine the application of that particular term. The court is still then upholding Parliamentary intent, exercising its supervisory function, but allowing a degree of (controlled) autonomy for the regulatory body. It is on this basis that the US Supreme Court held in the seminal *Chevron* case[53] that if the statute is unambiguous, then the court must give effect to it; if however a statute is silent or ambiguous as to a particular issue, the court will consider, not "what is the correct interpretation?", but rather "is the agency's interpretation one of a range of permissible interpretations?". A court may not substitute its own construction of a statutory provision for a reasonable interpretation made by the administrator of an agency.[54] This "rationality" test is still open to manipulation by the courts,[55] but the approach is one which would address more satisfactorily the tension between control and autonomy, and which moreover can be broadly justified within even conservative constitutional theory.

That theory nevertheless is struggling in the face of the hybrid nature of the regulatory state, and it is the challenges posed by such bodies which demand its revision. If judicial review of the interpretation of regulatory instruments is

---

[53] *Chevron USA v. NRDC*, 467 US 837 (1984) 84.

[54] At 844. See further Note, (1985) 90 *Harvard LR* 247; C. Sunstein, "Law and Administration after *Chevron*" (1990) 90 *Columbia LR* 2072; J. Pierce, "Chevron and its Aftermath: Judicial Review of Agency Interpretations of Statutory Provisions" (1988) 41 *Vand. LR* 301; C. Farina, "Statutory Interpretation and the Balance of Power in the Administrative State" (1989) 89 *Colum. LR* 452.

[55] Empirical research on the effect of the *Chevron* decision on lower courts did however indicate that there had been a dramatic decrease (40%) in decisions which overturned an agency's interpretation of the law: P. Schuck and D. Elliott, "To the *Chevron* Station: An Empirical Study of Federal Administrative Law" (1990) 90 *Duke LJ* 984; but see T. Merrill, "Judicial Deference to Executive Precedent" (1992) 101 *Yale LJ* 969; and further L. Cohen and M. Spitzer, "Solving the Chevron Puzzle" (1994) 57 *Law and Contemp. Prob.* 65.

rooted in the idea that courts have a monopoly on the interpretion of law, and is so justified in the public law context by the doctrine of Parliamentary sover eignty, then the courts are faced with difficulties in deciding what is a legal instrument and what is not. This may not always be clear, indeed indications of judicial uncertainty when faced with guidance and directions were noted above. The problem is exacerbated when faced with non-statutory regulators. The justification of parliamentary sovereignty and parliamentary intent cannot apply if Parliament has not acted. Nor does the test which the courts have adopted for distinguishing public from private bodies (that bodies are public if they are sufficiently integrated into a govermental system of control)[56] of itself provide a justification. Here the issue of exactly how review should therefore proceed is open to question: should it be on the basis of rationality, of legitimate expectations or, as is suggested here, should the court go further and start to recognise, and develop, constitutions for such bodies, of which the body's rules can be a clear and integral part, to which it requires them to adhere?

HYBRID REGULATION AND JUDICIAL REVIEW

As noted above, the forms regulatory bodies can take and the nature of their relationship with those that they regulate, with government and with statute, are multifarious. They may be set up by Charter,[57] by statute,[58] incorporated under the Companies Acts,[59] or be unincorporated associations.[60] Their rules may be a species of delegated legislation,[61] contractual,[62] or without legal basis.[63] They may have to conform to legislative requirements,[64] or be drawn up in consultation with government.[65] Their rules may perform the government's obligation to implement EC Directives;[66] compliance with them may confer exemption from or be deemed to be compliance with legislative requirements[67]; their breach may be subject to legislative sanctions,[68] regulatory sanctions or no

---

[56] See further Black, n. 3 above.
[57] E.g., the BBC, the Jockey Club, the Law Society.
[58] E.g., the General Medical Council.
[59] The Securities and Investments Board and self-regulatory organisations (SROs).
[60] The Advertising Standards Authority; the Takeover Panel.
[61] E.g., the rules of SIB and the Law Society.
[62] E.g., the rules of the SROs, and sporting bodies such as the Jockey Club, the Football Association and the Boxing Board.
[63] E.g., the Codes of Practice of banks, building societies, the Takeover Panel and the Advertising Standards Authority.
[64] E.g., some provisions in the rules of the Institute of Chartered Accountants of England and Wales.
[65] The Code of Practice of the British Pharmaceutical Association was the subject of consultation with the (then) DHSS.
[66] The Stock Exchange is a competent authority under EC law; the ASA's Control of Misleading Advertisements Regulations 1988 implements the EC Directive.
[67] Rules of exchanges, professional bodies and self-regulatory organisations recognised under the Financial Services Act 1986.
[68] E.g., the Advertising Standards Authority.

legal sanction at all. Finally, there may be networks of associations, demanding compliance with each other's self-regulatory rules.[69] This section will consider the position of the courts in reviewing the interpretation and validity of rules issued by such "self regulatory" bodies.

The discussion below focuses on the court's answers to two central questions which arise when considering the rules of such bodies: first, if the challenge is whether the body has interpreted its own rules properly or acted within them, how will the court approach the issue of interpretation, and, secondly, on what basis, if at all, could a rule of a non-statutory body be struck down as invalid?

Regulators' Interpretations of their Own Rules: "Errors of Law" or Matters of Rationality?

Review of the interpretation of regulatory rules occurs in two broad contexts, depending on the exact nature of the self-regulatory body and the statutory framework in which it operates. These are, first that of rules which are made within a wide set of powers granted to that body by statute, and secondly, rules made by a body not acting under any direct grant of statutory power at all.

Rules made Under Statutory Powers

Widespread delegation of rule-making powers to regulatory agencies is in fact relatively rare in the UK, in contrast to the US, although the system of financial regulation is an important exception. In terms of the legal issues which arise the situation has been treated as being akin to the "plain vanilla" case of a statutory (or prerogative) body making decisions in accordance with secondary or tertiary rules. The courts recognise that regulatory rules may not be drafted with the same degree of precision as would be the case with primary legislation or statutory instruments, and that less strict standards of interpretation apply,[70] but interpretation is still as much a matter for the court to determine as it is in the case of primary legislation.

Interpretation of rules made under grants of legislative powers raises slightly different issues from the interpretation of primary legislation, however. This is so even if one adopts the orthodox parliamentary sovereignty approach to the issue, and does not argue for a "rationality" test to be applied to the interpretation of statutory provisions. The difference between the two situations is that, while it is at least coherent to argue that if a body misinterprets a statute and steps outside the "four corners" of the Act, it steps outside the powers given to it by Parliament, it could be the case that the "misinterpretation" by a body of

[69] SIB requires regulated firms to comply with the Code on Takeovers and Mergers; Stock Exchange Listing Rules require compliance with Code of Best Practice produced by Committee on the Financial Aspects of Corporate Governance.
[70] R. v. *Criminal Injuries Compensation Board, ex p. Schofield* [1971] 2 All ER 1011.

its own rules did not take it outside the "four corners" of the legislation. The body may, in other words, have the legal power to make the rule that it thought that it had made; the issue is not what rules it has the power to make, but the interpretation of the rules which it has made.

However the court has taken the same approach to interpretations of rules made under statutory powers as it does to interpretations of primary legislation itself, even where there is no question that in misinterpreting its rules the body has acted outside the "four corners" of the legislation. Where it would be within the broad grant of statutory power for the regulatory body to have made the rule which it (mistakenly) thought it had, the court has not shown any indication of adopting the principles of rationality in reviewing a regulator's interpretation of its own rules, rather errors in interpretation have been approached on the basis that they are errors in law.

Nevertheless, the interpretations which have then been given have themselves afforded considerable latitude to the regulator, although it is a latitude which has been given through imaginative or purposive constructions rather than through the adoption of the rationality approach. An example is provided by the case of *R. v. ITC, ex p. Virgin*.[71] The case concerned the interpretation of the ITC's own rules for invitations to bid for the Channel 5 licence. The terms of invitation stated that no amendments nor any new material could be introduced to an application subsequent to its delivery nor would any applicant be allowed to enhance its application once it had been submitted. The Broadcasting Act 1990, under which the powers were exercised, however provided that during the period between receipt of the application and grant of the licence the commision could require the applicant to furnish such additional information as the ITC might reasonably require as to its financial position (section15(4)). On their face, therefore, it appeared that the ITC had imposed on itself a self-denying ordinance. However the court held that the proper construction of the rules governing the invitation to bid was that they applied only to programming proposals, not to financial information. To hold otherwise would have made the statutory powers redundant. The rules cannot therefore have meant what they appeared to say.

The ITC is a statutory body, but the courts have not shown any difference in approach to self-regulatory bodies acting under statutory powers. The court maintains the "correctness" approach to interpretation and has not shown any indication of allowing the body greater room to interpret its own rules, even when no issue of statutory *vires* is raised. Nevertheless, cases concerning the interpretation of the Investors' Compensation Scheme's (ICS) rules illustrate that the court has explicitly adopted highly purposive interpretations, using purposes which in fact conflict.

Thus when faced with what they considered was an unjust conclusion arising from the ICS's application of its rules, the court simply adopted a construction

---

[71] [1996] EMLR 318 (QB).

of the rules to reach the conclusion it felt was appropriate. So in *R. v. ICS, ex p. Bowden* Mann LJ held that an investor's right to compensation was transmissible on death to his personal representative.[72] Although personal representatives did not fall within the definition of "eligible investor[s]", the court held that it would be absurd if personal representatives could not claim on behalf of the deceased, and that the rules should be construed so as to avoid absurdity. As Mann LJ stated:

> "Death is inevitable but its occurrence before an application or before determination is accidental. The scheme is for the compensation of small investors and ordinarily they will have regarded their saving as a benefit of their family. They would be surprised if the moment of death was to injuriously affect the inheritance. . . . [T]he law does not require so unjust a conclusion."[73]

In *R. v. ICS, ex p. Weyell* a similar approach to the construction of the rules was adopted.[74] In making the declarations which it did in *ex p. Bowden*, Cresswell J held that the Divisional Court applied "a sensible and purposive construction to the rules which, though intended to benefit small investors, are in some respects not clearly drafted".[75] The court held that the right to claim under the scheme was transmissible on death even if death occurred before the claim had arisen. It was further held that even if there were no transmissible rights, the rights of a surviving spouse should not be restricted to claiming half the amount of compensation where they remained wholly responsible for liabilities incurred as a result of the breach of the rules. Such a restriction would be "extraordinary".[76]

However, the range of approaches that the court will adopt to the interpretation of rules which are clearly within the body's power to make is indicated by the path of *ex p. Bowden* itself through the appeal courts. The principal issue at these stages concerned the basis of compensation given under the scheme.[77] The scheme affords compensation to private investors for loss caused by breach of the rules by an authorised firm where the firm has gone into default, up to a maximum of £48,000.[78] The scheme is set up under section 54 of the FSA, and section 54(2)(d) permits rules to be made which "specify the terms and conditions on which, and the extent to which, compensation is to be payable and any circumstances in which the right to compensation is to be excluded or modified". The rules of the scheme provided that compensatable claims were those

---

[72] [1994] 1 All ER 525 (DC). This point was not appealed.
[73] *Ibid.*, at 539.
[74] [1994] QB 749.
[75] *Ibid.*, at 774F.
[76] *Ibid.*, at 775A.
[77] There were two subsidiary issues: whether the decisions that the applicants had to give credit for money received by them and spent, to limit to £500 the amount recoverable for professional fees, and not to pay damages for inconvenience, illness, distress and anxiety, were lawful and rational. The last point was dropped on appeal to the House of Lords.
[78] 100% of claims up to £30,000, and 90% of claims thereafter up to a maximum of £50,000: r.2.07.

arising for property held and transactions remaining uncompleted, and that compensation for any other claim was to be met "where the Management Company considers that this is essential in order to provide fair compensation to the investor".[79] The rules further provided that "a claim is not a compensatable claim unless it relates to a liability which has been established before a court of competent jurisdiction or which the Management Company is satisfied would be established if proceedings were brought before such a court".[80]

The requirement that the only claims to be recognised were those which would be recognised in common law clearly limited the discretion of the ICS, and required the scheme to operate in parallel to the common law at least in terms of the types of claim which could be compensated. The issue was whether under its rules the ICS had to operate effectively in the same way in which a court would and provide exactly that compensation that could have been obtained in common law with respect to the different types of claim, or whether it had a discretion to award compensation on a different basis with respect to those types of claims (i.e. under different heads of claim). The point to note is that either rule would have been within the statutory powers.

In the Divisional Court, Mann LJ held that such a discretion was plainly afforded by the rules, and the consideration of how much compensation to award in order to provide fair compensation was a matter for a judgement which could only be impugned if it were irrational.[81] Overturning his decision, the Court of Appeal held[82] that the basis of compensation should be that which would be given by a court; the ICS had no discretion to limit that compensation except for those types of claims clearly excluded by the rules, subject only to the overall limit of £48,000. Further, to impose any type of limit at all on the amount that could be claimed by way of compensation for professional fees was irrational, although the court gave no reasons for this part of its decision. Their decision was in turn overturned in the House of Lords by a majority of four to one, Lord Steyn dissenting.[83] Lord Lloyd, giving the leading speech, held that the phrase "an application for compensation relating to any other claim" in rule 2.04 fitted better with a broad discretion to include within the definition of a compensatable claim either the claim as a whole or those elements of it which the ICS considered essential in order to provide fair compensation, and to exclude those elements which did not meet that requirement.[84] How that discretion was exercised, and thus on what basis compensation was given, was thus subject to the principles of review for irrationality. Lord Steyn dissented on the point of construction of the rule, on the basis that the rule had to be interpreted in accordance with its context. The rule did not contain language which was apt

[79] R.2.04(1).
[80] R. 2.04(2); further exclusions in r.2.04(3). Private investors have the right to bring a civil action for loss or damage caused by breach of the rules under s.62 FSA.
[81] [1994] 1 All ER 525 at 534.
[82] *R. v. ICS, ex p. Bowden* [1995] QB 107 (CA).
[83] *R. v. ICS, ex p. Bowden* [1995] 3 All ER 605 (HL).
[84] *ibid.*, at 611.

to provide a discretion to reduce compensation, and within the context both of the particular rule and of the rules as a whole the phrase could not be read as conferring such a discretion.

In considering the judicial approach to the construction of the ICS rules, the point to be made here is not so much whether or not the construction which was finally given to the rules was correct; as Lord Lloyd stated, they were drafted with "such confusing and needless obscurity"[85] that either interpretation was supportable. It is rather to note the courts' lack of reticence in engaging in the exercise of the rules' interpretation, and the conflicting approaches to that interpretation which were adopted. In considering the board's decision under the ICS rules, there was no question that the FSA did not allow SIB the power to make rules for a compensation scheme which would have enabled compensation to be given which was less than that which would be given at law, or which would have left the determination of compensation to the discretion of the ICS board; the issue was simply whether that was what had been done. There was no suggestion that the rules were thus outside the statutory powers, or that in misconstruing them the ICS board went beyond its statutory jurisdiction. Nonetheless, there was no indication that the issue was other than a matter for the court to decide; there was no implicit or explicit adoption of a view that where the issue was unclear, and either interpretation was clearly within the statutory boundaries, as long as the interpretation was reasonable then the court should not intervene.

Further, in interpreting those rules, the courts adopted explicitly purposive constructions, but according to conflicting purposes which, if consistently adopted, would themselves have led to opposite results. The purpose adopted in considering the rights of personal representatives and spouses to claim, to advance the objective of investor protection and to meet investors' expectations of their rights, was not adopted when considering the issue of the ICS board's discretion to determine the amount of compensation payable. Rather, in construing that part of the ICS rules, Lord Lloyd argued that he could "envisage no sensible *commercial* reason" why the ICS should not have a discretion to award an amount in compensation that would be lower than that which the investor would be given at common law.[86] "If the management company may disregard unmeritorious claims which would nevertheless have succeeded in court, why may it not disregard the unmeritorious elements of meritorious claims?"[87] Why the decision had to be based on such a commercial reason is not clear.[88] Moreover, it is not clear why, if it should be so based, it would necessarily lead to this conclusion. As Lord Steyn noted, the rules already impose limits on the

---

[85] *ibid.*, at 608J, *per* Lord Lloyd.
[86] *ibid.*, at 611G (emphasis added).
[87] *ibid.*
[88] Although the objectives of the Financial Services Regulation do combine efficiency, flexibility, competitiveness and investor protection, these were not referred to: DTI, *Financial Services in the UK: A New Framework for Investor Protection*, Cmnd. 9432 (HMSO, London, 1985).

amount of compensation which may be claimed, in that there is no power to pay greater compensation than is recoverable at law, and that there is a maximum limit on the amount of compensation payable. Given these limits, Lord Steyn argued, "one is not entitled to start with any a priori view that it would be surprising if r.2.04.1 did not confer a general discretion to reduce such claims".[89]

Lord Steyn in fact eschewed any adoption of an explicit purpose, and opted for a contextual approach to interpretation. However, if the same investor-protection purpose had been adopted by the majority of the Lords in construing the rules as to the basis of compensation as was adopted by the Divisonal Court with respect to determining the eligibility of personal representatives to claim, or even if the investor-protection rationale had been given equal force with the commercial, then it could equally have been argued that, given those limits on compensation, the rules should be interpreted so as to afford the investor as far as possible the same compensation as he could have obtained at law.

Rules not Made under Statutory Powers

Given that the ICS rules are made under statute and are items of subordinate legislation (broadly defined), it is not perhaps surprising, although as argued above not desirable, to see the courts engaging in detailed exercises of their interpretation.[90] Where the courts have shown greater uncertainty as to their role is with respect to the rules of bodies which are not creatures of statute and which have not been written pursuant to any statutory power. This situation raises a particular problem. We have seen that the justification given by the courts for exercising a monopoly power over the interpretation of statutory provisions is rooted in the principle of parliamentary sovereignty: review occurs on the basis that a body acting under statute cannot be allowed to determine its own jurisdiction; it has to be kept within the boundaries imposed by that statute. There is no room for permissible errors of law, even if they fall within a spectrum of reasonable interpretation. Where there is no question of *vires* raised, however, this basis falls away. The issue which consequently arises is, on what basis are the courts intervening, and therefore what should their approach be? Do we, and should we, see a continuation in effect of the operation of the jurisdictional/non-jurisdictional distinction when the courts are considering such rules, or do the courts approach the issue as one of rationality or on some other ground?

The issue was well recognised by Lord Donaldson MR in *Datafin*,[91] where he noted that there was little scope for applying the principle of *ultra vires* in the

---

[89] [1995] 3 All ER 605 at 613H.

[90] If the courts were to take a similar approach to the interpretation of SIB's Principles, for example, this would defeat their purpose entirely: one of the main reasons for removing the Principles from the scope of s.62 was to avoid court involvement in their interpretation and so facilitate the use of broader and vaguer rules in the furtherance of a diverse set of regulatory goals: see further J. Black, "'Which Arrow?' Rule Type and Regulatory Policy" [1995] Public Law 96 and n. 49 above.

[91] *R. v. Take-over Panel, ex p. Datafin plc* [1987] 1 QB 815; see also *R. v. Take-over Panel, ex p. Guinness* [1990] 1 QB 146.

context of an alleged misinterpretation of its own rules by a body which under the scheme is both legislator and interpreter.[92] When it came to interpreting its own rules, the Panel had to be given considerable latitude, partly because as legislator it could properly alter them at any time, and partly because of the form the rules took, that is, laying down principles to be applied in spirit as much as in letter in specific situations.[93]

A similar reticence has been evidenced with respect to the Press Complaints Commission,[94] and to the interpretation of the Code of the Independent Committee for the Supervision of Standards of Telephone Information Services (ICSTIS).[95] In the latter, leave was sought to challenge the ICSTIS's interpretation of its own code; Kennedy J refused on the ground that the ICSTIS had in fact adopted the interpretation which the applicants advanced, but also on the basis that, given that the code was not based on any statutory provisions, it was difficult to say that its misinterpretation meant that the body had acted unlawfully. While this case may suggest that cases concerning the interpretation by a body of its own self-regulatory code will be difficult to challenge,[96] it is suggested that such a conclusion should not be too quickly drawn. Although the court may hesitate to intervene for what it may term "technical" breaches,[97] it is by no means clear that judicial reticence will be evident where the breach appears to be more serious.

It nevertheless appears that when non-statutorily-based rules are in issue, the court is giving greater leeway to the body in the interpretation of its own rules. What is not clear is the basis on which this is being done. Is the court providing this leeway by adhering to an even older orthodoxy and by re-introducing[98] the distinction between jurisdictional/non-jurisdictional errors and allowing "errors"? That does not appear to be the case; rather, if the dicta of Lord Donaldson in *Datafin*[99] are adopted, the courts would intervene only if the interpretation which a non-statutory body gave to its own rules was "so far removed

[92] At 841B.

[93] At 841D–E.

[94] *R. v. Press Complaints Commission, ex p. Stewart Brady*, The Times, 22 Nov. 1996. On refusing an application for leave for judicial review of the PCC's decision not to censure the publication of a photograph of the applicant, Lord Woolf found that the PCC had been entitled to come to the conclusion that it did under the Code, and that if there had been a breach it did not warrant censure.

[95] *R. v. ICSTIS Ltd, ex p. Telephone Entertainment Service and others*, 6 Feb. 1992, unreported (transcript: Marten Walsh Cherer). Although note that if the body fails to follow the procedures set out in its own code and in doing so acts unfairly, the courts will find procedural impropriety: *R. v. ASA, ex p. Insurance Service plc* [1990] Admin LR 77; *R. v. General Council of the Bar, ex p. Percival* [1991] 1 QB 212.

[96] See, e.g., Scott in this volume.

[97] In *ex p. Stewart Brady* Lord Woolf held that while it was arguable that the PCC was liable to review, if the court did have jurisdiction over the PCC it was important that the jurisdiction should be reserved for clear, rather than technical, breaches of the code.

[98] Or continuing it: those bodies excluded from the operation of the distinction in *Page* were tribunals and inferior courts. As noted above, the distinction was maintained for bodies exercising a jurisdiction which was purely "domestic", as indeed in *Page* itself, although the meaning of "domestic" is unclear.

[99] [1987] 1 QB 815 at 841E.

from the natural and ordinary meaning of the words of the rules that an ordinary user of the market could reasonably be misled".[100] If it is assessing them on the basis of rationality, is this because it has suddenly abandoned the "correctness" approach entirely? On what basis can it justify any intervention at all, however? As noted, although non-statutory, governmental bodies may be held to be public; the non-statutory basis means the usual "four corners" justification for the control of interpretation is not available.

A number of grounds are potentially available, but it is not clear which, if any, are being adopted. The first is that of legitimate expectations. The argument here would be that while non-adherence by a body to its own rules may not be unlawful in what Lord Reid would term the narrow sense,[101] it may breach the legitimate expectations that those subject to the rules have that they will be adhered to. As noted above, that published rules can create such expectations in public law is well established.[102] Moreover, the ground of legitimate expectations may also interact with that of rationality, *viz*, that in interpreting the rules the body will not adopt interpretations which are totally absurd, in that they depart completely from the normal meaning of the words, and thus what the person could have expected would have been the meaning which would be given to the rule.

Alternatively, or in addition, the rules could be seen as setting the constitutional framework of the body, and the courts' role as ensuring that the body acts within them. The extent to which the courts would need to look to the body's own rules and the extent to which they could look at extraneous principles would perhaps depend on the degree to which the body was woven into a statutory system. If it is closely woven into a statutory system, then at present the court may draw on that as a source of principles against which to assess the validity of regulatory rules.[103] If it is not, then the body's rules themselves have to be relied upon as indicators of its purpose and objectives, and as defining the relationship between it and its members and between the members *inter se*. A loose analogy could be drawn between such an approach and that of ensuring that a company acts within its memorandum and articles, with similar approaches to the construction of those rules being taken as are to the construction of articles.[104] The notion that the court may have a role in keeping a

---

[100] Normally by way of declaratory judgement: [1987] 1 QB 815 at 841E.

[101] *Anisminic v. Foreign Compensation Commission* [1969] 2 AC 147.

[102] *R. v. Home Office, ex p. Khan* [1985] 1 All ER 40, and see n. 33 above.

[103] In the case of financial services SROs, the court has suggested that it will draw on the surrounding legislation to determine the rationality of those rules or whether they pursue an improper purpose: *R. v. Lautro, ex p. Kendall*.

[104] On the need to adopt a commercial approach to the construction of articles see *Holmes v. Keyes* [1959] Ch 199; *Mutual Life Insurance Co v. Rank Organisation Ltd* [1955] Ch 143. As the issues which arise in company law indicate, however, for example as to when personal rights arise for breach of the articles, or the instances in which actions in accordance with the articles will still be held to be unfairly prejudicial under s.459 Companies Act 1985, the court may, if it pursues this line, find itself developing a law for the internal regulation of regulatory associations in a manner akin to its role in incorporated business associations.

body within its self-adopted constitution is evident in *Datafin*, where Lord Donaldson held that the principle of *ultra vires* could perhaps be applied were the Panel to violate its own self-proclaimed principle of doing equity between one shareholder and another.[105] Moreover, it may be that where a body is incorporated the courts may take a stricter approach to ensuring that it stays within its self-adopted constitution than where the body is unincorporated.[106]

It is not clear which, if any, of these approaches are being used with respect to the interpretation of rules of self-regulatory bodies. However, what is clearer is that if the nature of the body or the rules is such that they take the form of a contract, then the court may approach issues of their interpretation in the same way as any contract.[107] In the judicial debate over what is public and what is private, the presence of contract is almost always determinative: if there is a significant contractual element, notwithstanding considerations such as exercise of monopoly power or integration into a governmental system of regulation, then the body and its decision are deemed to be private.[108] The basis for the court's role in interpreting rules issued by a self-regulatory body could simply be that in misinterpreting the rule the body has acted in breach of an agreement reached between the parties, and thus is acting in a way to which the other party did not consent. However, it is questionable whether the rules of a self-regulatory body, particularly one exercising a monopoly jurisdiction, can really be said to have been fully consented to in the same way as contracts which are the outcome of bargaining between parties, or whether it is more accurate to see the analogy to be more with contractual models of the state than with instruments of economic exchange.[109] In any event, it seems difficult to base the court's supervision of a body's interpretation of its own rules on the basis that it is giving effect to the agreement entered into between the parties in the same way as in the case of commercial contracts.

Whichever of the approaches it adopts leads the court down different paths. The legitimate expectations approach, with or without the rationality twist, enables it to remain more clearly within the existing principles of judicial review. Moreover, the doctrine is sufficiently vague and context specific to give the courts considerable freedom of manœuvre in approaching the question of interpretation of or adherence by a body to its own rules. The "associational constitution" route could prove to be more imaginative and lead potentially to the development of principles of internal conduct of regulatory organisations analogous to those formed (albeit largely by statute) for incorporated or unincorporated but commercial associations (companies and partnerships). This could be fruitful, although its full implications cannot be worked through here.

---

[105] [1987] 1 QB 815 at 841D.

[106] See *ibid.*

[107] See further below.

[108] See further Black, n. 3 above.

[109] On the issues raised by the increased use of contractual powers see further M. Freedland, "Government by Contract and Public Law" [1994] *Public Law* 86 and I. Harden, *The Contracting State* (Open University Press, Buckingham, 1992).

The final route, that of simply treating regulatory rules as species of contract, is the least defensible in principle for, as noted, it simply sidesteps the question and fails to recognise the true nature of the contract and the circumstances surrounding its formation and use.

Reviewing the Decisions of Regulatory Ombudsmen

The review of the decisions of regulatory ombudsmen provides an additional example of the nature of the confusion which surrounds the question of review of interpretation, and which illustrates the point made above that, in adopting the correctness approach, the courts are in effect allowing appeal on a point of law. The function of dispute-resolution or redress may form part of the general functions of a regulator or association. Thus in telecommunications regulation, the Director General of Telecommunications has a role in determining disputes between licence-holders and others as to the terms on which they should conduct business. In electricity regulation, the Director General of Electricity Supply has a role in determining disputes between suppliers and those they are supplying.[110] Alternatively (or in addition), there may be a distinct body whose role it is to perform this function. The form these bodies take varies considerably: they may be statutory (Pensions Ombudsman, Building Society Ombudsman), contractual (Insurance Ombudsman, Banking Ombudsman, PIA Ombudsman), they may be entirely non-legal/consensual, and the system of regulation they are woven into may or may not have a statutory element.[111]

In considering the issue of the review of the body's interpretation of the rules in determining disputes, whether the courts will review on the basis of correctness, rationality, or indeed will use the jurisdictional/non-jurisdictional distinction appears to depend on the nature of the body doing the interpreting rather than the nature of the rules being interpreted.[112] Provisional findings are not subject to review,[113] an approach consistent with the attitude taken to provisional decisions in the context of review on the grounds of procedural fair-

---

[110] S.23 Electricity Act 1989. The scope of the jurisdiction has been widely construed: *R. v. DGES, ex p. Redrow Homes (Northern) Ltd*, *The Times*, 21 Feb. 1995. See also the powers of the Director General for Gas Supply under the Gas Act 1985, and those of the Director General for Water Services under the Water Industries Act 1991. See generally *Report by the Comptroller and Auditor General, The Work of the Directors General of Telecommunications, Gas Supply Water Services and Electricity Supply*, HC 645 (HMSO, London, 1996).

[111] On the jurisdiction and operation of different regulatory ombudsmen see generally R. James, *Private Ombudsmen and Public Law* (Dartmouth, Aldershot, 1997); R.W. Hodgin, "Ombudsmen and other Complaints Procedures in the Financial Services Sector in the United Kingdom" (1991) *Anglo American LR* 1.

[112] There is an obvious overlap here with the review of the ICS rules, discussed above, where, as noted, the correctness basis was used.

[113] *R. v. PIA Ombudsman and PIA, ex p. Burns-Anderson Independent Network plc*, 21 Jan. 1997 (CA) official transcript, Smith Bernal Reporting). The case concerned the Ombudsman's provisional determination that the sale of holiday time-shares in a particular scheme was a collective investment scheme and so investment business under the Act, a determination based on matters of fact and on a particular construction of the relevant statutory provisions (s.75(6)(g)).

ness,[114] and as long as the Ombudsman stands open to hear debate on issues of jurisdiction, there will be no unfairness in him proceeding.[115] The Ombudsman has the right to determine, in the first instance, whether he has jurisdiction to adjudicate on a matter brought before him; the legal "cleanness" or clarity of a challenge to jurisdiction or its likely consequence should not normally be a reason for depriving him of that right.[116] "If it were otherwise", Auld LJ held, "it would be possible for respondents to complaints before him, by raising apparently substantial issues of law or of precedent fact, readily to subvert or frustrate the efficient and speedy working of the Ombudsman scheme".[117]

Although the court showed an awareness of role of the Ombudsmen, recognising that they provide alternative fora for dispute-resolution, there is no indication that the court will review their final decisions on anything other than a basis of correctness. They may be an alternative venue to the courts for resolving disputes, but those disputes are to be resolved on the basis of interpretations of rules which are ultimately for the courts to determine—at least, as long as the dispute resolver is a public body. For the courts adopt a different approach from ombudsmen or others exercising dispute-resolution functions whom they deem to be public, and those who are private. The issue is of particular relevance in commercial regulation because of the plethora of such bodies which exists, and an important case in this context is that of *Aegon Life*, which concerned the reviewability of the Insurance Ombudsman.[118] The case is discussed more fully in Martyn Hopper's chapter in this volume, but to reiterate briefly the body was held to be private. Rose LJ held that even if the Ombudsman was integrated into the FSA system of regulation, the facts that the source of powers was contractual and that decisions were of arbitrative nature meant that the Ombudsman was a private body, not susceptible to review. The presence of contract was decisive and sufficient to remove the IOB from the realm of public law.

The correctness of the decision has been questioned[119] but, right or wrong, significant consequences flow from it. Not only is the right to challenge decisions of such Ombudsmen limited by privity of contract (which may in certain circumstances exclude those with whom the insurers have contracted), but if their status is simply that of a private arbitrator, their determinations and in particular their interpretations of the regulators' rules, will not automatically be subject to any challenge in the courts.[120] This narrow focus on the type of body interpreting the rules, as opposed to a wider recognition of the general framework in which it operates, may however mean that when the rules are interpreted by the Insurance Ombudsman their interpretation will be assessed on the

---

[114] *Wiseman* v. *Borneman* [1971] AC 297.

[115] *Ex p. Burns Andersen*, at 10F.

[116] At 8E (*per* Auld LJ).

[117] At 9A.

[118] *R.* v. *Insurance Ombudsman Bureau, ex p. Aegon Life, The Times,* 7 Jan. 1994.

[119] See, e.g., Black, above n. 49, and Martyn Hopper's ch. in this volume.

[120] *Norwich Union Life Assurance Society* v. *P & O Property Holdings Ltd* [1993] 1 EGLR 164 (CA); *Jones* v. *Sherwood Computer Services Ltd* [1992] 1 WLR 277 (CA).

148   *Julia Black*

basis of the jurisdictional/non-jurisdictional principle; where they are interpreted by a public body, the distinction does not apply. Thus whether or not a person has a right to challenge a particular interpretation of a regulatory rule depends, it appears, not on the public or private nature of the rules, but on the public or private nature of the body that happens to be interpreting or applying them.

The question of the public/private categorisation of regulatory instruments and their interpretation also arose in *Mercury Communications* v. *DGT*.[121] From this case it seems that even if the instrument is "private", the "public" nature of the body doing the interpretation will be determinative of the question whether that interpretation will be reviewed.[122] The immediate issue was whether a challenge by Mercury to the Director General's interpretation of a provision in BT's licence could proceed in the commercial court. The issue at the root of the case, however, concerned the nature of the BT licence and the nature of the DGT's function in issuing determinations under that licence.[123] Part of the question essentially was, where the function forms part of the overall activity of a statutory regulator, does that function operate in public or private law, or some combination of both? The context of the challenge was that under BT's licence, BT is obliged to enter into agreements with other operators which allow it to use its network (interconnection agreements). Those agreements have to conform to certain provisions in BT's licence. If BT and the other operator cannot agree terms then under BT's licence the DGT determines what they should be. The arrangements are complex, but the point to note is that the DGT has a role in determining the terms on which BT and other operators do business, when those parties cannot agree between themselves, such determinations having to be made in accordance with the conditions set out in BT's licence. It has this role by virtue of a provision in BT's licence, issued under the Telecommunications Act.[124] The issue arising in the case was that MCL and BT had been unable to agree the pricing structure for their interconnection agreement, the DGT had therefore made a determination, and MCL was challenging it on the basis that it did not conform to the terms set out in BT's licence. The House of Lords held that the case could proceed in the commercial courts. Lord Slynn characterised BT's licence as being analogous to any commercial contract entered into by a Department; however, the DGT's role in interpreting that contract was subject to review by the courts, for failure to interpret that contract correctly would be an error of law.

The judgment finds an uneasy relationship between public and private: on the one hand, the licence is akin to a normal commercial contract, and yet errors in its interpretation are reviewable as errors in law. Thus although the DGT was

[121] *Mercury Communications Ltd* v. *Director General of Telecommunications*, 9 Feb. 1995 (HL).
[122] See further A. McHarg, "Regulation: A Private Law Function?" [1995] *PL* 551.
[123] See further Colin Scott's ch. in this volume.
[124] S.7 TA 1984.

acting in what could be characterised as a dispute-resolution role, in determining the meaning of what was held to be a private contract both in nature and for
purposes of procedure, the leeway which would be given to private arbitrators
to determine disputes was not given; rather, errors in interpreting the licence
would be corrected by the court. It is suggested that the fatal confusion in
Mercury was not the procedural point, but that which flowed around it. The
licence was on the one hand seen as a normal commercial contract for services
which Departments can enter into and the dispute as one between economic
actors as to terms on which they should conduct their business; on the other, the
licence was seen as akin to statute or subordinate legislation in terms of who had
sole jurisdiction to determine meaning of its terms.

The Validity of Regulatory Rules

Turning from the question of interpretation to that of the validity of regulatory
rules, the question which arises is: when will rules issued by a regulator be struck
down as invalid, and do those circumstances depend on whether the body which
issued the rules is held to be public, and so subject to public law principles of
rationality and procedural impropriety, or private?[125]

The simple answer is that if the body is held to be public then it is subject to
the principles of rationality as set out in *Kruse* v. *Johnson*,[126] to the principles of
procedural impropriety, notably the position as to consultation,[127] and to the
doctrine of legitimate expectations; and if it is private, then contract law.[128]
Things, however, are rarely that straightforward. The regulatory forms we are
looking at are characterised by their commingling of public and private. In these
circumstances, the interesting issues arise of whether the public-law principles
applied are themselves affected by this institutional hybridity, and how the principles of one branch of law, public law, interact with those of another, contract
law,[129] where, for example, there is a regulatory rule which takes the contractual form. The questions posed are thus: how do the two different realms of law
interact within these amalgams, and does the nature of the interaction depend
on the "public" or "private" characterisation of the body issuing the rule?

With regard to the application of public-law principles to self-regulatory
bodies, it may be that the formal categorisations of illegality, irrationality and

---

[125] With respect to the *vires* of the rules, then in the case of non-statutory bodies the courts will
either draw on the body's own implicit or explicit constitution to set the limits of its powers (as suggested in *Datafin*), or if the body operates within a broader statutory framework, it may look to that
to set the limits and purposes of its powers: see the suggestions in *R.* v. *Lautro, ex p. Kendall*, 14 Apr.
1992, Lexis transcript.
[126] [1898] 2 QB 91. As Henry J stated, "an irrational rule should be one that hits you between the
eyes": *R.* v. *Lautro, ex p. Kendall*, Lexis.
[127] *R.* v. *Lautro, ex p. Kendall*, 14 Apr. 1992, unreported, Lexis transcript.
[128] On the position as to the *vires* of the body to the issue of the rule's validity, see above n. 97.
[129] This issue is also addressed below.

procedural impropriety are eschewed. As Lord Donaldson MR indicated in *Guinness*,[130] the court may approach self-regulatory bodies "more in the round". This may be not so much out of concern about the impact that the application of judicial review would have on the operation of such bodies, as of a concern for the impact which that application could have on the principles themselves. Indeed it was because of this potential impact on public law principles that Rose J resisted their extension to bodies such as the Football Association, saying that it would be a "quantum leap" which public law should not, and could not, make.[131]

Nevertheless, it appears that public and private law are interacting in this area. The application of public-law principles or, perhaps more accurately, principles familiar in public law, to what would under the courts' current test, be "private" bodies, is well noted,[132] and there is some basis for suggesting that the courts are requiring such bodies to act in accordance with principles of rationality, fairness and non-discrimination. Thus it appears that where the rules of a body are discriminatory or arbitrary that the court will strike them down, even if the body is not subject to review. Although many of the examples are provided by the pre-*O'Reilly* cases concerning the rules of sporting bodies[133] and it would seem, following *Aga Khan*, that these bodies would not now be public so as to be subject to review, it appears that those principles of rationality will still be applied to them,[134] and, further, that principles of fairness will be seen as implied terms of the membership contract.[135] Given that the courts have imposed standards of due process on non-public bodies,[136] it is only a relatively small step for the courts to find that procedural impropriety in forming a rule may lead the court to find the rule invalid even where it is formed by such a non-public body.

The process is not all one way: self-regulatory bodies may be subject to the burden, as some might see it, of such principles of "good administration", but they may also find that private-law principles are adjusted in their application to them. An example which has arisen recently, again in the context of sporting bodies, is the application of the contractual doctrine of restraint of trade. The doctrine is imposed in contract law in the public interest, that of freedom to trade, yet conflicts with the public-law interest in regulation, which might

---

[130] *R. v. Take-over Panel, ex p. Guinness* [1990] 1 QB 146.
[131] *R. v. Football Association, ex p. Football League* [1993] 2 All ER 833 at 849C.
[132] For a recent statement see D. Oliver "Common Values in Public and Private Law and the Public Private Divide" [1997] *Public Law* 630.
[133] E.g., *Nagle v. Fielden* [1966] 2 QB 633.
[134] See the dicta of Farquharson LJ in *Aga Khan* [1993] 2 All ER 853 at 873, and indeed the *Stevenage* case.
[135] *Ibid.*, at 87B, per Hoffman LJ.
[136] *Enderby Town Football Club v. Football Association* [1971] Ch 591; *Dickson v. Pharmeceutical Society* [1970] AC 403; *Breen v. Amalgamated Engineering Union* [1971] 2 QB 175 (explained by Rose LJ as "examples of the courts injecting principles of natural justice into the decision making processes of domestic bodies" in *R. v. Football Association, ex p. Football League* [1993] 2 All ER 833 at 842H); *Jones v. Welsh Rugby Union Football, The Times*, 6 Mar. 1997.

require such restraint. The question which has arisen is whether regulatory rules which are contractual and which restrict entry into and conduct within particular markets, can be struck down as offending against the contract law doctrine of restraint of trade. The answer which the courts have given is that if they are issued by a body which is acting as a regulator in what the court may broadly find to be the public interest, they cannot. This is clearly the position with respect to rules made pursuant to statute. So in *R. v. General Medical Council, ex p. Colman*[137] Ralph Gibson LJ held that:

> "If a restriction imposed by the GMC is within the statutory powers so given, and is not unreasonable, and is in accordance with the policy and purpose of the Act, there is no room for the court to treat the restriction as prima facie contrary to public policy and as requiring proof to the court's satisfaction that it is no more than is reasonably required in the public interest."[138]

It is also the case with respect to rules made by SROs acting within the FSA framework. *Colman* was followed in *ex p. Kendall*, where leave was refused to challenge a provision in Lautro's rules on the grounds of restraint of trade.[139] The rule prohibited members from appointing a person as a company representative if that person was indebted to another authorised person. Henry J held that as long as the rule was within Lautro's powers, as defined by the broad statutory framework of the FSA, then it could not be struck down. This decision in turn was to be made according to principles of irrationality.

The position is thus almost certainly that if a body is sufficiently integrated into a statutory system of regulation so as to be exercising a public function its rules will not be struck down for restraint of trade. However, it has also been held that, even where the body is not acting within a statutory framework, but rather where it is performing a regulatory function in the public interest (albeit one which apparently does not make it sufficiently public for the judicial review procedures to be required), then the normal contractual rules of restraint of trade do not apply. Thus in *Stevenage Borough Football Club* v. *The Football League*,[140] where Stevenage sought an injunction against the Football League restraining it from imposing its criteria for membership to the league on Stevenage so as to refuse it admission, Carnwath J stated that the rules were not part of an ordinary contractual situation where the purpose of restriction was to protect a private commercial interest. Rather, they were part of a system of control imposed by a body exercising regulatory powers in the public interest. Different considerations therefore arose. The onus in those circumstances was on those seeking to challenge the system of control to show that the particular rules under attack were unreasonable in the "narrow" sense. If the admission criteria were shown to be arbitrary or capricious, whether because of the way in

---

[137] [1990] 1 All ER 489.
[138] At 509.
[139] *R. v. Lautro, ex p. Kendall*, 14 Apr. 1992, unreported, Lexis transcript.
[140] *The Times*, 1 Aug. 1996.

which they were formulated or the way in which they were applied, they were open to challenge; but the onus was on the challenger to make out its case. So where a body is found to be regulating in the public interest (even if it is not found to be "public"), any restraints on trade which its contractual rules may impose are *prima facie* justified, in a reversal of the normal contract law position. Carnwath J in fact held that although the rules were an unlawful restraint of trade, relief should be refused as a matter of discretion.[141]

In sum, therefore, as regards the issue of the rules' validity, then SRA rules may be struck down on the basis that they are outside the body's statutory powers or, if there are none, then outside its actual (in the case of incorporated bodies) or deemed (in the case of unincorporated ones) constitution, or outside the scope and purposes of the broad statutory framework in which it operates. Rules may be struck down on the basis that they are arbitrary or discriminatory, apparently regardless of the public or private nature of the body; alternatively they will not be held to be *prima facie* invalid as restraints of trade, again, apparently regardless of the public or private nature of the body. However, as *Guinness* suggests, as the "private" is infused with the "public", so it may be that the public does not remain immune from the effects of the hybridity of the institutional structures.

REGULATORY AND CONTRACTUAL NETWORKS

Issues concerning or relating to regulatory rules may also arise in the context of networks of regulatory rules and contractual arrangements. Continuing the theme of review of rules in situations where public and private are mixed, the particular question which may be asked in this context is whether we are seeing a development of new principles in both private and public law which reflects the hybridity of the institutional structure of the regulation.[142] What here is the relationship between the regulatory rules or instruments and the operation of common law principles? This relationship can be examined in two broad contexts: that of franchising and licensing regulation, and that of the relationship between regulatory systems and the common law.

Franchising and Licensing Regulation

The particular issue which arises in the context of franchising or licensing regulation is what impact do those licences or franchises have on the contractual

---

[141] An attack by Stevenage on the exercise of this discretion failed: see (1996) 9 Admin. LR 109 (CA).

[142] There are clearly areas in which no such "fusion" of public and private law is occurring, notably as regards the issues of void and voidable acts, as shown by Christopher Clarke's and Cathy Otton-Goulder's ch. in this volume.

relationships entered into by those operating in the regulated field? This framework of regulation through licence or franchise differs from that of regulation through a body, be it a statutory body or an SRA, issuing rules to guide and direct the behaviour of a wide range of persons and which apply generally to all those operating within the area being regulated. Provisions concerning standards of service, pricing, etc. are set out, not in rules but in each individual licence or franchise, and licences or franchises issued to a number of operators may or may not contain common terms. The form of regulation thus differs considerably: notably changes in the terms of regulation usually have to be made by modifications to each individual licence, and consent is frequently required for modification.[143] There are thus no rules, in the sense of generally applicable norms; rather a network of individual agreements which themselves form the framework for the activities and legal relationships of those operating in the area. This network does not simply consist of the licensor and a number of licensees, but of those with whom the licensee itself enters into commercial agreements.

The structure of these commercial and regulatory relationships raises issues which are only just starting to be explored. These include the difficult issue of the degree to which those who are not parties to the franchise or licence arrangement should be consulted on proposed changes to it[144]; and the tension between the individuated nature of the relationship between regulator and regulated and the generality of the system of regulation in terms of assessing the need for consistency of treatment of regulatees and the rationality of regulatory decisions.[145] The issues which I want to focus on here, however, concern the public or private nature of such licences and the reviewability of actions relating to them, and the impact that the framework of licence-regulation has on the relationships between licence-holders and their commercial counter-parties.

The fact that the license or franchise takes the form of an agreement between two parties gives it the appearance of being analogous to a contract. Thus, as noted in the *Mercury* case above, and also in the case of *Rank*,[146] such an analogy has been the basis of decisions that issues arising from their interpretation or as to their alteration are not public-law issues. This approach misses a crucial point. Such licences and franchises are not simply commercial agreements between economic actors; they are instruments of regulation, of the exercise of state power, function and control.

It may be, however, that in considering such networks, we are seeing two conflicting trends, and that in some instances the regulatory character of such licences is being recognised, with significant results. Again in the telecommunications sector, there have been cases in which the contracts concluded between

---

[143] With, in the utilities sector, referral to the MMC in the event that agreement cannot be reached.

[144] See further J. Black, "Talking about Regulation" [1998] *Public Law* 77.

[145] See further C. Scott, "Regulatory Discretion in Licence Modifications" [1997] *Public Law* 400 and further in this volume.

[146] *R. v. IBA, ex p. Rank*, 26 Mar. 1986, Lexis transcript.

BT and commercial counter-parties have been held to be affected by the regulatory framework in which those agreements are concluded. In effect, that regulatory framework has been held to affect the operation of normal principles of contract law, infusing them with principles familiar from public law. Thus the ability of BT to exercise its power under its standard terms and conditions to terminate its service on giving one month's notice was held not to be determined in accordance with classical principles of contract law.[147] In considering the termination clause, the court held that the contract had to be seen in the overall context of BT's position as an operator licensed by the SST and regulated by the DGT. Given that BT was a dominant supplier, closely regulated to ensure that it operated in the interests of the public, the court doubted whether the classical approach to the implication of terms should be used. Rather, there were strong grounds for the view that in the particular circumstances BT should not be permitted to exercise a potentially drastic power of termination without demonstrable reason or cause for doing so.[148] It thus appears from these cases that in some areas at least the hybridity of new institutional frameworks is affecting the operation of the substantive doctrines of law, in this case contract law.

Regulatory Rules and Common Law: Separate Spheres of Operation?

A second significant example of where the question of the relationship between regulatory rules and common law arises is in the context of regulatory rules issued by regulatory bodies, and the question in this context has two aspects: first, does a regulator have to have express statutory authority to modify common law principles (as is the case for the abrogation of fundamental rights), or can a regulator have implicit authority to issue rules which are contrary to common law (as long as this is within the general statutory purposes, where there are any)?; and, secondly, if the regulator is held to have that implicit authority, what is the relationship between the rules which are then written and the common law?

It is clear that many ombudsmen and compensation schemes envisage that compensation may be given on a basis different from that under general law (although their terms of reference generally require them to take the provisions of general law into account),[149] and, moreover, the approach of the courts in *ex p. Bowden* indicates that there does not have to be any express statutory authority for this to be so. The question then arises as to the relationship of those regulatory systems and that of common law.

---

[147] *Timeload Ltd* v. *British Telecommunications plc*, 30 Nov. 1993, unreported (transcript: John Larking).

[148] To an extent, BT's contracts with its operators also viewed in context of overall regulatory position in *Megaphone International Ltd* v. *BT plc*, Independent, 1 Mar. 1989.

[149] And they will not normally be permitted to insist on payments, for example, which it would otherwise be *ultra vires* for a body to make: *Westminster CC* v. *Haywood and Pensions Ombudsman*, *The Times*, 12 Mar. 1996.

In the case of Ombudsmen or compensation schemes, it is not normally the case that a person has to use the regulatory scheme rather than go to common law,[150] and indeed the regulatory scheme may provide redress where the common law would not.[151] These systems therefore do not really raise the possibility of a "clash" between regulatory provisions and common law, at least for those seeking redress, as it is open to the parties to use either channel to get redress. The more difficult situation is where the regulatory system and the common law conflict as to the duties which are imposed.

Although it has not materialised in litigation, the potential for such a conflict was seen as a real one with respect to the initial FSA system of regulation, and the Law Commission was asked to consider relationship between regulatory rules and fiduciary duties.[152] The Commission's provisional conclusion was that there were probably gaps between the requirements of fiduciary law and the provisions of the regulatory rules, such that compliance with the rules would not necessarily amount to compliance with fiduciary law.[153] In considering what the judicial response should be were the issue ever to come before the court, the Commission considered three possible models.[154] First, the "private law" model: in the absence of express statutory authority, regulatory rules had to be formulated in accordance with fiduciary duties; rules made contrary to fiduciary law are invalid, and thus any issue of a clash does not arise.[155] Secondly, the public-law model: regulatory rules cannot be held invalid simply because they conflict with fiduciary duties; the authority for the regulator to make the rules is limited only by the statutory provisions or provisions in the regulator's own constitution. Because the rules are presumptively valid (and validity depends on conformity with statutory purposes, not conformity with the common law), the issue of a potential clash between them and fiduciary law does arise.[156] There are then three possibilities. Under the "public-law" model the regulatory rules are presumed to modify fiduciary duties. Alternatively, the regulatory rules and the common law simply operate in completely separate spheres: fiduciary duties do not affect the operation and interpretation of the regulatory rules, and the regulatory rules do not affect the content of fiduciary duties.[157] Finally, under the third, "hybrid" model, which the Commission

---

[150] There is a right of appeal on a point of law from the Building Societies and the Pensions Ombudsmen.

[151] Or, in the case of the ICS, where there would be no real likelihood of recovery as the firm is in default.

[152] Law Commission, *Fiduciary Duties and Regulatory Rules: A Consultation Paper*, CP No.124 (Law Commission, London, 1992); *Fiduciary Duties and Regulatory Rules*, LC No.236 (Law Commission, London, 1995).

[153] Consultation Paper, paras 3.4.39, 4.5.25.

[154] *Ibid.*, paras. 5.4–5.5, 6.1–6.22.

[155] *Ibid.*, paras. 5.4.5, 5.4.8–5.4.12.

[156] *Ibid.*, paras. 5.4.13–5.4.22.

[157] *Ibid.*, paras. 5.4.12, 6.19.

provisionally favoured,[158] the rules do not necessarily override fiduciary duties, but the court may take the regulatory requirements into account in determining what the precise content of the fiduciary duty is in any particular instance.[159]

In the light largely of subsequent developments in the case law on fiduciary duties, the Commission decided that there was no need for legislation to clarify the matter.[160] It is however likely that the "hybrid" model in fact represents the legal position.[161] The interaction between the different systems of law, in which one serves to shape and modify the other, echoes that seen in the situations examined above, and it is suggested, is to be preferred to a rigid demarcation between the different areas of regulatory and common law.

CONCLUSIONS AND ISSUES RAISED

The review of regulatory rules and other instruments of regulation thus raises issues which touch the core both of the debate concerning the appropriate role of the courts in exercising their judicial review jurisdiction in areas which are incontestably "public", and of the nature of the legal response to the changes which are occurring in the institutional structure of regulation.

Some of these responses evidence a degree of flexibility by legal principles in the face of such hybrid structures; more usually, the response is structured in the "either/or" terms of the public/private divide. So it appears, for example, that the extent to which a regulator will be permitted to make errors in interpreting its own rules depends both on the status of those rules and the public or private nature of the body interpreting them. Where the body is public, and the rules characterised as subordinate legislation, then review will be on the basis of the correctness of the interpretation; where it is operating without any statutory source of power and/or its rules are not subordinate legislation, then on the basis of rationality. A preferable approach, it has been suggested, would be to adopt the principle of rationality in reviewing all interpretations by regulators of their own rules and of general statutory provisions. There is moreover a grey

---

[158] Consultation Paper, para. 5.5.3. This is the Commission's third model, although, as it depends on the validity of the regulatory rules, it may be more appropriately be seen as a version of the second, public-law, model.

[159] *Ibid.*, paras. 5.4.23–5.4.29.

[160] The Commission had provisionally recommended legislation to provide an explicit defence for breach of fiduciary duties that the person had acted in conformity with regulatory rules (*ibid.*, paras. 7.18–7.23). This was rejected in the final Report, para. 14.20.

[161] See *Swain* v. *Law Society* [1983] AC 598 (rules can authorise a breach of fiduciary duty, no private law remedy); *Dunford & Elliot Ltd* v. *Johnson & Firth Brown Ltd* [1977] 1 Lloyd's Rep. 505 (non-enforcement of stipulation of confidence where such a stipulation was in breach of the Code on Take-overs and Mergers); *Lloyd Cheyham & Co. Ltd* v. *Littlejohn & Co.* [1987] BCLC 303; *Dawson International Plc* v. *Coats Paton* [1989] BCLC 233, affirmed [1990] BCLC 506 (compliance with guidance of Consultative Committee on Accountancy Bodies as to auditor's liability contributed to finding that there was no "unreasonable" or "unfair" conduct); *Re a Company* [1986] BCLC 382 (non-compliance with the Take-over Code indicated unfair prejudice under s.459 Companies Act 1989). See further Consultation Paper, paras. 5.4.26–5.4.27.

area between these situations, and it is by no means clear where the line between them falls.

With respect to the validity of the rules, then it appears that rules can be struck down on the basis of *vires*, procedural impropriety (although likely to be rare) and extreme irrationality regardless of the public or private nature of the body. It may be, however, that in applying those public law principles to either public or private bodies, the courts may apply either slightly different forms of those principles, or those principles in a different way, as suggested in *Guinness*.[162] Conversely, normal principles in contract law, notably of restraint of trade, may not operate where the body is deemed to be performing a regulatory function, albeit that the body is not "public".

It does appear that the hybridity of the bodies and instruments which are involved in regulating is being echoed in the interaction of principles in private and public law, although, as noted, we are some way off seeing a united set of substantive public and private-law principles. Thus it appears that the operation of private-law principles and the nature of the duties imposed in private relationships can be affected by the presence or content of regulatory principles which operate in the same area, and further that private bodies can be subjected to principles which are familiar in public law. Exactly what the effect of the hybridity of regulatory instruments and frameworks is on the operation of public-law principles is somewhat harder to gauge: the fluidity of those principles themselves can make it difficult to establish exactly what the "formal" categorisations themselves require in any particular instance. However, it is suggested that some differences in the application of those principles can nevertheless be seen. That interaction between the principles of private and public law is occurring prompts the final observation: that there is perhaps a danger in being obsessed, or at least diverted, by the question of what is "public" and what is "private". Instead of using a classification based on a body's institutional relationship with the state to determine the legal principles that should apply to it, we should rather start by looking at the type of function being exercised, asking what duties and responsibilities should accompany the exercise of such functions and to whom should they be owed, what degree of autonomy should those exercising them have and what degree of judicial supervision should be exercised over them, and use that, not a narrow public/private dichotomy, as the basis for determining the legal principles which should apply.

---

[162] [1990] 1 QB 146.

7

Irrationality and Commercial Regulators

PAUL WALKER*

INTRODUCTION

Lord Diplock in *Council for Civil Service Unions* v. *Minister for the Civil Service*[1] described the grounds on which administrative action is subject to control by judicial review. One of those grounds he called "irrationality", and said of it:[2]

> "By "irrationality" I mean what can now be succinctly referred to as "Wednesbury unreasonableness" (*Associated Provincial Picture Houses* v. *Wednesbury Corporation* [1948] 1 KB 223). It applies to a decision which is so outrageous in its defiance of logic or of accepted moral standards that no sensible person who applied his mind to the question to be decided could have arrived at it."

The term "irrationality" is not an altogether satisfactory label for this ground of review. The 5th edn. of de Smith criticises it for casting doubt on the mental capacity of the decision-maker[3]; moreover the label wrongly suggests that any illogicality may vitiate a decision, and it obscures the moral element which Lord Diplock himself identified.[4] But it is a convenient shorthand for the purposes of this chapter.

In 1992 I wrote an account of irrationality as a ground of review in English administrative law.[5] I saw no reason then to suggest that any special principles applied to judicial review of commercial regulators. Indeed 3 years earlier the then Chairman of the Takeover Panel had affirmed that "the broad principles of

* Barrister, Brick Court Chambers, London; formerly director of the New Zealand Institute of Public Law. I thank the participants at the LSE Seminar series in Spring 1997 for valuable comments on a paper which was the forerunner to this chapter.

[1] [1985] AC 374.

[2] [1985] AC 374 at 410.

[3] S.A. de Smith, H. Woolf and J. Jowell, *Judicial Review of Administrative Action* (5th edn. Butterworths, London, 1995) p. 550, citing Lord Donaldson M.R. in *R.* v. *Devon County Council ex p. G* [1988] 3 WLR 49, 51; see also Sir John Laws in [1996] JR at p.50.

[4] See P. Walker, "What's wrong with irrationality?" [1995] PL 556 at p. 566.

[5] See chapter 6 of M. Supperstone and J. Goudie (eds), *Judicial Review* (Butterworths, London, 1992), now revised in the second edition (1997).

administrative law should apply consistently across the board".[6] However, in 1995 Richard Gordon Q.C. asserted that the present body of commercial case law was not consistent with that view, in particular because:[7]

> "The courts afford an extremely wide margin of appreciation to those bodies which are concerned with the regulation of commercial activities."

In this chapter I shall look at some of the more recent cases to see whether commercial regulators are benefiting from any special principle. I shall suggest that the concept of "irrationality" as a ground of review requires the court to be willing, where necessary, to identify limits to the exercise of power, limits which are dictated by fundamental values. The analysis which I put forward in 1992 included some propositions which I hope I may be forgiven for repeating here:[8]

> "Reasonable people may differ about moral standards, and about the rigour with which logic must be applied. An assertion that a decision is illogical or fails to meet moral imperatives must be weighed against the needs of good administration, recognising that administrators will sometimes find themselves confronted with a Gordian knot, and must not shirk from applying a common sense solution. Only if the solution strays so far from logic or accepted moral standards that no reasonable administrator could have thought it right will it be condemned as irrational. This involves a value judgment by the Court: but it is a judgment of a very limited kind.
>
> The fact that the test is so stringent places a high burden upon an applicant. This does not mean, however, that an administrative body may render itself immune from judicial review on rationality grounds by simply asserting that it weighed all relevant factors and formed its own value judgment."

The nature of this exercise, whether the court is examining the decision of commercial regulators, immigration officers or Secretaries of State, does not differ. It is an exercise of last resort. The court must begin with the question of legality: if the decision-maker proceeded on an incorrect understanding of the relevant discretionary power, then that will usually be an end of the matter. Only if the decision-maker proceeded on a correct understanding of the law, and what was implicitly or explicitly required to be regarded or ignored, does the court normally need to proceed to consider whether what was done went beyond what a reasonable administrator, *properly directed in law*, could have thought appropriate. What may be noted in this exercise of last resort is that there are features of commercial regulation which suggest that a reasonable decision-maker will for good cause often (but not always) be able to give less weight to rigorous logical analysis or rigorous moral examination. This may seem an

---

[6] "Judicial Review and City Regulators" (1989) 52 MLR 640.
[7] R. Gordon, "Declaratory Judgments and Judicial Review", Conference Paper 29 September 1995.
[8] Text referred to at n. 5 above, at page 121; these propositions were cited with approval by Beaumont & Hill JJ. in *Minister for Primary Industries and Energy* v. *Austral Fisheries* (1993) 40 FCR 381 at 400.

unsatisfactory answer to those who lament a lack of principle in this area[9]: but there is a danger that any attempt to capture the principle by categorising particular types of activity, or grounds of unreasonableness, will lose vital flexibility and will encourage "boundary-dispute" litigation without offering any concomitant predictability of court decisions.

BACKGROUND

As Julia Black has observed[10], the regulation of commercial (and professional) activity is not new. Nor is supervision of such regulation by the courts. In 1768 the Court of Kings Bench dealt with an application for mandamus to compel the College of Physicians to admit Dr. Letch to membership. Lord Mansfield said that while the Court should not interfere with the judgment and discretion of the College, nevertheless the College in the exercise of its powers ought not to accede certain limits. Among those limits, the College ought not to reach a decision which was arbitrary or capricious.[11] In setting out the limits within which the College might exercise its powers, Lord Mansfield was proceeding on the basis that he was merely applying to the College the principles which flowed from the Court's "jurisdiction over corporate bodies, to see that they act agreeably to the end of their institution".

Turning to the first half of the 20th century the *Wednesbury* decision itself concerned the regulation of commercial activity. It is elementary that Lord Greene M.R. was speaking perfectly generally when he said:[12]

"It is true to say that, if a decision on a competent matter is so unreasonable that no reasonable authority could ever have come to it, then the courts can interfere. That, I think, is quite right; but to prove a case of that kind would require something overwhelming, ..."

Of course the "regulator" in that case was a local authority with power to licence cinemas,[13] not the sort of sophisticated bodies which we find in the financial services and utilities fields today. And modern commentators[14] have criticised the failure to find something "overwhelming" in the decision that children could not attend cinema performances on Sundays, even if accompanied by an

---

[9] Among them Lord Browne-Wilkinson, who asked in the Foreword to M. Supperstone and J. Goudie, *Judicial Review*, "Above all, is it possible to extract a more principled approach to determining the legality of administrative action than the rather pragmatic concept of *Wednesbury* unreasonableness?"

[10] J. Black, "Constitutionalising Self-Regulation" (1996) 59 MLR 24.

[11] *R. v. Askew* (1768) 4 Burr 2186 at 2188.

[12] [1948] 1 KB 223, 230.

[13] An excellent account of the background is given by Sir Robert Carnwath, "The reasonable limits of local authority power" [1996] PL 244.

[14] e.g. *ibid.* at p.247; Lord Cooke of Thornden has speculated that the town of Wednesbury may have had strong ecclesiastical traditions: see "The struggle for simplicity in administrative law" in Taggart (ed.), Judicial Review of Administrative Action in the 1980s, p. 13.

adult: but I wonder whether such critics have taken account of the very different moral atmosphere (at least in relation to religious observance of Sundays) which prevailed in 1948.

Certainly when referring to older cases one must bear in mind that since the 1960s there has been a "sea-change in attitudes towards administrative law".[15] Sir Stephen Sedley has described his perception of changes in our "moral economy" which have rendered the legitimacy of government heavily contested, and have conferred legitimacy upon the court's willingness to adapt and expand old principles to new and different administrative structures.[16] In considering the extent to which review for unreasonableness has been adapted to deal with the new structures of commercial regulation, I shall look at three fields: financial services, broadcasting and utilities.

FINANCIAL SERVICES REGULATION

Lord Bingham, speaking extra-judicially, has said in the context of the court's discretion to refuse relief:[17]

> "Had the courts declared the field of financial regulation a no go area that would, I think, have been regrettable, but they have not done so. On the other hand, it would seem to me wise for the courts to venture into this uncharted minefield with considerable circumspection lest the cure be more damaging to the wider investing public than the disease. I would expect the developing case law to define with greater precision the grounds on which the Court will exercise its discretion to refuse relief, but for the moment perhaps the courts have got the balance about right."

Has the same circumspection been applied to review for unreasonableness?

Gordon rightly observes[18] that while many practitioners look to the court of Appeal decision in R. v. *Panel on Takeovers and Mergers, ex p. Datafin Plc*[19] as an illustration of judicial expansionism, in fact the approach taken by Lord Donaldson in that case and in R. v. *Monopolies & Mergers Commission, ex p. Argyll Group Plc*[20] was a cautious one. What was envisaged for the Takeover Panel in *Datafin* was that, save in the case of a breach of natural justice[21], the court should permit contemporary decisions to take their course and grant declaratory relief only. The reasons for this were the special nature of the Panel and its functions, the market in which it operated, and the need to safeguard the

---

[15]   de Smith, Woolf & Jowell, n. 3 above p. 8, para. 1-011.
[16]   S. Sedley, "The moral economy of judicial review" in Geoffrey P. Wilson (ed.), *Frontiers of Legal Scholarship* (Wiley, Chichester, 1995).
[17]   T. Bingham, "Should public law remedies be discretionary?" [1991] PL 64, 75.
[18]   Paper cited at n. 6 above, paragraph 1.03.
[19]   [1987] 1 QB 815.
[20]   [1986] 1 WLR 763.
[21]   See [1987] 1 QB at page 842B.

position of third parties trading on an assumption of the validity of the Panel's rules and decisions.[22]

This self-imposed restraint means that the relationship between the Panel and the court is expected to be "historic rather than contemporaneous". It was designed to avoid the perils that—if judicial review were to have its ordinary, contemporaneous, consequences—applications would often be made which were unmeritorious, dislocating the operation of the market during dependency of proceedings, creating uncertainty in areas where it is vital that there be finality. The "historic" approach described by Lord Donaldson in *Datafin* is not one which involves altering the grounds of review;[23] instead it relies upon the court's discretion to refuse leave to apply for judicial review, and if leave is granted, to refuse relief. On this "historic" basis, the Master of the Rolls' judgment in *Datafin* does not suggest that any special rule for the determination of an allegation of "unreasonableness"—indeed in relation to the Panel's interpretation of its own rules, the Master of the Rolls contemplated that legitimate cause for intervention by the court could exist if the interpretation were so far removed from the natural and ordinary meaning of the words of the rules that an ordinary user of the market could reasonably be misled.

The first suggestion that "unreasonableness" as a ground of review might require modification in relation to the Takeover Panel came not in *Datafin*, but in the second case to come before the court of Appeal involving the Takeover Panel, *R. v. Panel on Takeovers and Mergers, ex p. Guinness Plc*[24]. Lord Donaldson contemplated that, in relation to the Panel, the tripartite classification of the grounds of review in *CCSU* might no longer be appropriate:

> "It may be that the true view is that in the context of a body whose constitution, functions and powers are sui generis, the court should review the Panel's acts and omissions more in the round than might otherwise be the case and, whilst basing its decision on familiar concepts, should eschew any formal categorisation. . . . In the context of the present appeal [Lord Diplock] might have considered an innominate ground formed of an amalgam of his own grounds with perhaps added elements, reflecting the unique nature of the Panel, its powers and duties and the environment in which it operates . . . In relation to such an innominate ground the ultimate question would, as always, be whether something had gone wrong of a nature and degree which required the intervention of the court and, if so, what form that intervention should take."

Specifically in relation to "irrationality" as a ground of review, the Master of the Rolls said:

> "Irrationality, at least in the sense of failing to take account of relevant factors or taking account of irrelevant factors, is a difficult concept in the context of a body which is itself charged with the duty of making a judgment on what is and what is not

---

[22] Page 842C to D.
[23] At page 842F the Master of the Rolls adopted the tripartite classification in *CCSU*.
[24] [1990] 1 QB 146.

relevant, although clearly a theoretical scenario could be constructed in which the Panel acted on the basis of considerations which on any view must have been irrelevant or ignored something which on any view must have been relevant."[25]

This passage contains an important recognition that, even in the absence of any statutory guidance, review for irrationality may be available where a decision-maker has taken a view on the relevancy of a particular matter which no reasonable decision-maker could have thought right.[26]

Lloyd L.J. did not comment directly on the Master of the Rolls' suggestions; instead, he affirmed that in questions of fair procedure the Court should enforce the principles which it had developed over many years, making no exception for the Panel.[27]

Woolf L.J. agreed with the reasons given by the Master of the Rolls. He expressly recognised that the Panel's non-statutory basis, and self-determining scope of activity, created constraints as to the manner in which the courts could intervene. For example, subject to certain qualifications, the Panel was under no duty to carry out its investigations in any particular way and it must be for the Panel to decide to what extent it is appropriate for it having regard to its resources to engage in extensive investigations. Further there were no statutory obligations on the Panel equivalent to the statutory obligations which made it possible to identify considerations for statutory bodies which must be taken into account or ignored.[28] That said,

> ". . . In the public law field, if the Panel, without being under any enforceable duty to do so, engages in an activity which can have consequences to a third party, then the Panel by so doing can impose on itself legally enforceable obligations of a similar nature to those to which it would be subject if it were carrying out that activity pursuant to a statutory duty. However, this does not mean the obligations are identical to those which would exist if it were under a statutory duty. In the normal case a body such as the Panel will retain a very wide discretion as to how it performs the task it sets itself and the Court will regard its role as being one of last resort reserved for plain and obvious cases."

Woolf L.J. then added that it was appropriate for the court to ask, in relation to the Panel's activities as a whole, whether something had gone wrong in nature and degree which required the intervention of the courts. In the context of the

---

[25] Page 159; the first part of this passage, referring to the identification by the court of relevant and irrelevant factors, would now be regarded as part of the investigation of the legality of the decision-maker's approach: see per Lord Bridge in R. v. *Secretary of State for the Environment, ex p. Hammersmith & Fulham London Borough Council* [1991] 1 AC 521 at 597 disapproving the view to the contrary expressed by the Court of Appeal in that case (at [1991] 1 AC 562).

[26] For cases in which this approach was applied to treaties, see *Ashby* v. *Minister of Immigration* [1981] 1 NZLR 222, and *Tavita* v. *Minister of Immigration* [1994] 1 NZLR [1994] 2 MZLR 257(CA). A discussion of cases involving the Treaty of Waitangi will be found in Philip A. Joseph, "Constitutional Review Now" [1988] *New Zealand Review* 85.

[27] At 185E to F.

[28] At 193.

instant case (the issue was whether an adjournment should have been granted):[29]

> ". . . It is more appropriate to use the term which has fallen from favour of "natural justice". In particular in considering whether something has gone wrong the court is concerned as to whether what has happened has resulted in real injustice. If it has, then the court has to intervene, since the Panel is not entitled to confer on itself the power to inflict injustice on those who operate in the market which it supervises."

I make two general comments. First, insofar as special principles apply to the Panel, this is not merely because the Panel is a commercial regulator. Lord Donaldson in *Guinness* stressed that the historic approach to review arose because:[30]

> "When the takeover is in progress the timescale involved was so short and the need of the markets and those dealing in them to be able to rely on the ruling of the Panel so great, that contemporary intervention by the court will usually either be impossible or contrary to the public interest. Furthermore, it is important that this should be known, as otherwise attempts would undoubtedly be made to undermine the authority of the Panel by tactical applications for judicial review."

He put forward the innominate ground because the Panel's constitution, functions and powers were sui generis[31] and Woolf L.J. likewise stressed the lack of statutory power and self determining scope of activity of the Panel.[32]

Second, I draw attention to the limited nature of any qualification on the test of "unreasonableness". The judgment of Lloyd L.J. puts forward no such qualification—he viewed the case as solely concerned with procedural propriety. Lord Donaldson M.R. and Woolf L.J. looked at the conduct of the Panel as a whole and concluded that nothing had occurred such as would warrant intervention by the court. Here we may note that, in the words of Woolf L.J. quoted earlier, the Panel retains a very wide discretion as to how it performs the task it sets itself, and the court intervenes only in plain and obvious cases.

These remarks certainly suggest that, if one were to adopt the European law concept of "proportionality", the "margin of appreciation"[33] afforded to the Panel was considerable. In the context of review for unreasonableness I think one can say that the courts have recognised that the need for speedy and effective regulation of takeovers is such that very great caution should be exercised before concluding that an apparent departure from logic or accepted moral standards has gone beyond the limits of reasonableness.

[29] At 194A.
[30] At 158.
[31] At 159H.
[32] At 192.
[33] See the decision of the European Court of Human Rights in *Markt Intern & Beerman* v. *Germany* (1989) 12 EHRR 161, 174, cited by Lord Ackner in *R.* v. *Secretary of State for the Home Department, ex p. Brind* [1991] 1 AC 696. I have discussed elsewhere the temptation for an English lawyer to equate the doctrine of the "domestic margin of appreciation" with the fundamental English doctrine that there may be a range of reasonable responses open to a decision-maker under domestic principles of judicial review: see Supperstone and Goudie (eds) n. 5 above, pp. 6.49 to 6.50.

Cases concerning other financial regulators suggest that, where appropriate, the courts will identify features of the financial markets which generally call for caution before intervening on rationality grounds: and this flows from a strong appreciation by the courts of the importance of the performance by regulators of their public duty to ensure that commercial activities are conducted fairly and in accord with proper standards. The Financial Services Authority (formerly the Securities and Investments Board) and the bodies recognised under the Financial Services Act are, of course, in a different position from the Panel in that their regulatory mandate can be found in statute. This means that review for illegality is more straightforward than is the case in relation to the Panel. In the context of review for irrationality, however, the courts have maintained a cautious approach. This is epitomised by the Court of Appeal decision in *R. v. Securities & Futures Authority, ex p. Panton*[34] where at an ex parte hearing (and thus in the absence of representation of the Securities & Futures Authority) the Court of Appeal refused a renewed application for leave to move for judicial review. It was said[35] of the financial regulators that they were amenable to judicial review:

"but are, in anything other than very clear circumstances, to be left to get on with it."

R. v. Securities & Investment Board, ex p. Independent Financial Advisers Association[36] is an exceptional case where, in one respect, the court found irrationality on the part of a financial services regulator. The Securities & Investment Board gave guidance in a statement to self regulatory organisations on action which it considered appropriate to ensure that independent financial advisers ("IFAs") addressed the problem of mis-selling of personal pensions. The main ground of challenge—that the SIB had asserted a power to enforce the statement—failed; but in one respect the Court intervened:[37]

"In our judgment the statement ought to say that notwithstanding paras 41 and 42, IFAs are not to be required to take any step which will invalidate their insurance cover without their insurers' consent. To the extent that it does not say that, the statement is wholly irrational."

At first sight this seems surprising. Why should there be a logical or moral imperative which requires any reasonable supervisory body to include a statement about the need to avoid invalidating insurance cover? The answer has, I believe, been rightly identified by Martyn Hopper[38]: a vital practical aspect of the provision of compensation for investors was that, in the case of many smaller IFAs, their professional indemnity insurers remained "the one source of funding which could be relied upon to provide compensation for investors". Taking a realistic and common sense view, there was a paramount need to

---

[34] Unreported, 20th June 1994, Court of Appeal.
[35] by Sir Thomas Bingham MR at p. 7 of the transcript.
[36] [1995] 2 BCLC 76
[37] [1995] 2 BCLC at 90.
[38] See chapter 2 above, p. 000.

ensure that insurance cover was not invalidated: no reasonable supervisor could fail to give priority to this when giving guidance to regulatory organisations.

This examination suggests that the court's exhortation in *Panton* that financial regulators should, in anything other than a very clear case, "be left to get on with it" is no more than a reiteration in relation to financial regulation of the more general principle that the views of those who exercise decision-making power are entitled to respect.[39] If regulators take a stance which on any view ignores a relevant matter (even in the absence of statutory guidance on the point), or if they lose sight of practical reality, their actions may be quashed for unreasonableness.

BROADCASTING

The leading judicial review case in relation to the regulation of broadcasting is *R. v. Independent Television Commission, ex p. TSW Broadcasting Limited*[40]. The Broadcasting Act 1990 introduced a new regime for Channel 3. Licences were to be allocated by secret competitive tender in each region, subject to certain conditions imposed by the Act. One of these conditions was that under section 16(1)(b) the ITC were obliged to reject an application unless it appeared to them that the bidder would be able to maintain the promised service throughout the period for which the licence would be in force. TSW Broadcasting Limited had held the licence for the South West region since 1981; however, the ITC rejected its bid for a new licence on the grounds that TSW had not met the section 16(1)(b) condition.

The leading speeches in the House of Lords were delivered by Lord Templeman and Lord Goff. Lord Templeman rejected TSW's claim that a "slanted" and "unfair" briefing paper vitiated the ITC's decision. He stated[41]:

> "Where Parliament has not provided for an appeal from a decision maker the courts must not invent an appeal machinery. In the present case Parliament has conferred powers and discretions and imposed duties on the ITC. Parliament has not provided any appeal machinery. Even if the ITC make mistakes of fact or mistakes of law, there is no appeal from their decision. The courts have invented the remedies of judicial review not to provide the appeal machinery but to ensure that the decision maker does not exceed or abuse his powers. . . . But the rules of natural justice do not render a decision invalid because the decision maker or his advisers make a mistake of fact or a mistake of law. Only if the reasons given by the ITC for the decision to reject the

---

[39] For expressions of a similar view in other contexts, see *R. v. Secretary of State for the Environment ex p Nottinghamshire CC* [1986] AC 240, 267 (local government finance) and *R. v. Secretary of State for Health ex p ER. Squibb & Sons Ltd* (1997) 10 Admin LR 145, 152 (licensing of medicines).

[40] House of Lords 26th March 1992; reported some years later in [1996] JR 185 and [1996] EMLR 291.

[41] At 191.

application . . . disclosed illegality, irrationality or procedural impropriety . . . could the decision be open to judicial review."

Having noted that this was not a case in which TSW could rely on any breach of the principle of proportionality or could require a close scrutiny of possible threats to human rights of fundamental freedoms, he continued[42]:

> "Judicial review does not issue merely because a decision maker has made a mistake . . . An applicant for judicial review must show more than a mistake on the part of the decision maker or his advisers. Where a decision is made in good faith following a proper procedure and as a result of conscientious consideration, an applicant for judicial review is not entitled to relief save on one of the grounds established by Lord Greene MR in Associated Picture Houses v. Wednesbury Corporation [1948] 1 KB 223".

In the concluding section of his speech, he added[43] :

> "Of course in judicial review proceedings, as in any other proceedings, everything depends on the facts. But judicial review should not be allowed to run riot. The practice of delving through documents and conversations and extracting a few sentences which enable a skilled advocate to produce doubt and confusion where none exists should not be repeated."

These observations by Lord Templeman are not specifically directed at judicial review of regulators. They are quite general (save only that they reserve the position where considerations of proportionality or human rights may be relevant). Both Lord Templeman and Lord Goff also examined an assertion that TSW were entitled to rely on a legitimate expectation that certain criteria would be used by the ITC. In rejecting this assertion, neither of their Lordships suggested that they were applying any special principle to the ITC as a regulatory body.

The reasoning of Lord Templeman was relied on by the Divisional Court in a subsequent challenge to the ITC's decision over the Channel 5 licence. In *R. v. Independent Television Commission, ex p. Virgin Television Ltd*[44] Virgin complained that the ITC had acted irrationally in concluding that Virgin's bid did not meet quality and diversity requirements in the Act. The Divisional Court (Henry L.J. and Turner J.) cited the passages from Lord Templeman's speech quoted above, and added:

> "The submission was that since, in this case, the Commission had explained the factual basis of its decision, if that decision was truly based on erroneous fact, then the decision itself was flawed. As to that, we would say, plainly so. But, as Lord Templeman made clear in TSW, mistakes of fact may be made provided that the mistakes are not grave enough to undermine the basis of a multi-faceted decision. And even this is not necessarily the end of the matter. The reason is this. The factual part of the Commission's decision necessarily involved consideration of evidence presented to it. It was for the Commission to evaluate that evidence, and no one else. We think

[42] At 192.
[43] At 195.
[44] [1996] EMLR 318 (Divisional Court).

that Mr. Scrivener's submission fails to make adequately, or at all, the important distinction between evidence and the facts which it was the function of the decision making body to find from that evidence."[45]

Having set out details of the expertise of the ITC and the approach which the ITC had adopted, the Court continued[46] :

"It is quite plain that the Commission approached its task of evaluating the application and the evidence provided by Virgin to support it with model care. There must accordingly be a natural, as well as judicial, reluctance to conclude that the decision was flawed. This is not a consequence of judicial conservatism or intellectual disinclination. It is a logical consequence of the perceived care and meticulous approach which the Commission brought to bear on its task of assessment and evaluation in accordance with what Parliament has entrusted to it. It is also a consequence of the limits which the Court is required to observe in determining whether or not the decision maker has arrived at a decision which has a sufficient factual basis."

Again it seems to me that these observations are quite general, and are not confined to review of commercial regulators. Javan Herberg suggests[47] that the case illustrates the extreme difficulty of challenging a decision of a "specialist" body on any but the most narrow ultra vires grounds. To my mind, the difficulty for the applicant was that the evidence of great care taken by the ITC made it less likely that they had reached a view of the facts which was not reasonably open on the basis of the material before them.

UTILITIES

Colin Scott[48] has drawn attention to the effect of the separation of operation and regulation, combined with liberalisation of the market. This has resulted not merely in an increased incidence of litigation, but also in the introduction of legal values which bring about a shift in relations between utility companies and regulators.

There are difficult questions here as to whether the utility companies themselves may be subjected to judicial review, and if so on what grounds.[49] But there is no reason to doubt that the regulators themselves are subject to judicial review, which includes review for "unreasonableness". This is illustrated by the decision of the Court of Appeal in *R. v. Director General of Electricity Supply,*

---

[45] Javan Herberg points out ("JR of the ITC: The labours of sisyphus (continued)" [1996] JR 123, 125) that the Court is presumably proceeding on the basis that an erroneous finding of fact may ground a challenge where that finding is irrational or because there is "no evidence" for it.

[46] At 43.

[47] [1996] JR 123; he also suggests that expansion of the doctrine of mistake of fact may enable the presentation of a challenge other than by direct reliance upon an allegation of irrationality, both the *TSW* and the *Virgin* decision seem to me to point the other way.

[48] See chapter 1.

[49] See Lidbetter, "Privatised Utilities and Judicial Review" [1996] JR 249, discussing *Mercury Energy Limited* v. *Electricity Corporation of New Zealand* [1994] 1 WLR 521 and other cases.

ex p. Scottish Power Plc[50]. In broad outline, the Court of Appeal (Staughton & Morritt LJJ and Sir Ralph Gibson) held that the Director General of Electricity Supply ("DGES") acted irrationally in refusing to modify the pricing conditions of Scottish powers' licence. The pricing condition contained a number of elements, one of which was a "Great Britain Yardstick" common to both SP's licence and the licence granted to Scottish Hydro-Electric Plc. The DGES referred the terms of HE's licence to the MMC, and accepted their recommendation that the definition of the Great Britain Yardstick should be modified as part of a number of alterations to HE's pricing formula. However the DGES refused to use the new definition of the Yardstick in SP's licence, on the grounds that the increase in price which would otherwise have flowed to HE from the revised definition was broadly offset by the MMC's recommendations of reductions in other aspects of HE's pricing. But the DGES did not form a view on whether such offsetting reductions ought also to arise in SP's case. The court held that :

> "The simple refusal to propose the modification of the definition of G.B.Y in the licence of S.P., to which on the grounds of fairness S.P. was entitled, cannot be justified, in our judgment, by the reasons advanced."

It is noteworthy that the Court of Appeal did not suggest that any special principle came into play such as would restrict review for irrationality.

THE DANGERS OF CATEGORISATION

A beneficial development in administrative law in recent years has been the recognition that the courts may intervene to prevent unfairness amounting to abuse of power. The view which I took in 1992 was that this was an example of review for unreasonableness: those cases where the court had contemplated such interventions were cases where no rational decision maker could think it right to act in the manner proposed.[51] Lawyers, with their longing for certainty and predictability, have a natural desire to try to pigeon-hole potential sets of facts, seeking to achieve an ideal world in which one can advise with precision which circumstances may lead to a particular result. Consistently with this desire, it was argued in R. v. *Inland Revenue Commisssioners ex p. Unilever plc* that "unfairness" could not be found to exist outside those forms of unfairness which had already been recognised by the courts—for example, conduct akin to breach of contract. In that case both the taxpayer and the Revenue had for many years shared an honest error as to the applicability of a time limit. When the Revenue sought without notice to rely upon the time limit (departure from

---

[50] Court of Appeal, 3rd February 1997, unreported. For discussion, see C. Scott, [1997] PL 400 and A. McHarg (1998) 61 MLR 93. The decision is remarkable for a further reason: the English Court of Appeal (absent any contention by the parties to the contrary) assumed jurisdiction to decide the validity of action taken by a regulator which had effect only in Scotland.

[51] See the text cited at n. 5 above, p. 135.

which had caused no prejduce to the Revenue) the Court of Appeal held that reliance on the limit was an abuse of power. Sir Thomas Bingham MR said[52]

> "The categories of unfairness are not closed, and precedent should act as a guide not a cage. Each case must be judged on its own facts, bearing in mind the Revenue's unqualified acceptance of a duty to act fairly and in accordance with the highest public standards."

The danger of the categorisation proposed by the Revenue was that it would prevent the court from recognising a potential abuse of power. The flexibility of review for unreasonableness has enabled the courts to proceed, with caution, where appropriate, to identify cases where unfairness is such as to call for intervention: it has enabled constructive discussion of the way in which legitimate expections of a particular result should be handled by the courts[53] and it enables courts to ask, where a decision interferes with basic human rights, whether a reasonable decision-maker could have concluded that there was a competing interest sufficiently strong to warrant that interference.[54] Precedent in all these fields must be taken as a guide, but if it is used to categorise, then attention will naturally be focussed on the issues used to draw the line (e.g. has there been reliance to detriment?) and will be diverted from the central question of unreasonableness as a long-stop limit on governmental action.

A preferable categorisation is the recognition by courts of the appropriateness of judicial deference. That is not to say that the court should abdicate responsibility where a decision-maker is "expert". Professor Cranston has suggested an intermediate position which would accord deference if earned.[55]

> ". . . this would depend on factors such as the public authority's expertise and experience, whether its position is consistent and plausible, whether its position has been formulated thoroughly and in detail, whether the issue is a technical one, and whether (when the matter is one of construction) the public authority participated in the drafting of the measure."

The recent cases on financial services, broadcasting and utilities suggest that many of these factors are being respected by the courts in their approach to questions of unreasonableness.

CONCLUSION

Bishop has observed[56] that the independence and autonomy of judges insulate them from political pressures to a greater degree than regulatory agencies. Such

---

[52] At 690.
[53] Difficulties remain in this area as observed by Cranston ("Reviewing Judicial Review" in G. Richardson and H. Genn (eds.) *Administrative Law and Government Action* (OUP, Oxford, 1994) there is an important public benefit in the general right of government to change its mind.
[54] See the cases cited by M. Fordham, "Anxious Scrutiny" [1996] JR 81.
[55] N. 53 above, at p. 80.
[56] W. Bishop, "A theory of administrative law" (1990) 19 J. Legal Stud. 489, 491–492.

independence and autonomy is, to my mind, a vital part of the legitimacy of judicial review of administrative action, and in particular review of administrative action for unreasonableness. This does not mean that the Judges provide a regime of substantive accountability for regulators. The courts are right to adopt a cautious approach to substantive review. As Ogus points out[57] :

> "If the gates are open too widely, the administrative costs of regulation may escalate and private interests will have an incentive to exploit the process for tactical purposes, thereby frustrating the implementation of public interest goals."

Moreover, insofar as the Judges play a role in the setting of standards of good administration, there is a danger that the use of the courts for this purpose may bring with it potential problems of uncertainty and inconsistency.[58] This danger is recognised by the courts, and clearly justifies the degree of circumspection. Such circumspection may be particularly important in fields such as commercial regulation. But it does not and should not prevent the courts from carrying out their constitutional role as a long stop, to identify that which society regards as imperative and that which society regards as completely unacceptable. As was said by Simon Brown L.J. in the context of challenges which assert unfair behaviour by administrators:[59]

> "Of course legal certainty is a highly desirable objective in public administration as elsewhere. But to confine all fairness challenges rigidly . . . . would to my mind impose an unwarranted fetter upon the broader principle operating in this field: the central *Wednesbury* principle . . . that an administrative decision is unlawful if "so outrageous in its defiance of logic or of accepted moral standards that no sensible person who had applied his mind to the question to be decided could have arrived at it. (See *Council of Civil Service Unions* v. *Minister for the Civil Service* [1985] AC 374 and 410 per Lord Diplock). The flexibility necessarily inherent in that guiding principle should not be sacrificed on the altar of legal certainty."

---

[57] A.I. Ogus, *Regulation: Legal Form and Economic Theory* (Clarendon Press, Oxford, 1994) p. 117.
[58] R. Baldwin & C. McCrudden, *Regulation and Public Law* (Weidenfeld, London, 1987) p. 70 to 77; in R. Baldwin, *Rules and Government* (Clarendon Press, Oxford, 1995), at p. 86 to 106 Baldwin examines the uncertainty found in the Court's approach to "tertiary rules" (i.e. rules other than primary or delegated legislation).
[59] R. v. *Inland Revenue Commissioners, ex p. Unilever* [1996] STC 681.

Index